Congratulations! Possession of this handbook entitles you to valuable online resources!

1. The Self Study Guide, a companion to your handbook

2. Registration for the weekly SubSuggestions eNewsletter

3. STEDI.org's monthly "Subinars", a series of free webinars that address key tactics in the management of classrooms, special education, teaching strategies, and other relevant topics chosen to help you improve your professionalism and overall skills in the classroom.

4. Access to STEDI Profiles, a tool designed to help substitute teachers promote their skills and experience to permanent teachers and school district personnel, and

5. The Bus Stop Blog: Join the hundreds of substitute teachers that visit and contribute to the Bus Stop blog daily. At the blog you will find tips and suggestions about classroom management, professionalism, and great fill-in activities. The Bus Stop blog has endless amounts of information for those who want to excel at substitute teaching.

Visit www.stedi.org and register to take advantage of these benefits!

Enjoy your experience in the classrooms!

http://STEDI.org

© Copyright 2009

Substitute Teaching Division, STEDI.org

ISBN: 978-0-9821657-8-2 • Substitute Teacher Handbook • 7th Edition

What It's All About

Substitute teaching is an important educational component in our schools. It is a rare teacher who never needs a substitute for either personal or professional reasons. Research has shown that in the United States a student spends over one full year with a substitute teacher before graduating from high school. Principals, teachers, parents, and students value good substitute teachers who have a significant and positive impact on the quality of education while the permanent teacher is away.

You can become an expert in substitute teaching even though you may not be a certified teacher. Successful teachers are those who have either consciously, or subconsciously, developed the skills that make them effective in the classroom. In other words, by learning certain skills, techniques, and methods, you can be a successful teacher.

Considerable time has been devoted to researching, documenting, and field-testing the ideas and strategies presented. Most of the theory behind these skills and strategies has been intentionally left out. The content has been compressed to specific do's and don'ts for successful teaching. Applying and improving these skills and strategies are key to your enjoyment and satisfaction with substitute teaching.

Research conducted by the Substitute Teaching Institute has identified the following:

- *The number one request by substitute teachers is that they learn skills to successfully manage classroom/behavior situations.*

- *The number one trait of a successful substitute teacher is the use of a **SubPack** or resource kit.*

- *The number one request by permanent teachers and school personnel is that substitute teachers be prepared and professional.*

- *The number one request by students is that substitute teachers present stimulating lessons and exciting fill-in activities.*

For information on substitute skills visit: www.stedi.org

Useful Icons

The icons (pictures) throughout the book are used to give visual recognition to tips, activities, and chapters. These icons will enable you to quickly locate each section and better understand what you are reading.

One Professional to Another

This icon presents key points in the section you are reading. By reviewing each box, you can quickly identify topics covered in the chapter.

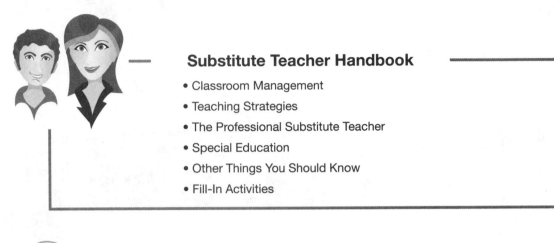

Substitute Teacher Handbook

- Classroom Management
- Teaching Strategies
- The Professional Substitute Teacher
- Special Education
- Other Things You Should Know
- Fill-In Activities

Remember

The remember sections point out important items or ideas you need to retain and take into consideration as you acquire new skills.

Handbook Overview

Preface

The preface is an introduction to this handbook, its purpose, and contents.

Chapter One:
Classroom Management

Learning takes place as teachers systematically and skillfully manage the learning environment. This chapter contains the four principles of human behavior and the five key skills necessary for success in the classroom. Included in the chapter are ideas for starting the day, maintaining a risk free environment, and suggestions for managing challenging scenarios.

Chapter Two:
Teaching Strategies, Skills, and Suggestions

Chapter two contains methods for presenting the permanent teacher's lesson plans. Suggestions are given for how to approach unfamiliar topics and how to involve students in active learning. There are also ideas for low cost/no cost rewards and motivators, and suggestions for building a resource kit or *SubPack* with teaching aids.

- Brainstorming
- Concept Mapping
- K-W-L
- Questions for Higher Level Thinking
- Cooperative Learning
- Using Audio Visual Materials Effectively

Chapter Three:
The Professional Substitute Teacher

Permanent teachers and district personnel unanimously request that substitute teachers be professional. Chapter three outlines aspects of being a professional substitute teacher that begin well before the bell rings.

- At Home
- Prior to Entering the Classroom
- In the Classroom Before School
- Throughout the Day
- At the End of the Day

Chapter Four:
Special Education

The special education setting is varied and can be very rewarding. The substitute teacher in special education classrooms can experience success by understanding and implementing the skills outlined in chapter four.

- Having an Attitude of Respect
- Working with Paraeducators
- Being Familiar with Special Education Laws and Terms
- Instructional Consistency
- Adapting Lessons and Activities
- Knowing Students and Meeting All Their Needs

Chapter Five:
Other Things You Should Know

Other things you should know about include:

- Safe Schools Policy

- First Aid and Safety

- Legal Aspects of the Job

- Child Abuse Reporting

- Sexual Harassment

- Evacuation and Other Out-of-Classroom Activities

The information in this chapter should only be used to supplement local school district policies and procedures.

Chapter Six:
Fill-In Activities

This chapter provides many lesson and activity ideas for your *SubPack* that provide hours of meaningful learning. A detailed *Reference Guide for Activities* listing individual activities is found on pages 104-106. Chapter six has been divided into three sections according to the type of activity:

Five-Minute Fillers

Whole-class critical thinking activities for those extra five minutes that occur throughout the day.

Early Finishers

Independent activities for students who finish assignments early.

Short Activities

Teacher-directed activities and lessons. This section is organized by subject and includes lessons that can be taught in an hour or less.

- Art
- Critical Thinking
- Foreign Language
- Geography
- Government / History

- Language Arts
- Math
- Music
- Science
- Speech / Drama

Special Needs

Special Needs Adaptation

This icon highlights suggested adaptations for Short Activities that address the unique learning requirements of students with special needs.

Accelerated Adaptation

This icon suggests modifications to accommodate the needs of advanced learners.

Accelerated

Contributing Authors

Geoffrey G. Smith

Mr. Smith founded the Substitute Teaching Institute (STI) at Utah State University (USU) in 1995 to research best practices in substitute teaching management. STI spun off from USU in 2008 as the Substitute Teaching Division, STEDI.org which continues the mission of "Revolutionizing the Role of Substitute Teaching into an Opportunity of Educational Excellence," with Mr. Smith as its Director.

Cynthia Murdock

Ms. Murdock served as the curriculum development director at STI/USU. Her teacher-leader ability, along with experience as a substitute and permanent teacher provided a plethora of ideas and materials for teaching. She has written and edited the SubExchange newsletter, several Substitute Teacher Handbooks, and has also been a professional development instructor.

Max L. Longhurst

Mr. Longhurst, is an elementary education specialist at Utah State University. He writes, field-tests, and develops materials for teachers and conducts training for permanent teachers. He is the former director of the Elementary CORE Academy for the state of Utah.

Glenn Latham

Dr. Latham was a professor emeritus of special education at USU and served as a principal investigator at the Mountain Plains Regional Resource Center. His internationally acclaimed work is founded on a system of principles, strategies, and skills developed, tested, and proven in his 35 years of continuous research and trial. Dr. Latham defined this behavior model in over 250 technical research papers, reports, journal articles, presentations, books, and chapters in books relating to behavior management at home and in schools.

Michelle Ditlevsen

Ms. Ditlevsen has a bachelor's degree in special education and has demonstrated her skills in education as both a permanent and substitute teacher. Currently, she is a special education teacher in northern Virginia. She has contributed to numerous projects for Utah State University through research, editing, writing, and training.

Special thanks to: Diane Iverson, Barbara Haines, Blaine Sorenson, Robert L. Morgan, and Jessica Smith. Graphics and formatting by Donny Merrill

Remember

The information in this handbook is not intended to replace the rules and regulations of the district. Use only those suggestions and activities from this handbook that do not conflict with the district's policies and established practices.

Table of Contents

Classroom Management

Classroom and behavior management skills are essential for success in the classroom. Chapter One explains four principles of human behavior, five management skills, and various strategies to help you effectively manage student behavior. The behavior management skills and strategies outlined are also effective in at-risk and special needs classes. Developed by Dr. Glenn Latham, the skills presented are statistically proven to prevent 94 percent of inappropriate student behavior and provide strategies to handle the remaining 6 percent.

As you come to understand and implement the skills and strategies presented, you will increase your ability to:

- Effectively get and keep students on task

- Maintain a risk-free environment

- Communicate expectations

- Respond non-coercively to negative student behavior

Take notice that learning this material is not easy, at least at first. It takes time and practice like learning any new skill. Does knowing the state motor vehicle rules of the road mean you can drive a car safely? No, it takes effort and training. Just like with driving, classroom management will not come naturally or be easy at first, but it can become second nature and it is worth the effort.

"Every learner who enters our classroom should leave a better and more able person. When the learning environment is managed properly, this is more a possibility than it is a simple ideal."

– Dr. Glenn Latham, Professor of education and a behavior analyst

Register for free at STEDI.org to gain access to online resources for substitute teachers.

Four Principles of Human Behavior

Principles are truths not bound by age, time, location or situation. Once familiar with these specific principles, you will see them illustrated all around you – between parents and children, among adults, in retail stores, in schools, in churches, on playgrounds, and at family events. It is impossible to write a book that covers each classroom scenario an educator may encounter. However, when an educator knows and applies principles, the likelihood of appropriate student behavior will increase.

Principle One:
Behavior is largely a product of its immediate environment.

Students behave or misbehave due to what is happening in the classroom more than the influence of outside factors. If the teacher changes the environment in the classroom, the behavior of the students will change.

Too often in public education, teachers blame a student's inappropriate behavior on inalterable variables. The first principle of human behavior states that it doesn't matter if a student comes from a bad home life or was diagnosed with a behavioral disorder. If a student is acting out, there is something in the classroom environment that is influencing his behavior. You as the teacher control that environment.

Example:

Outside the Classroom: If a car (student) travels along the same bumpy road everyday and results in needed repairs, then no matter how much money or time is spent fixing the car, unless the road is fixed (teacher skills), the car (student) will always need repairs.	**Inside the Classroom:** The same students can behave perfectly for one teacher and completely disrespect another teacher.

Principle Two:
Behavior is strengthened or weakened by its consequences.

We do what we do, because we get what we get when we do it.

When students are persistently disruptive or not paying attention, examine what the immediate consequence is. Teacher attention is a powerful motivator for most students. If a teacher pays more attention to students who are misbehaving than students who behave properly, inappropriate behavior will likely continue, and even increase.

Example:

Outside the Classroom: At the grocery store a child doesn't get the candy he wants and throws a temper tantrum. His mom gives him the candy to make him be quiet. The child has now learned a valuable lesson: he knows if he doesn't get what he wants; he can throw a tantrum and get it.	**In the Classroom:** A student yells out the answer to a question and the teacher acknowledges his answer, the next time a student wants to answer a question, he will most likely yell out the answer again. However, if a student yells out the answer and the teacher doesn't acknowledge it and calls on a student who is raising her hand, the first student will know he needs to raise his hand in order to get the teacher's attention.

Principle Three:
Behavior ultimately responds better to positive than to negative consequences.

People respond better to positive encouragement than negative processes.

By genuinely reinforcing appropriate behavior many undesirable behaviors will become extinct and appropriate behaviors will increase. Think of the tasks you do every day; if someone thanks you for what you do or compliments you on how well you did it, it's more likely you'll continue similar behavior.

Example:

Outside the Classroom: In athletics there is a phenomenon called: home field advantage. When an athletic team is playing in their own stadium, court, or field and in front of their own fans, they have an increased likelihood of winning the game.	**In the Classroom:** A teacher was trying to line up her students. She kept asking Caden to get in line. He wouldn't go. After asking three times, she changed her tactic. She thanked Sophia and Mark for getting in line quickly. After watching the exchange Caden jumped in line almost immediately. After 30 seconds, she then thanked Caden for standing quietly in line.

Principle Four:
Whether a behavior has been punished or reinforced is known only by the course of that behavior in the future.

If an appropriate behavior is repeated, it has been reinforced. If a negative behavior is repeated, it too has been reinforced. If a negative behavior has discontinued, it has been properly disciplined.

The only way to tell if a response to a behavior is punishing or reinforcing is to watch what happens to the behavior in the future. What is a punishment to one person may reinforce and perpetuate a behavior in another person.

Example:

Outside the Classroom: Robyn walked into the bathroom to find her husband cleaning it. She immediately gave her husband a huge hug and thanked him for making the bathroom look so good. The next Saturday the bathroom was cleaned again.	**In the Classroom:** Two students are talking in the back of the classroom and not working on their assignments. The teacher moves closer to the students. One student stops talking and begins working. The other student keeps talking. The teacher realizes that proximity wasn't a punishment to the second student and tries another strategy. The teacher quietly says to the student, "*What do I expect you to be doing now*?" The student replies that she doesn't understand the assignment. The teacher then assists the student, as the rest of the class continues working.

These four principles of human behavior are essential for success in the classroom. It will take practice to gain a full understanding of these principles. For educators, this is a call to action. As we get better at controlling our own behavior, student behavior will improve.

Five Skills for Effective Behavior Management

The following skills for managing student behavior are based on the four principles of human behavior previously discussed. Understanding and effectively implementing these skills will help prevent unnecessary classroom management problems and prepare you to handle challenging situations that may occur.

Skill One: The ability to get and keep students on task.

Skill Two: The ability to maintain a high rate of positive teacher-to-student interaction and risk-free student response opportunities.

Skill Three: The ability to teach expectations.

Skill Four: The ability to respond non-coercively.

Skill Five: The ability to avoid being trapped.

Skill One:
The ability to get and keep students on task.

Students cannot learn if they are not actively engaged in learning activities. To be actively engaged in assigned activities is commonly referred to as being on task. When students are on task, they will learn more and create fewer classroom management problems. Getting and keeping students on task can usually be accomplished by using two simple strategies:

1. Begin instruction or activities immediately.

2. Manage student behavior by walking around.

Starting the Day

- Greet students at the door

- Direct students to a starter activity

- Take roll based on the seating chart while students are working

- Introduce yourself as the teacher

- Proceed with the written lesson plan

Begin Instruction or Activities Immediately

Some permanent teachers may leave instructions for a starter activity for students to complete at the beginning of class. If such an activity is not outlined in the lesson plan, prepare an activity that students can work on as soon as they walk into the classroom. Many effective substitute teachers start the day by having students make name tags, help construct a seating chart, if one was not left, write in a student journal, engage in silent reading, or participate in one of the Five-Minute Filler activities found in Chapter Six.

Starter activities serve two purposes in the classroom: first, they get students actively engaged in a learning activity, thereby decreasing the opportunity for inappropriate behavior. Second, they provide the time for you, as the substitute teacher, to take roll and get materials ready so you have a smooth transition to the next activity.

The shorter the time between the beginning of class and when students are actively involved in a productive activity the better. This eliminates down time/wasted time when opportunities for students to engage in inappropriate behavior increases.

Nametags

Nametags may be worn or kept on students' desks throughout the day. Using commercial name tags, adhesive file folder labels, or strips of masking tape are all effective possibilities. Name tags are a tremendous help when facilitating class discussions and managing student behavior.

Seating Chart

A seating chart is a valuable tool you can use throughout the day to take roll and assist you in calling students by name. Sometimes you may not be able to locate a seating chart, or the seating chart left by the permanent teacher may not be current. If this is the case, quickly make a seating chart using small Post-It Notes® and a file folder from your *SubPack*. Distribute Post-It Notes® to students and have them write their name on it. After students have done this, arrange the names on the file folder in the same configuration as the desks in the classroom. The few minutes it takes to establish an accurate seating chart at the beginning of class is well worth the benefits it provides.

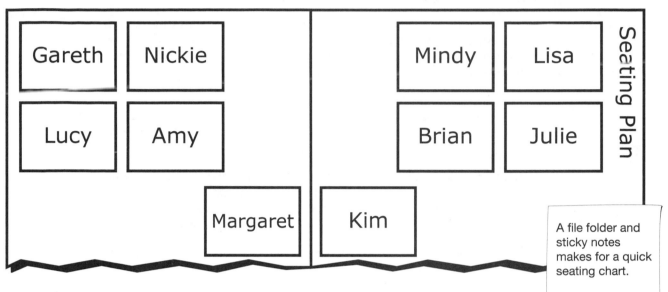

A file folder and sticky notes makes for a quick seating chart.

During the starter activity, try to minimize the time spent on procedural matters such as taking roll and lunch count. Dragging these activities out simply provides time for students to get bored and start behaving inappropriately. After students have had time to complete their starter activity, outline for students the schedule of activities for the day.

Now is the time to quickly review expectations, explain consequences of student behavior, and introduce any incentives or early finisher activities you will be using. Share any information left by the permanent teacher regarding what they should accomplish during the day, and then get students involved in the next learning activity as quickly as possible.

The sooner you get students on task, the easier it is to keep them actively engaged in constructive activities. Do not allow yourself to be led off task by student protests and long, useless discussions.

If students complain, respond with empathy, understanding, and firmness. Don't, however, compromise your expectations or waste instructional time being overly sympathetic.

Students Getting the Teacher Off Task

Teacher: *"Please take out your reading books and read silently at your desk for the next 20 minutes."*

Students: *"Reading is boring. We never read before lunch time."*

Teacher: *"You know, when I was your age, I thought reading was boring too. Sometimes I used to just sit at my desk, hold my book open, and pretend to read. Have any of you ever done anything like that?"*

Teacher Getting Students On Task

Teacher: *"Please take out your reading books and read silently at your desk for the next 20 minutes."*

Students: *"Reading is boring. We never read before lunch time."*

Teacher: *"I understand that silent reading may not be your favorite activity and this may not be the way Mrs. Jones does it, however, today we are going to read silently, at our desks, for the next 20 minutes. Please take out your reading books and begin."*

Manage by Walking Around

The easiest and most effective strategy for keeping students on task is for the teacher to walk around the classroom in a random pattern. By moving about the room, you can observe the progress of students, acknowledge and reinforce appropriate behavior, and manage off-task behavior with proximity.

There is a direct relationship between how close a teacher is to students and how well students behave. Wear comfortable shoes and plan to be on your feet all day monitoring, assisting, providing positive reinforcement, and using proximity, or nearness to students, to keep students on task.

Do not underestimate the power of the proximity strategy; you will be amazed at how many negative behavior problems will be taken care of just by placing yourself nearer to a student. In most cases, talking to the poorly behaving student will not be required. However, what is required is continually reinforcing on-task behavior with verbal praise.

By walking around the classroom, instead of reading a book at the permanent teacher's desk, you are showing the students that it is important to be on task, not just telling them. The teacher should be the most on-task person in the classroom.

Other On-Task Strategies

In some circumstances additional strategies are needed to get and keep students on task. Sometimes an event outside the classroom, such as an assembly, fire drill, or rousing game of soccer at recess, makes it difficult to get and keep students on task. On other occasions the entire class may be off task or out of control for no apparent reason at all.

Most times the permanent teacher may have techniques, such as silent signals or prompt/ response procedures that can be implemented to get the attention of, or refocus, the class. If such techniques have been outlined in the lesson plans or explained by a student, don't hesitate to implement them. If this is unsuccessful, or you don't know what the permanent teacher usually does, the following strategies will get the attention of the entire class.

STRATEGY ▶   ### Refocusing the Class: Captivate and Redirect

Often the best way to deal with major disruptions such as assemblies or a fire drill is to minimize the event by capturing and redirecting students' attention. For example, complete an activity that requires mental concentration, such as a Five-Minute Filler or Critical Thinking Activity from this handbook. Involving students in an exciting and mentally challenging learning activity will help them settle back down into the routine of the day.

STRATEGY ▶   ### Whisper

Your first instinct in a situation where the entire class is noisy and off task may be to raise your voice above the noise level of the room and demand attention. However, this can incur some unwelcome side effects, such as the students hearing you speak loudly and assuming it is all right for them to raise their voices as well. A productive strategy is to whisper.

Move to the front of the room and begin giving instructions very quietly. As students hear you, they will need to become quiet in order to understand what you are saying. Soon students who are still inattentive will focus and listen to the instructions also. When you have the attention of the entire class, you can then give instructions or directions as needed.

Write and Erase

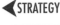

If students are between activities and talking among themselves, one way to get their attention and give further instructions is to begin writing and erasing the student instructions on the board, one word at a time. For example, if you wanted them to get their science books out of their desks, you would write the word "Get" on the whiteboard then erase it. Then you would write the word "your" and erase it. Then write "science" and erase it, etc. Students soon become involved in trying to figure out what you are writing and that they are missing the instructions. You will quickly have the undivided attention of the entire class.

> **Tip:**
>
> When erasing a board, use vertical strokes; your hips will show the least amount of movement. Horizontal strokes make hips shake, which students may find humorous and thus distracting.

Lights Out

This strategy should only be used when you need the attention of the entire class and when you will not be unnecessarily interrupting students who are on task. Quickly turn the classroom lights off then on again. Be prepared to begin speaking in the moment of surprised silence, when you have everyone's attention. If you wait too long to start talking, the class will begin talking about the lights going out and the event itself will become a real distraction.

Skill Two:
The ability to maintain a high rate of positive teacher-to-student interactions and risk-free student response opportunities.

Positive Teacher-to-Student Interactions

The most powerful consequence of any student behavior is teacher attention. The behavior you are providing attention to, is the behavior that is going to prevail in the classroom. On average, teachers allow 98 percent of all appropriate student behavior to go unrecognized and are two to three times more likely to recognize inappropriate behavior. If teachers spend their time reinforcing only negative or bad behavior in a classroom, it is more likely students will behave poorly.

Rather than trying to weaken undesirable behavior using adverse or negative processes, research has shown that strengthening desirable behavior through positive reinforcement does more to make a classroom favorable to learning than any other skill.

In general, positive verbal praise, a smile or nod, and other appropriate gestures, are among the very best ways to interact in a positive manner with students. Negative and corrective interactions should be outnumbered by positive interactions; a ratio of one negative interaction to eight positive interactions is recommended. For ideas of positive things you can say to students, see the list of 101 Ways to Say "Good Job!" in Chapter Two.

Remember

The behavior you are trying to control is your own.

To become more positive in challenging situations, you must identify and practice positive interaction skills. One way to do this is to determine situations in which you are most inclined to be negative by creating an "Anticipate a Problem" form (see page 26). On the left side of the paper, describe a problem or inappropriate behavior that is most likely to elicit a negative response from you. On the right side of the paper, write a possible proactive, positive response that could be used instead. Remember that you are learning a new skill and need to practice several times in order for it to become natural and you to be proficient.

At times, situations will arise that will be so annoying and unnerving that every positive interaction you have ever practiced will completely escape your recollection. When you can't think of an appropriate way to respond and are overwhelmed with the urge to react in a negative manner, **don't do anything!** Unless what you are about to say or do has a high probability for making things better, it is better to do nothing at all.

STRATEGY ▶ *Positive Interaction Strategy: The Designated Problem Student*

On occasion, a teacher may leave a note about a problem student, or a neighboring teacher may warn you about a trouble maker. In such situations, you can often gain the compliance of the student and prevent potential problems by being proactive and positive.

When the students arrive, determine who the identified student is and request that student be a helper for the day. Ask her help with special jobs that keep her positively occupied. Be positive in your interactions and thank her for her assistance.

STRATEGY ▶ *Positive Interaction Strategy: The 'You vs. Them' Class*

Sometimes you may get the feeling that the whole class, or at least several students have secretly planned to make the day as difficult for you as possible. Most 'You vs. Them' scenarios turn out to be a lose-lose situation for everyone involved.

You might try an activity from the Five-Minute Filler section of this handbook, such as Mystery Box, A Silly Story, or Number Phrase. Interact with the students early in the day – let them get to know you better and see that you have a sense of humor. Chances are, once you break the ice and establish rapport with the students; the remainder of the day will go more smoothly. Making the classroom a battleground for control will usually make things worse.

STRATEGY ▶ *Risk-Free Student Response Opportunities*

Student response opportunities and active participation in the learning process play an important role in student achievement. When students are engaged in appropriate responses to learning activities, they have neither the inclination, nor the time to be engaged in inappropriate behavior. Lecture little, if you have to lecture at all, and question much. Provide opportunities for risk-free student responses immediately. Let students answer questions that illustrate or explain the point you are trying to get across.

Remember

Attention is to behavior what profits are to business.

Also, be sure to provide all students with opportunities and invitations to respond and inquire. There are always students with their hands raised continually, anxious to say just about anything. On the other hand, there are also those students who sit in class, never asking a question or making a comment. As a teacher, it is easy to get in the habit of calling on students who are attentive, interested, and willing to volunteer information.

A simple way to ensure that all students have a chance to respond, while at the same time maintaining the students' attention, is to place the names of all the students in a container and draw them out randomly. After a student has responded put his name back in the container, otherwise he will lose interest and stop paying attention because he won't be called on again.

Another component of risk-free student response is to maintain a learning environment where students are not afraid to respond – an environment that is free of failure and criticism. This can be accomplished by:

- Asking the student to repeat what has been said.

- Calling on students who you think know the answer.

- Asking students to respond to questions by writing answers on a piece of paper.

- Having students answer in pairs or small groups (limit students to 30 second discussions).

Failure is a negative, ineffective, and poor teacher. In order to establish and maintain a risk-free classroom environment, do everything possible to help students have successful experiences. As you provide opportunities for students to give correct responses, you are also setting up opportunities to positively acknowledge these successes.

Handling Wrong Answers: Echo the Correct Response

◀ STRATEGY

Suppose you asked a student a question expecting a correct response, but for whatever reason the student didn't give the right answer. In such situations, don't dwell on the failure of the student or the incorrectness of the answer. Instead, direct the question and the student's attention to another student who you are quite sure is familiar with the answer. Once the question has been answered correctly, come back to the original student and ask the question again, allowing her to echo the correct response. By doing this, you can create a successful experience for the student.

Teacher: *"Jenni, how do you spell the word 'symphony'?"*

Jenni: *"S - Y - M - F - O - N - Y"*

Teacher: *"Very good, Jenni. You are very close. Is there any one else that thinks they know how you spell symphony? Gabe, why don't you give it a try?"*

Gabe: *"S - Y - M - P - H - O - N - Y"*

Teacher: *"That is correct. Good job, Gabe. Jenni, will you please spell symphony again?"*

Jenni: *"S - Y - M - P - H - O - N - Y"*

Teacher: *"Very good! That is exactly right."*

Occasionally students will respond inaccurately or inappropriately on purpose. Do not allow yourself to be drawn off target and into their control. Even though the student response was inappropriate, it is inconsequential and thus can be ignored. Move on to a student who is likely to respond correctly and appropriately. Provide positive reinforcement for the correct response, and then continue with the discussion. Responding to the inappropriate comment will most likely reinforce the behavior and prompt other students to engage in such responses.

Skill Three:
The ability to teach expectations.

Teaching expectations involves communicating to students the behaviors that are expected in the classroom. Expectations should provide boundaries and establish standards for student success. Types of expectations include:

- Classroom Expectations – Rules

- Instructional Expectations

- Procedural Expectations

As a substitute teacher, your first objective should be to model the expectations of the permanent teacher. Locate the classroom rules posted in the classroom and try to determine the procedures and strategies used by the permanent teacher to get the attention of the class. Reviewing the lesson plans and talking to students can accomplish this. Be sure to find out the permanent teacher's expectations about mp3 players and cell phones and follow them, even if you don't agree. If there are no rules or procedures in evidence, be prepared to implement appropriate expectations.

Class expectations should be concise, specific, instructive, operational, and must convey an expectation of student behavior. Phrases such as "be cooperative," "respect others," and "be polite and helpful" are too general and take too much time to explain. Effective expectations such as "Follow directions the first time they are given," are direct, provide specific standards, and are appropriate for any grade level. The number of expectations should correlate with the age and ability of the students; in general, it is recommended they be limited to five or less.

Once general classroom behavior expectations have been taught they should be displayed somewhere in the room. Hopefully the permanent teacher has already done this. If not, you can write them on the board or on a poster-sized sheet of paper you carry in your *SubPack*. In primary grades, using pictures in addition to words is a good way to convey your expectations.

Each assignment and activity throughout the day will have its own set of instructional and procedural expectations. **Instructional and procedural expectations** need to be communicated to students in order for them to successfully complete their assignments.

As you develop and explain instructional and procedural expectations, realize that students need four things in order to successfully meet the expectations you establish:

1. They need to know exactly what it is they are supposed to do.

2. They need to know how they are expected to do it.

3. They need to have the necessary tools to accomplish the expected task.

4. They need to know exactly how much time they have to complete the task.

Example: *"When I say begin, stop reading and quietly put your reading book away. Get out your math book and paper. Open the book to page 112. You have one minute to do this, please begin."*

Remember

You should never repeat something a student already knows.

Explaining instructional and procedural expectations in the form of a step-by-step process often makes it easier for students to remember the expectations and complete the corresponding task appropriately. Just telling students what your expectations are is often not enough. Expectations should be explained, restated by the students, demonstrated, and even role-played until you are sure the students understand what is expected of them.

Questioning students can help determine if this has been accomplished. Having students respond as an entire group and act out behaviors, such as raising their hand, is also a good idea because it requires every student in the class to understand and acknowledge the expectation.

Have Students Restate Expectations

Having students restate expectations is one way to ensure that they understand and acknowledge the expectations. The few minutes it takes to communicate expectations for each activity are well worth the time to prevent inappropriate behavior. Once you have established your expectations, stick with them! Students will remember what you have said and expect you to follow through. Firmness, fairness, and consistency are the keys to classroom management. Praising students when expectations are met reinforces and perpetuates appropriate student behavior.

Teacher:	(Calling on attentive student) *"Robbie, thank you for paying attention. What do I expect you to do when you want to answer a question or say something?"*
Robbie:	*"You want me to raise my hand."*
Teacher:	*"That's right Robbie. I expect you to raise your hand."*

Having students restate expectations is also a great way to find out what a permanent teacher's expectations are. For example:

Teacher:	*"Ella, what is your teacher's expectation when it comes to cell phones?"*
Ella:	*"He lets us use them whenever we want."*
Teacher:	(Without hesitation) *"Max, what is your teacher's expectation when it comes to cell phones?"*
Max:	*"We can use them whenever we want."*
Teacher:	(Without hesitation) *"Rana, What is your teacher's expectation when it comes to cell phones?"*
Rana:	*"They can't be out during class."*
Teacher:	*"Max, Ella, What is you teacher's expectation when it comes to cell phones?"*
Max, Ella:	*"They can't be out during class."*
Teacher:	*"That's right, thank you. It is the same for today as well. Thank you to those who have their cell phones put away and are ready for the next activity."*

Again, this will take some time, but it is a strategy that can be used to find out a permanent teacher's expectations, without having to raise your voice. The students know exactly what expectations are set, they can then teach each other instead of you being the enforcer. Later in the class when a student has her cell phone out, you can go up to her and ask her what the expectation is. Because you spent a few minutes clarifying the expectation, each student should be clear on what is expected.

Skill Four:
The ability to respond non-coercively.

Any time a student behaves inappropriately you will probably find it annoying. However, the type of behavior, rather than the annoyance level, should be your guide for implementing an appropriate teacher response strategy. Inappropriate student behaviors can be classified as either consequential or inconsequential.

Consequential behaviors are those that have a significant negative effect on the learning environment and interfere with the rights of other students to learn.

Inconsequential behaviors are those that the classroom environment would be better off without, but their negative impact on student learning is minimal. Inconsequential behaviors, such as tapping your pencil on the desk, can become consequential if they escalate or persist over a period of time.

Ignore Inconsequential Behavior

Most inappropriate student behavior, regardless of how annoying it is, is inconsequential. This means that it is not life threatening and it isn't going to destroy the building or its contents. A substitute teacher responding, whether verbally or through body language, to inconsequential student behavior is providing reinforcement and the frequency of these behaviors will likely increase.

A better approach is to ignore inconsequential behavior and respond positively to appropriate behavior with a smile, verbal praise, a nod, or other appropriate gestures.

Example: When asking a question of the class, a student responds without raising his hand for permission to speak or speaks out of turn.

Step One: Do not respond to the disruptive student. Look at those who are raising their hands and call on one of them saying, "*Thank you for raising your hand,*" then allow her to answer the question.

Step Two: If the student continues to speak without raising his hand when you ask the next question, continue to reinforce the students who are behaving appropriately, using the proximity strategy, move closer to the student who is not cooperating.

Do not acknowledge the student who is speaking out of turn. If you give in and respond to that answer, it will be reinforcing the inappropriate behavior, and would then be considered a negative interaction. Generally after steps one and two, a noncompliant student will cooperate and the inappropriate behavior will have stopped. It is important to quickly recognize and reinforce the appropriate behavior of students as they comply with expectations.

Respond Non-coercively to Consequential Behavior

While most student behavior is inconsequential, there are inappropriate student behaviors that are of consequence and need to be addressed. Consequential behavior can be defined as behavior occurring when:

a. A student persists in and is being disruptive.

b. A student increasingly destroys the learning environment.

c. Students are physically or verbally abusive to one another.

Teachers commonly respond to consequential behavior using coercion. Coercion involves attempts to achieve compliance through the use of threats or force. The intent is to compel students to behave out of fear of what will happen to them if they do not behave properly. Coercion makes a student want to escape or avoid the coercer; it does nothing to address the problem.

At best, coercion instills a sense of fear in students that prevents them from acting out. While on the surface the problem seems to have gone away, in reality you have threatened the student's self-confidence and destroyed the atmosphere of risk-free student response opportunities.

For example, teachers often use sarcasm to make a student comply. They do this by making fun of or embarrassing the student in front of his friends. The reason teachers adopt this dreadful form of discipline is because it looks like it works; however, you are destroying the student's confidence and any rapport you may have established with that student is ruined.

Redirect Student Behavior

Instead of being coercive, a better way to handle consequential behavior is to stop the student behavior, then redirect it. This should be done as privately and quietly as possible. The following are six steps for stopping and redirecting inappropriate student behavior:

1. Say something positive to the student or class.

2. Briefly describe the problem behavior.

3. Describe the desired alternative behavior.

4. Give a reason why the new behavior is more desirable.

5. Check for understanding.

6. Provide positive feedback.

An example of how this would be done in the classroom setting:

1. Say something positive.	*"Charlotte, I enjoy having you in class. You have a lot of very creative ideas."*
2. Describe the problem behavior.	*"Just then when I asked you to stop talking to Adam and read your book, you continued to talk to him."*
3. Describe the desired behavior.	*"When I ask you to do something, I need you to look at me, say 'OK,' or nod, and follow my instructions immediately."*
4. Reason the new behavior is desirable.	*"If you will stop talking to Adam, the class will be quieter and everyone, including you, will be able to finish the reading task more quickly."*
5. Check for understanding.	*"Charlotte, what are the three things you should do when I give you instructions?"* (Charlotte says, *"Look at you, say 'OK,' and do it."*) If Charlotte does not respond, prompt her. If she responds inappropriately, repeat the question without displaying anger.
6. Provide positive feedback.	When Charlotte responds correctly, the teacher says, *"Great! This time you looked at me, said 'OK,' and picked up your book. Well done!"*

Though this process may seem complicated, it actually takes less than two minutes and becomes quite natural when regularly practiced. At this point you might be thinking, *"Well that's all right for young students, but not for the kids I work with."* It may interest you to know that this strategy was developed at Boys Town in Omaha, Nebraska, and is used daily with boys and girls of all ages, including high school. This strategy demonstrates the best that research has to offer for stopping and redirecting inappropriate behavior.

More Non-coercive Strategies

The following are examples of other non-coercive response strategies that can be used to respond to inappropriate consequential student behaviors. Remember, the main objective of all response strategies is to stop inappropriate behavior by getting the full attention of the student, then redirect student actions to an appropriate activity.

STRATEGY ▶ ### *Reevaluate the Situation*

One of the first steps you should take when a student or group of students is behaving inappropriately is to reevaluate the situation. If you have a group of students who will not stop talking, step back and see if you can determine why they are talking. Perhaps they do not understand the assignment and are trying to work it out together. If you find that this is the case, you may need to deal with the disruptive event, re-teach the objective, or perhaps even restructure the assignments to be completed as a class or in small groups.

STRATEGY ▶ ### *Reinforce Appropriate Behavior*

Recognition and praise reinforce students who are behaving appropriately. Phrases such as, *"Thank you for putting your hand up, Andy,"* and *"I appreciate that Jose, Su-Ling, and Monica followed my directions so quickly,"* are great motivators for appropriate student behavior. A teacher might also try tangible rewards, such as points or tickets, to provide motivation for behaving appropriately. Overlooking inconsequential off-task behaviors and giving attention to students who are meeting expectations creates a positive classroom atmosphere where all students have a reason to behave appropriately.

STRATEGY ▶ ### *Proximity*

Proximity is an easy-to-use strategy for dealing with many inappropriate behaviors. If a student or group of students is off task or disrupting the class, move closer to the student or group of students in incremental steps. As you move toward the problem, often behavior will change, and students will comply with expectations without your saying a word.

STRATEGY ▶ ### *Restate Expectations*

Sometimes students are off task or behave inappropriately because they do not fully understand your expectations or the related consequences. Often restating the expected behavior, motivators, and consequences, followed by a check for student understanding, is all it takes to get a class back on task.

> Example: *"It is important for everyone to behave appropriately as you work on this task. Please listen as I restate the expectations for the activity. The expectations are: put your feet on the floor, turn your bodies facing forward, and work silently. If you have a question or need help, please raise your hand and I will come to your desk. Students who meet these expectations will receive a ticket (or other motivator). Tobin, please repeat for the class the behavior that is expected during this activity."*

STRATEGY ▶ ### *State the Facts*

In some situations, stating the facts motivates students to behave appropriately. For example, if you suspect students aren't sitting in the right seats, tell them that you are writing a list of students who are working and on task based on the seating chart.

Acknowledge and Restate

Some students may vocally express negative opinions, inappropriate views, and frustrations. Verbally acknowledging a student's comment validates him as a person and often diffuses an emotionally-charged situation. Phrases such as, "*I understand,*" or "*I can tell that you…*" and "*It is obvious that…*" can be used to acknowledge what the student said without getting emotionally involved yourself. Transition words such as "however" and "nevertheless" bring the dialogue back to restating the expected behavior.

> Example: "*I can tell that you are not very interested in this topic, nevertheless, the assignment is to construct a timeline for the industrial revolution and you are expected to have it completed by the end of class.*"

"I Understand"

There are two words that can stop most protests from any students and let you take control of the situation. These words are "*I understand.*"

If a student says, "*But that's not fair!*" you can say, "*I understand, however, these are the expectations for today.*" If a student says, "*I hate you!*" you can say, "*I understand, however, I am the teacher today and you are expected to follow my directions.*"

If a student says, "*This assignment is stupid,*" you can say, "*I understand, nevertheless, you will need to have it completed for class tomorrow.*"

Remove, Identify, and Redirect

In some instances, it is best to remove the student from the situation before addressing the behavior. Since it is necessary for you to maintain supervision over all of the students in the class, removal of the student should take her out of earshot, but allow you to maintain visual contact with the rest of the class. Calmly ask the student to go to the front or back of the room or into the doorway. Direct the class to resume working, and then approach the student.

Stay calm and in control of the situation. Identify the expectation that was broken or explain that his behavior was unacceptable. State the consequences and go on to explain the consequences if the behavior continues. Express your confidence in the student's ability to behave appropriately, have the student restate what is expected of him, and then return to his desk and continue working.

Consequences

Another aspect of responding non-coercively to inappropriate behavior is the implementation of consequences. Many times you will teach in classrooms where the permanent teacher has already established consequences for inappropriate behavior. Using these established consequences helps maintain continuity of the learning environment for students and means that you do not have to develop consequences of your own. In situations where you do have to devise and implement consequences, keep the following in mind:

- When possible, consequences should be a natural outcome or directly related to the behavior. For example, if a student is off task and does not finish her assignment, the consequence could be that she has to continue working on her assignment while the rest of the class is participating in a fun activity.

- Consequences and their implementation should not provide undue attention to misbehaving students.

- What is a negative consequence to one student may be reinforcing to another student. If the consequence does not change the behavior in time, change the consequence. See the fourth principle of human behavior.

- Consequences should be administered quickly and quietly without getting emotionally involved.

- All consequences should be reasonable, appropriate, and in accordance with district or school guidelines and policies.

Consequences should always be made known to students before they are administered. In other words, consequences should not be sprung on students out of nowhere after the behavior has already taken place.

Students need to know in advance what they can expect as a result of their behavior, both positive and negative, so they can make informed choices about how to behave. Consequences should be communicated to students as predetermined outcomes of behavior rather than threats. It is a good idea to discuss consequences in conjunction with explaining expectations for the classroom or particular activity.

Effective Discussion of Expectations and Consequences

Teacher: *"During today's science lesson, you will be using water and working with syringes at your desk. I expect you to use the syringes, water, and other materials appropriately as outlined in the activity. Anyone who uses these materials inappropriately will be asked to leave their group and observe the remainder of the activity in a seat away from the lab area."*

Teacher: *"Jordan, what is it that I expect during this activity?"*

Jordan: *"To use the syringes, water, and other materials correctly as outlined in the activity."*

Teacher: *"Shelley, what are the benefits of using these materials correctly?"*

Shelley: *"I can remain with my group and complete the activity."*

Teacher: *"That is right. What will be the consequences if someone uses the materials inappropriately, Tyrel?"*

Tyrel: *"He will be asked to leave the group and watch the rest of the activity from a seat away from the lab area."*

Responding Non-coercively to a Refusal to do Work

In some classrooms you may have a student or students who refuse to complete an assignment or participate in activities. Your first response should be recognition of students who are on task and positive encouragement for the noncompliant student. If, after you encourage the student to complete the assignment, she makes a statement such as, *"You can't make me,"* an appropriate strategy would be to acknowledge and restate. Disarm the student by acknowledging that she is correct, you cannot force the student, and then restate your expectations and consequences if they are not met.

Example: *"You're right, Daniela, I can't make you complete this task. I can, however, expect you to have it completed before recess. If it is not finished by then, you will have to take it home and work on it. I also expect you to remain quiet and not disrupt the other students who are choosing to complete the assignment at this time."*

It is important to note that many times a refusal to do work is an indication that students don't know how to complete the task. They would rather appear bad than stupid. If this is the case, you may need to restate the concept or provide extra assistance to the student. Emphasize what the student can do or has already accomplished and recognize student effort.

Responding Non-coercively to Inappropriate Language or Derogatory Remarks

Students, at times, may use obscene language or make a derogatory remark about you, another student, or the permanent teacher. In such situations it is important that you don't take the remarks personally. Respond to the behavior in a professional manner and don't let your emotions override your behavior management skills.

The classroom expectations and consequences established at the beginning of the day have provisions for dealing with this challenging situation – implement them! You might say something like, *"Ben, you chose to break the classroom rule regarding using proper language. What is the consequence?"*

The student should then state the consequence and it should be carried out. Do not ask the student why he said what he did (you don't really want to know), just acknowledge that the student chose to break a rule or behave inappropriately and implement an appropriate consequence. Dismiss the incident as quickly as possible and resume class work.

Responding Non-coercively to a Fight

Should you see two students yelling at each other or poised for a fight, respond quickly and decisively. Do not hesitate to get help from another teacher if needed.

Verbal jousting can usually be extinguished by a firm command as you move toward the problem saying, *"Stop this right now and take a quiet seat against the wall."* Your calm, authoritative voice combined with an instructive statement, will most often yield compliance to your directive.

If students are engaged physically, you must act quickly and with authority. Tell them to step back away from each other. Placing yourself between the students may stop the engagement, but can be dangerous for you. Do not get angry, excited, or show a lot of emotion – this compounds the situation. When given firm and instructive directions, students usually respond and comply as requested.

Responding Non-coercively to Threats

Threats are difficult to handle – the best strategy and response varies with each situation. However, should a student threaten you or another student, the most important thing you must do is stay calm and emotionally detached so you can evaluate and manage the situation professionally. It is also important to note that the school may have a policy on how to handle such situations. You may want to ask the neighboring teacher what you should do if you are ever in one of these situations.

Remember

Remember to punish at an individual student level rather than punishing the whole group. Punishing the entire class for the misbehavior of a student usually results in two negative outcomes. First, the student receives a lot of attention as he is singled out and recognized as the cause for the class consequences.

Second, any trust you had established with the remaining students is lost due to unfair actions. By correcting and applying consequences to an individual, that student receives direction and is not unduly recognized for his negative behavior.

Threat Strategy One: Acknowledge and Redirect

A threat is often the result of an emotional response. Ignoring the student will probably evoke more threats, and perhaps even aggression. Responding with threats of your own may accelerate the confrontation. The sooner the threat is acknowledged and the situation diffused, the better.

Once the student has calmed down, you can then direct her actions to something constructive. If you feel the student needs to discuss the situation, it is often wise to wait until after the lesson, later in the day, or refer the student to a school counselor so that emotional distance and perspective on the situation can be achieved.

> Example: *"I understand that you are very angry right now. However, I need you to sit down and begin completing page 112 in your math book. We will discuss the situation after lunch."*

Threat Strategy Two: Get Help!

If you feel that you or any of the students are in danger of physical harm, stay calm and immediately send a student to or call the office to elicit the help of a permanent teacher or principal. After help has arrived and the situation is under control, document the occurrence. Record what happened prior to the threat, what you said and did, what the student said and did, as well as the actions of anyone else involved in the situation.

Each of the strategies presented in this handbook assists teachers in remaining calm and in control. By implementing these strategies you will inspire respect and compliance; you will also demonstrate your ability to deal with the facts of reality and not emotions. These are two very important aspects of leadership in stressful situations.

Skill Five:
The ability to avoid being trapped.

There are seven traps in which educators, including substitute teachers, often get themselves caught. Once trapped, teachers lose some of their power to be effective educators. Recognizing and avoiding these traps helps you provide students with a better learning environment and avoid a lot of classroom management stress.

Trap One:
The Criticism Trap

Students require attention. Whether they get attention for good behavior or bad, they will get attention. The criticism trap refers to a situation where the more students are criticized for their inappropriate behavior, the more likely they are to behave inappropriately, in order to continue getting attention from the teacher.

Criticism or Negative Interactions

> Example: *"This generation, all you can do is listen to your mp3 players and text on your cell phones. You have no consideration for people in the same room as yourself."*

Remember

There are two words that can stop most protests from any students and let you take control of the situation. These words are "*I understand.*"

How to Avoid the Criticism Trap

By recognizing and providing reinforcement for appropriate behavior, the need for students to act out in order to get attention is virtually eliminated. As a general rule, teachers should never have more than one negative or critical interaction with a student for every eight positive interactions.

Positive Interactions

Example: *"I'm impressed with how hard some of you are working. Thank you for keeping cell phones away while you are working; it makes for a better learning environment."*

Trap Two:
The Common Sense Trap

The common sense trap is also known as the reasoning or logic trap. It is a situation where common sense, reasoning, and logic are used to try and persuade students to change their behavior. The reason this strategy is ineffective is that students neither learn anything new nor are offered reasonable incentive to change the behavior.

Getting Caught in the Common Sense Trap

Example: *"Nicki, let's go over this again. As I explained earlier, you should have your assignment completed by the end of class. Look at how much you have left to do. You keep telling me that you will finish in time, but unless you hurry up you never will. It's up to you to get it done. If you don't complete your assignments, you're going to have a lot of homework."*

How to Avoid the Common Sense Trap

Avoiding the common sense trap involves creating a positive environment where there are incentives to change and where positive consequences reinforce that change.

Avoiding the Common Sense Trap

Example: *"Nicki, you have done the first four problems right. However, I can see that you still have a lot of this assignment left to complete. In order to participate in the end of the day activity, you will need to hurry up and finish your work. I'll be back in a few minutes to see how you are doing."*

Trap Three:
The Questioning Trap

For the most part, questioning students about inappropriate behavior is useless and unproductive. There are three reasons for not questioning students about their behavior. First, you really don't want an answer — you want to change the behavior. Students can answer your questions and still not comply with the way you want them to behave. Second, one question usually leads to more pointless questions that accomplish nothing and waste educational time. Third, as you question a student about an inappropriate behavior, you are actually calling attention to and reinforcing the behavior you want to eliminate. This attention may strengthen the behavior and increase the probability that it will occur again.

Answers to Questions that Don't Change Behaviors

Teacher: *"Why did you hit Doug?"*

Student: *"I hit him because he is ugly and I was trying to fix his face. You see my long-term goal in life is to be a plastic surgeon and make ugly people beautiful. Since I haven't yet learned the precise surgical skills needed to do this, I am doing the best I can for a boy my age."*

In this (admittedly absurd) illustration, the student answered the question but it didn't accomplish anything. The teacher gained no new information to help in changing the problem behavior and has probably been induced to ask further useless, infuriating questions.

One Pointless Question Leads to Another

Teacher: *"Why aren't you working on your task?"*

Student: *"Because I don't want to."*

Teacher: *"Why don't you want to?"*

Student: *"It's stupid."*

Teacher: *"What's stupid about it?"* Etc.

How to Avoid the Questioning Trap

As tempting as it may be, don't ask students questions about their inappropriate behavior unless you really need the information to redirect the behavior. A better approach is to restate the expected behavior, have the student demonstrate an understanding of the expectation, then positively reinforce the expected behavior as was discussed in Skill Four: Responding Non-coercively to Inappropriate Behavior.

Trap Four: The Sarcasm Trap

Probably nothing lowers a student's respect for a teacher more than does the use of sarcasm. Belittling students with ridicule destroys a positive classroom environment and may prompt them to lash out with inappropriate remarks of their own. The use of sarcasm suggests that you, as the teacher, do not know any better way of interacting and sets the stage for similar negative interactions between students themselves.

Getting Caught in the Sarcasm Trap

Teacher: *"My, my aren't you a smart class? It looks like by age 12 you have all finally learned to find your own seats and sit down after the bell, and to think it only took you half of the morning to do it. I don't know if there is another class in the entire school as smart or quick as you guys."*

How to Avoid the Sarcasm Trap

Avoiding the sarcasm trap is easy: do not use sarcasm! Better ways of communicating with students are discussed throughout this chapter.

Communicating Without Sarcasm

Teacher: *"One of the expectations of this class is to be seated and ready to go to work when the bell rings. I appreciate those of you who were quietly seated when the bell rang today."*

Trap Five: The Despair and Pleading Trap

The despair and pleading trap involves making desperate pleas to students and asking them to "have a heart" and behave appropriately. Teachers often become their own worst enemies when they communicate to students that they feel inadequate and incapable of managing the classroom and need help.

There will be days when nothing you do seems to work. As tempting as it may be to confide your feelings of inadequacy and frustration to the students and plead for their help in solving the problem, don't do it. It rarely accomplishes the desired outcome. More often than not students will interpret your pleas as an indication that you have no idea what you are doing and the inappropriate behavior will accelerate rather than diminish.

What the Despair and Pleading Trap Sounds Like

Teacher: (With a distraught expression and hopeless voice) *"Come on, class, can't you do me a favor and just be quiet for the rest of class? I've tried everything I know to get you to behave and nothing has worked. What do you think I should do? How can I get you to be quiet?"*

Student: *"Don't ask me, you're the teacher!"*

How to Avoid the Despair and Pleading Trap

The best defense against the despair and pleading trap is a good offense. Come to the classroom prepared with several classroom management strategies. For some classes, positive verbal reinforcement will be enough to gain compliance. In others, you may need to introduce tangible reinforcers such as point systems, end of the day drawings, or special awards (see pages 55-58 for ideas). When you find that one strategy is not working with an individual or class, don't be afraid to try something else.

An Option to the Despair and Pleading Trap

Teacher: *"Between now and the end of class, I am going to be awarding points to groups who follow my instructions and are on task. At the end of class, the group with the most points will get to choose a reward."*

Trap Six:
The Threat Trap

Threats are just one step beyond despair and pleading on the scale of helplessness. The majority of threats are either inappropriate or unenforceable. They are typically hollow expressions of frustration that tell students that teachers are upset and at a loss of what to do. Unreasonable and out-of-control threats may sound intimidating, but if students choose to call your bluff you will lose control of the situation because you can't carry out the consequence you have established. You should never threaten consequences that are unenforceable or unreasonable.

Getting Caught in the Threat Trap

Teacher: *"If you don't sit down and be quiet right this minute, I'm going to call your parents and have them come and sit next to you for the rest of class!"*

How to Avoid the Threat Trap

The best way to avoid frustrating situations that may evoke threats is to formulate and state both expectations and appropriate consequences in advance. Then reinforce appropriate student behavior and administer established consequences as needed.

Avoiding the Threat Trap

Teacher: *"During this group activity, you are expected to remain in your seat and work quietly with other group members. Should you choose not to do this, you will not be allowed to participate with your group in the review game at the end of the activity."* Wait several minutes for students to comply. *"The members of group number three are doing an excellent job of staying in their seats and working quietly."*

Trap Seven:
The Physical and Verbal Force Trap

The use of physical and verbal force, except in instances where life or property is at risk, is absolutely inappropriate. It is far less appropriate than the behavior that it is intended to stop. Physical force in the classroom as a behavior management tool is not only unproductive and inappropriate, in many states it is also illegal.

Example of Physical Force

Teacher: *"I told you to sit down."* Teacher pushes student into his/her desk. *"Now stay there until class is over."*

Avoiding the Physical and Verbal Force Trap

Concentrate on restating the expectation in a proactive way, then have the student restate and demonstrate the expectation. Keep your cool, count to ten, walk to the other side of the room, do whatever it takes to keep from resorting to force.

The Seven Traps Conclusion

The use of any trap-related management strategy is evidence of an unprofessional, frantic, desperate, even drastic, attempt at managing student behavior. While trap-related strategies may result in initial student compliance, over time they are certain to backfire and result in the steady deterioration of the school and classroom environment.

Behavior Management Summary

By gaining an understanding of basic human behavior and utilizing the skills discussed in this chapter, you will be better prepared to more effectively manage the behavior of students in the classroom. Reviewing this chapter often will assist you as you continue to develop and expand your repertoire of classroom and behavior management skills.

Remember

Classroom and behavior management involves using techniques and implementing strategies that foster appropriate student behavior in the classroom.

Other Management Suggestions

1. Know the teacher next door. Introduce yourself so you can call on someone to answer questions about schedules or material for the class throughout the day.

2. When students need to go to the restroom or the library, send only one student at a time. When the first one returns, a second one may go.

3. If a student does not respond when you call her by name, you may suspect the students have changed seats. Tell them it is better if you have their correct names so the right student gets recognized because you are writing a list of students who are working.

4. Do not let students start any name calling or rudeness directed to other students. It is much easier to stop a verbal disagreement than pushing or fighting.

5. Try to be in the hall between classes. If the students see a teacher, they are less likely to behave inappropriately.

6. Have a couple of extra pens or pencils with you for students who have "forgotten" and would rather go to their lockers and walk the halls than be in class.

7. If you give a student a pen or pencil and would like it back, be sure to ask the student for his lunch card, or something of value that he will be sure to remember. Many students just forget that it isn't their pen.

8. Try to identify the names of one or two trustworthy students who will tell you the truth and help out in class.

9. Always keep students in class the full amount of time. Never let a class go early for lunch or the break unless the teacher for whom you are covering or the teacher next door says it is okay. Some schools have very strict rules about the number of students in the cafeteria/ hallways at a time.

10. Never let a student have a pen without an ink cartridge. It might be used as a spit ball thrower.

11. Establish your rules and expectations very clearly at the beginning of the day.

12. Students should always use the phone in the office, not the phone in the classroom.

13. It is not professional to discuss a teacher's class with others, especially with individuals not associated with school. You also should not discuss individual students or problems.

14. If you need to talk to someone about a problem, talk to the principal.

15. Be neat in your appearance.

16. Follow the lesson plans the teacher has left. Be prepared with fill in activities if there is extra time.

17. Correct all the students' work for the day, if possible.

18. Even though a few students can upset your plans, try to find out the names of students who have been good or helpful and let the teacher know about them as well.

19. Most students will respect your leadership, but there will be some who will question your plans or authority. It is better not to argue. Instead say, "*I know this may not be the way Mr. Smith does it, but this is the plan for today.*"

20. If you are not sure how the teacher wants an assignment done, ask another teacher or develop your own plan. Then be sure to leave a note for the permanent teacher explaining what you assigned.

21. Be assertive so students don't feel they can manipulate your decisions and authority. Use statements such as:

    "I need you to start reading now."

    "I don't need..."

22. Don't let students manipulate you by protesting or saying, *"We never do that!"* Calmly tell them, *"I understand, but today we will read aloud instead of silently."*

23. Walk around the room. Never sit at your desk, especially during independent work, or an exam. Students will be less likely to talk or cheat when you are close to them.

24. Don't let students wear hats during a test — they have been known to write answers on the brim.

25. Don't try to catch a student by grabbing an arm or clothes. The student could fall and you could twist his/her arm, or tear his/her clothes.

26. Don't let any student possess a knife or any weapon. Report suspected violators to the principal's office or send a reliable student to the office.

27. Do not touch the blood of a bleeding child. Use a napkin, towel, or a cloth to cover the cut. Whenever possible, have the student treat the injury until the proper individuals have been notified.

28. If a teacher has classroom sets that are used by the students, make sure they are all returned before the entire class leaves. It is easier to locate one book or calculator in a classroom of 30 than trying to find it in the whole school. Hopefully, the calculators or books are numbered and have been assigned in a given order so you know who has the missing book.

29. Don't make statements lightly—*students remember*!

30. Know and understand each school's policy for electronic devices so you can be consistent. Also note that you need to follow the same policies yourself.

Remember

Reinforcers strengthen behavior and punishers weaken behavior.

Classroom Management

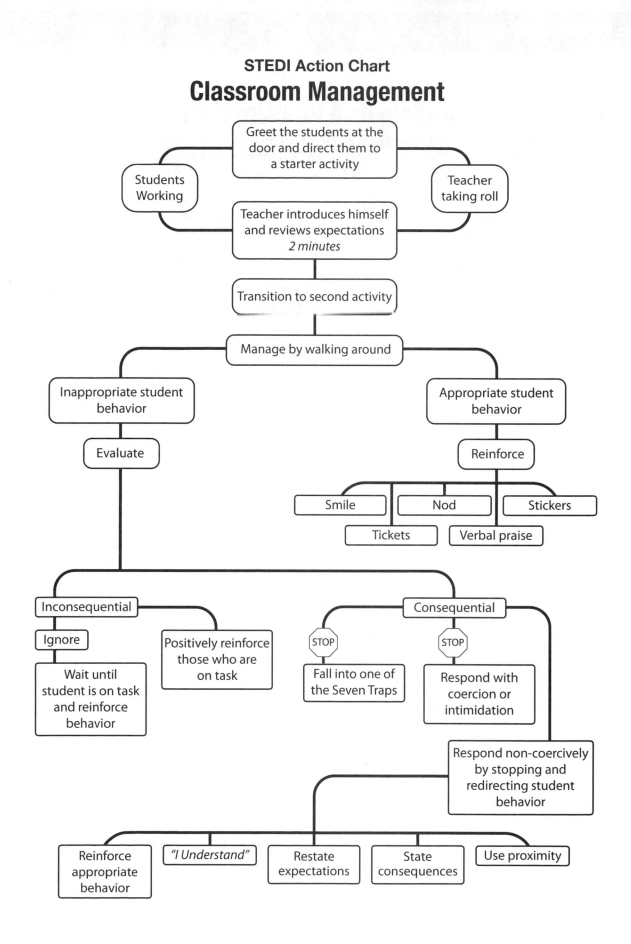

Anticipate a Problem Form

To become more positive and proactive in challenging situations, you must identify and practice positive interaction skills. This form will allow you to anticipate potential problem behaviors and how you can react to them. Remember: the behavior you are trying to control is your own.

Anticipate Problem	Positive, Proactive Response
I tend to scold or criticize students when they get noisy or out of control.	I'll reinforce a behaving student then look for an opportunity, 30 seconds to a minute later, to verbally reinforce the disruptive student for being on task.

Teaching Strategies

Chapter Two

Have you ever had difficulty following a lesson plan left by the permanent teacher, tried to lineup a class of thirty active second graders, or taken an assignment to teach a foreign language with fear and trepidation?

This chapter on Teaching Strategies is filled with tips and suggestions from the files of experienced substitutes and permanent teachers to help you succeed at all levels of substitute teaching. It includes strategies for presenting the permanent teacher's lesson plans:

- Brainstorming

- Concept Mapping

- K-W-L

- Cooperative Learning

- Questioning

- Effective Implementation of Audio/Visual Materials

This chapter also includes information about creating a *SubPack* as well as suggested items for the *SubPack*.

For additional information regarding Teaching Strategies, visit:

www.stedi.org

Brainstorming

Brainstorming is an essential part of teaching creativity and problem-solving processes that form the basis for active learning. With younger children, it makes sense to compare a brainstorm to a rainstorm.

> *Can you feel and count the individual drops of rain in a rainstorm when the rain begins to fall?* (Yes)
>
> *As the storm gets bigger and bigger, can you count the drops of rain?* (No)
>
> *A brainstorm is like that too, only we are going to use our creative minds to think of many, varied, and unusual ideas; so many that we will hardly be able to write them down quickly enough.*

There are four simple rules that help make the brainstorming process a peaceful and orderly one. Teach these "DOVE" rules to the students:

D Don't judge others' ideas — evaluation comes later.

O Original and unconventional ideas are encouraged.

V Volume of ideas — as many as possible in time limit.

E Everyone participates.

It is very common for students to run out of ideas in a short amount of time. This is called "hitting the wall." Help students keep thinking — the most interesting and unusual ideas often come after the immediate and obvious ones have been expressed. You may have a student read their list in order to help others start thinking of new ideas. Remind students that it is okay to "piggyback" on someone else's ideas. Often a really unique idea from one person can spark another good idea from someone else.

It is important in brainstorming to limit the time. A shorter time limit is better than one that is too long. One to three minutes is usually about right, occasionally up to five minutes might be needed. It is better to start with a short time and extend the activity than to have the students lose interest.

Brainstorming can be very useful when teaching students about creativity. Brainstorming new and crazy uses for an object teaches students to be flexible in their thinking. The following examples work well:

- Brainstorm uses for a pencil.

- Brainstorm uses for a set of keys.

- Brainstorm all of the things that would be in the perfect classroom.

Brainstorming at the beginning of a lesson is a good way to introduce the lesson and assess what students know about the topic, as well as being a method of channeling their thinking in a specific direction.

Depending on the topic of the lesson, brainstorm attributes or facts that relate to the lesson:

- Brainstorm things that are red (or read).

    . . .things in your home that are man-made, things that are natural.

. . .things in the classroom that are geometric shapes.

. . .things that live in the ocean, names of birds or flowers, insects, folktales, etc.

Brainstorming is also very effective as one of the steps in problem-solving and solution-finding situations:

- What problems might you have if you came home from school and were locked out of the house?

- What might happen if an earthquake destroyed your city?

- What are a variety of ways that you can prepare for an exam?

- What are some things you can say to friends who want you to smoke, drink alcohol, or take drugs?

Brainstorming can also be used to help children evaluate an idea. For example, brainstorm all of the possible consequences:

- What if a light bulb that lasted 20 years was invented?

- What if the sun did not shine for a year?

- What if students were required to wear school uniforms?

- What if school buses were allowed to have advertising on them?

- What if you ran for school president and won?

- What if your mother let you eat all of the junk food you wanted?

After many ideas have been generated, use those ideas to advance the objectives of the lesson. For example, if you brainstormed the consequences of eating all of the junk food you wanted, a lesson on nutrition might follow.

Evaluation of brainstormed ideas should not happen during the brainstorming process. If someone says *"That won't work"* or *"That's a stupid idea,"* then ideas are squelched and some students will stop participating. If evaluation is a step you want to use, it comes later after all ideas have been freely given.

Concept Mapping

Like brainstorming, concept mapping (webbing) can be used to introduce a topic. It can also be used to evaluate what students have learned at the end of a lesson.

As an introductory exercise, concept mapping provides you with information regarding what the students already know. You won't waste time covering the material they are already familiar with and can concentrate your efforts on presenting new information.

As a follow-up activity, concept mapping illustrates the learning that has taken place. It is fascinating to compare pre-lesson concept maps with post-lesson concept maps. Both you and the students will be amazed at how much they have learned.

Example of a Concept Map:

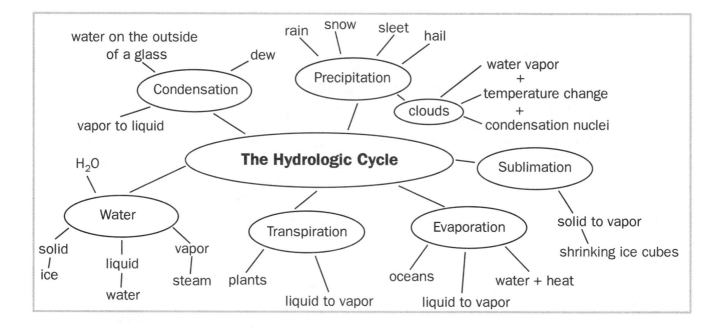

Concept mapping usually involves placing a word or idea in the middle of the board or on a piece of paper. Students then share what they know or associate with this concept. The information volunteered by the students is recorded with lines drawn to show how different concepts are related to one another. Concept maps can either be developed by the entire class, in small groups, or on an individual basis.

Concept mapping is also an effective method of reviewing information. It requires students to synthesize information they have read, heard, or observed and restate it in a concise manner using key words and terms that they understand. Once students have identified what they know in a concept map, another effective exercise is to have them incorporate examples and applications of the information into their map.

Other uses for concept mapping include organizing term papers, assignments, debates, and books. Once developed, prioritize the flow of the topics.

Both brainstorming and concept mapping can be used with any topic at any grade level. In either exercise, it is imperative that you, as the teacher, cultivate a risk-free class environment where students are not afraid to share their thoughts and ideas.

K-W-L Chart

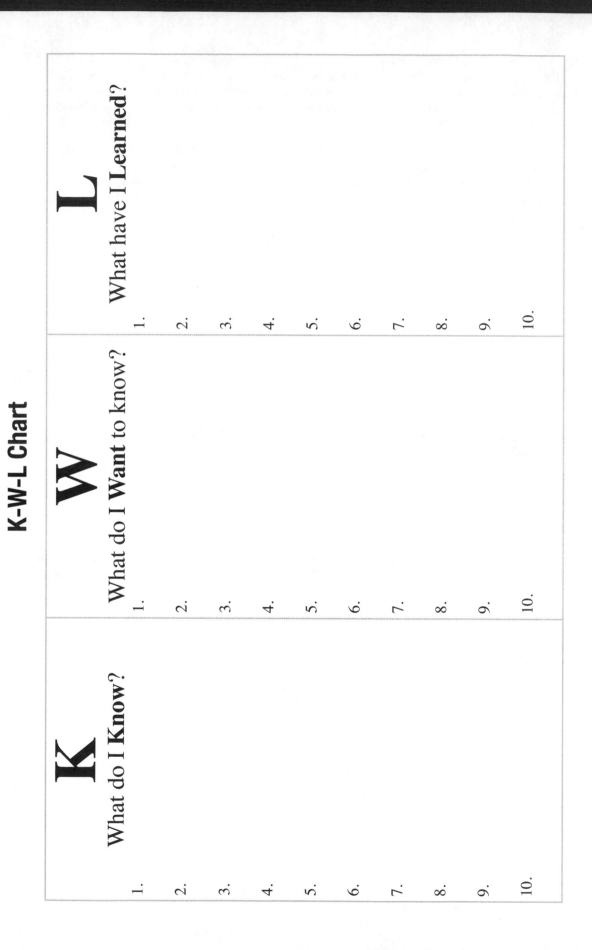

K
What do I **Know**?

1.
2.
3.
4.
5.
6.
7.
8.
9.
10.

W
What do I **Want** to know?

1.
2.
3.
4.
5.
6.
7.
8.
9.
10.

L
What have I **Learned**?

1.
2.
3.
4.
5.
6.
7.
8.
9.
10.

K-W-L

A major challenge of substitute teaching, particularly in the upper grades, is trying to teach a subject you know absolutely nothing about. One method of providing a meaningful learning experience in such a situation is the utilization of a K-W-L chart. K-W-L stands for:

- "What do I Know?"

- "What do I Want to know?"

- "What have I Learned?"

A K-W-L chart provides an outline for having students teach you. As you are being taught, the students will be teaching each other, and clarifying concepts in their own minds.

A lesson using K-W-L begins by the teacher listing the letters K, W, and L across the top of the board. Under the appropriate letter write, *"What do I know?" "What do I want to know?"* and *"What have I learned?"* Generated by the students, the teacher lists facts that students know about the subject in the first column. In the second column, the teacher lists things students want to know or understand. A brief look at a student textbook will help generate "want to know" topics and ideas that students are capable of addressing. Students are then asked to help answer and explain the items listed in the "W" column. Encouraging students to refer to their textbooks and other resources to answer your questions helps ensure that correct principles are being taught and explained.

At the end of the time period or lesson, the students and the teacher complete the final column, listing what they have learned during the class, with students checking to make sure the "learned" information is correct.

An example of a K-W-L chart used for learning about volcanoes:

K What do I **Know**?	W What do I **Want** to know?	L What have I **Learned**?
1. Lava comes out of volcanoes. 2. There are volcanoes in Hawaii. 3. Volcanoes erupt. 4. The lava from volcanoes is hot. 5. Volcanoes can be dangerous.	1. What is lava? 2. Where does lava come from? 3. Where are most of the volcanoes in the world? 4. Why do volcanoes erupt? 5. etc.	1. Lava is melted rock. 2. When lava is still under ground, it is called magma. 3. etc.

An adaptation of this teaching method is to have students complete individual K-W-L charts (see page 32). This works well with assignments such as reading science chapters or watching videos. Before the activity, students write down what they know and what they want to/think they will learn during the activity. At the end of the activity they complete the third column. A class discussion of the information students list in the third column helps clarify any confusing points and provides a review of the material covered.

Cooperative Learning

Many teaching strategies and activities call for students to work together in small groups. This is often referred to as "cooperative learning." In cooperative learning, the teacher acts as a facilitator rather than a presenter. Students learn as they interact with and teach each other.

Outlined below are instructions for a simplified version of cooperative learning developed by Dr. Carolyn Andrews-Beck.

1. Group students. Have students count off or form groups based on the seating arrangement. Do not let students self-select groups. Keep the groups small, usually between two and five students per group.

2. State the objective and instructions for the group work, then have students do the following:

   A. Circle – Arrange themselves in a small compact group so that they can all see everyone else's face.

   B. Introductions – Have students state their name to be sure everyone in the group knows each other.

   C. State the assigned task – *"The job is . . . ." "We will know we have finished when . . . ."*

3. Set a time limit for the activity.

4. Have students begin working together toward accomplishing the objective outlined in step two.

Assigning roles to students is also helpful in facilitating learning. Giving each member of the group a specific assignment guarantees their involvement. Students who are actively involved are more likely to learn.

Common Role Assignments

- **Director, Captain, Leader, or Manager:** The group leader responsible for keeping the group members on-task and working toward the objective.

- **Recorder:** Records information for the group's activities, fills out worksheets, or prepares written material from information provided by the group.

- **Materials Manager:** Responsible for obtaining and returning equipment, materials, and supplies necessary for the activity.

- **Procedure Director:** Reads instructions, explains procedures, makes sure the activity is being carried out correctly.

- **Cleanup Leader:** Supervises the cleanup of the group's area at the end of the activity or project.

Setting Up a Cooperative Learning Activity in the Classroom

1	Group Students	Teacher: Starting with Cherie and going up and down the rows please count off one through five. Cherie: One Next Student: Two Next Student: Three, Etc. Teacher: I would like all of the "ones" to bring a pencil and paper and form a circle by the door. I would like all of the "twos" to bring a pencil and paper and form a circle by the bulletin board in the back of the room. I would like all of the "threes"... Please move to your assigned location and form a circle now.
2	State the Objective and Instructions for the Group	Teacher: In your groups you are going to make up a two minute skit about one of the reasons we have listed on the board why young people should not start smoking. After you have made up the skit and had a chance to practice it, each group will present their skit for the rest of the class. Who can tell me what the assignment is? Noah? Noah: Use one of the reasons for not smoking on the board to make up a skit for the class. Teacher: How will you know when your group has finished? Trish? Trish: After we have practiced our play and are ready to present it to the class.
3	Set a Time Limit	Teacher: You will have 15 minutes to make up and practice your skit before we begin the class presentations.
4	Establish Roles and have Students Begin Working	Teacher: Identify the person in your group who is wearing the most blue. This person will be the skit director, they are responsible for selecting a reason from the board and making sure everyone has a part in the skit. The person sitting to the right of the director will be the time monitor who makes sure your skit isn't more than 2 minutes long and that your group is ready to present in 15 minutes. Everyone else will help develop the play and be actors. Are there any questions? . . . OK, you may begin.

Questioning

Good questions lead to good thinking — and good thinking leads to learning.

Good questions should:

- Be developed logically and sequentially

- Be adapted to students' abilities

- Cause students to think — not merely recite

- Encourage students to ask questions

Good questions will:

- Help keep students on-task and focused

- Help determine skill and knowledge levels

- Promote higher level thinking

- Encourage broader student participation

A Basic Rule . . . Ask, Pause, Call

Too often, good questions fail to be valuable because:

- Teachers don't allow enough time for the questions to be answered. Teachers frequently ask a question and then go ahead and answer it themselves — students quickly learn that they do not have to think or respond.

- Teachers fail to direct their questions to specific students. They give a question to the entire class that often makes it scary or "uncool" for any one student to volunteer to answer.

Using the *Ask, Pause, Call* method will increase the effectiveness of your questions.

ASK	A well thought out question to the class
PAUSE	Long enough for students to think about a response
CALL	On a specific student to respond to the question

Pauses Cause Them to Think

The 1st pause gives the entire class time to formulate an answer

The 2nd pause provides the student time to verbalize a response

The 3rd pause encourages the student and/or class to really "get into" the question

Do

✓ Be positive. Focus on what they DO know.

✓ Wait until the class is listening before asking a question.

✓ Ask questions in a clear direct manner.

✓ Expect an answer.

Don't

✗ Try to rush an answer (or simply answer it yourself).

✗ Use discouraging language (wrong, not true, incorrect, etc.).

✗ Call on the same students (give others a chance).

✗ Automatically repeat questions (teach them to listen the first time).

Questions to Promote Higher Level Thinking*

Effective questions keep students thinking and involved in the learning process. Questions range from simple knowledge to complex evaluation in the following order: knowledge, comprehension, application, analysis, synthesis, and evaluation. Each level involves a higher level of thinking and thus a greater degree of student involvement with the subject matter.

Higher level thinking questions can be used to help stimulate class discussions and give greater meaning to information or ideas students are studying. All students, despite their level, can respond to higher level thinking questions. By asking the right type of questions, you can help students progress from merely recalling facts and figures, to successfully applying and evaluating new information in a variety of situations.

Knowledge Level Questions

Knowledge level questions ask students to recognize, recall, and state facts, terms, basic concepts, and answers.

Sample Knowledge Level Questions

- Name the characters in the story.

- What is the capital of Wyoming?

- Define the word condensation.

- List the numbers between 23 and 45.

Comprehension Level Questions

Comprehension is the ability to understand concepts at a basic level. The student knows the meaning of the information, but does not relate or apply it to other situations.

Sample Comprehension Level Questions

- List three examples of plants.

- Describe the setting of the story.

- Classify the characters in the story as good guys or bad guys.

- Compare a cup of milk with a cup of water.

Application Level Questions

Application is the ability to use learned knowledge in particular and concrete situations. The student can apply rules, principles, and concepts in new and appropriate contexts.

Sample Application Level Questions

- Why is the sun important to life on Earth?

- Using what you have learned, how would you solve the following problem?

- How would schools be different without electricity?

- How much money would you have if you saved a dollar a day for seven years?

* Adapted from Bloom's Taxonomy, Dr. Benjamin Bloom.

Analysis Level Questions

Analysis is the ability to breakdown a concept into its component parts.

Sample Analysis Level Questions

- – Why did the boy in the story give away his gold coin?

- – Draw the parts of a flower.

- – Explain the differences between a raindrop and a snowflake?

- – Which characters in the film were necessary for the plot?

Synthesis Level Questions

Synthesis is the ability to put together elements or parts to form a whole. The student arranges and combines pieces to form a pattern, structure, or idea that was not clearly evident before.

Sample Synthesis Level Questions

- – How could you change the characters' personalities to make them more likable?

- – Design a new invention for . . .

- – Organize the books you have read this year into three categories.

- – Prepare a shopping list for Thanksgiving dinner.

Evaluation Level Questions

Evaluation is the ability to judge the value of materials, methods, or ideas. This level of thinking requires the highest level of intellectual functioning. It requires students to not only understand the material but to also make a judgment based on this understanding.

Sample Evaluation Level Questions

- – Should students be allowed to bring cell phones to school?

- – Would you recommend this book/film to a friend? Why?

- – How would the discovery of life on another planet affect the U.S. Space Program?

- – Does the protection of an endangered species justify the loss of job opportunities?

Verbs Often Used to Promote Higher Level Thinking

Level of Thinking	Typical Verbs Used		Example of Teacher Questions
Knowledge	define repeat label name	draw record identify list	**Name** the author of the book.
Comprehension	classify contrast explain give examples	compare translate summarize	**Compare** the weather today with the weather yesterday.
Application	apply complete illustrate solve predict	calculate demonstrate practice use show	**Complete** the sentence using a vocabulary word from the lesson.
Analysis	analyze discuss explain inspect	classify divide infer	**Explain** why it is important to have classroom rules.
Synthesis	arrange construct design generalize plan categorize	combine create develop organize predict rearrange	**Predict** what would happen if a law was passed that made commercials on television illegal.
Evaluation	assess estimate judge rate test justify	critique evaluate rank recommend value	What requirements for employing a new teacher would you **recommend** to the principal?

Effective Implementation of Audio Visual Materials

Many times the lesson plans left by a permanent teacher will include the presentation of audio visual materials such as videos, DVD's, CD's, interactive white boards, and LCD projectors. While audio visual presentations do not thoroughly captivate students as they once did, they can still be an effective means of presenting content material. The key to encouraging learning during the presentation is to involve students as active, rather than passive, viewers. Listed below are five strategies for involving students and conducting effective audio visual presentations.

Keep the Lights On

A darkened classroom is an invitation for problems. As it dulls your mental alertness, it will embolden students to try and get away with things they would never attempt in the light. A well-lit classroom is consistent with the traditional learning environment and makes it possible for students to take notes or complete assignments concurrent with the presentation.

Stand in the Back

Another critical aspect of audio visual presentations is what you as the teacher are doing. The students' job is to watch the presentation, your job is to monitor student behavior and learning during the presentation. Sitting behind the teacher's desk correcting papers or reading a book is not an effective means of doing this. Consider standing at the back of the room. Because you are already on your feet, you can easily move to problem areas in the classroom and, with proximity, stop problems before they start. By positioning yourself behind the students, they cannot see if you are paying attention directly to them; therefore, they must assume that you are and behave accordingly.

K-W-L

Use individual K-W-L charts such as the one found on page 32. Before the presentation, have students complete the first two columns indicating what they already know about the topic and what they think they will learn. As the video or filmstrip is presented, students write down information they are learning in the third column. After the presentation, have students share what they listed in the third column to create a comprehensive class list of the information that was presented.

Concept Mapping

Assign students to take notes during the presentation in the form of concept maps. Start by listing the topic of the video or filmstrip in the center of the page. As the presentation progresses, they should jot down key words and bits of information they are learning (see the example of a concept map on page 30). At the end of the presentation, have students turn in their concept maps for teacher evaluation or give a short test on the information, allowing students to refer to the concept maps they constructed.

Question Exchange

Either during or after the presentation, have students write three questions that meet the following two criteria:

1. the answer to the question must have been given during the presentation,

2. the student writing the question must know the answer.

At the conclusion of the presentation, students exchange questions and try to answer them.

How Should I Do That?

When substitute teaching, you are expected to cover the material outlined in the permanent teacher's lesson plan. However, sometimes lesson plan instructions are general and very nonspecific with regard to lesson presentation. Here are several techniques for presenting lesson plans that will cover the material in a positive and creative way.

Lesson Plan: *Have students read chapter 18 and answer questions.*

1. *Pre-test and Post-test*: Ask students to guess what will be covered before they start reading. Share ideas aloud and write down five facts or ideas as predictions. Afterward, conduct a post-test by checking the accuracy of the predictions.

2. *Togetherness*: Read the task out loud with students to find the answers. By making the task a class activity, you promote class cooperation.

3. *Group Effort*: Divide the class into groups and ask each group to report on part of the reading. This method is best used with material that does not require continuity to be meaningful.

4. *Quiz Board*: Give the assignment and tell the students that you will stop 15 minutes before the end of the class and establish a quiz board. Appoint three to five students or select volunteers to be members of the board. Ask them to come to the front of the room. The rest of the students pose questions to these students about the day's reading. After a certain number of questions have been answered, a new board may be selected. This technique works well for review. An added advantage is that you need not know the subject well in order to handle it.

Lesson Plan: *Have the class write a composition about X Y Z.*

1. *Sentence Starters*: To make any topic more meaningful, encourage students to relate to it personally. One way is to write sentence starters that use the students' natural speech pattern, such as, *"I wish," "I like," "I'm glad I'm allowed to," "I think."*

2. *Whole Class*: If the students are assigned to write a story, suggest that they first decide on a cast of characters, a setting, a time, etc., as a class. By doing the groundwork together, the students will be "into" the story before they lift a pencil.

3. *Brainstorm*: If the assignment is an essay, consider using a brainstorming technique. Ask students to say whatever comes to mind about the topic and write their ideas on the board in some quick, abbreviated form. When everyone has had a chance to study the list, students can begin to write using whatever brainstorming ideas they wish.

4. *Free Association*: Whatever the topic, propose that the students write free association word lists about it. Tell them to start with the given word, such as "freedom," "pets," or "winter," and then add up to ten other words that immediately come to mind about the key word. Now the students can write their own compositions.

5. *Clarify Values*: Before students start to write, initiate a values clarification exercise that will help students relate an abstract subject to their own lives. For example, if the topic is "conservation of electricity," have the students start by listing five electrical gadgets or appliances they use that they could do without. Record their answers on the board. From this specific exercise, the students can move on to the broader issue.

Lesson Plan: *The class has a test tomorrow. Have them review.*

1. *Games*: Try a game format for drill material, such as spelling, number facts, state capitals, and vocabulary. Use familiar games like tic-tac-toe, Jeopardy, baseball, etc.

2. *Model Tests*: Have pairs or small groups of students make up model tests. Assign one group true and false questions, another multiple choice questions, etc. Spend the last part of the class going over the questions. Ask each group to read their test while the rest of the class gives the answers.

3. *Students as Teachers*: Have the students teach each other:

   A. Give five minutes for students to write five to ten things they know about the material covered without opening their books or using their notes.

   B. Each student compares his/her list with the student next to him/her. In pairs, have them add additional items during the next ten minutes.

   C. Have the students remain in pairs and open their books and notes. Add to their lists using their notes and text during the next ten minutes.

   D. Allow each pair of students to join an adjacent pair. The groups of four compare their lists and add additional information during the next ten minutes. Encourage students to discuss and clarify their knowledge.

   E. In a full class discussion, have students consider all known knowledge. Allow students to ask questions of one another and have knowledgeable students clarify misunderstandings.

Lesson Plan: *Discuss topics A B C with class.*

1. *Students take Lead*: Have a student lead the discussion, or call on two or three students.

2. *Speak their Minds*: Have the class spill out all sorts of ideas related to the discussion topic. Do not judge the ideas — anything goes! Just encourage the students to speak their minds. After about five minutes, start the discussion again, this time arranging their ideas in a more orderly fashion.

3. *Debate*: If the topic is controversial, divide the class into sections, each representing a special-interest group. During the discussion, each group will give its point of view on the subject.

Lesson Plan: *Show the film or filmstrip, then discuss.*

1. *Pre-test and Post-test*: To heighten student interest in the audio visual materials, use the before and after technique. Introduce the activity with a comment such as, "If you were making a movie about crocodiles, earthquakes, or China, what would you include?" As they watch, have students check their lists against the film. How does the film compare to the students' expectations?

2. *Questions*: As students watch, have them write down three questions that are answered in the film or video, then discuss the questions with the class after the presentation.

SubPack

The number one trait of a successful substitute teacher is having a collection of resources in a *SubPack*. To be confident and prepared, a good substitute teacher will enter a classroom with a set of tools, much as a builder would enter a construction site. No one wants to begin a lesson plan and then discover that a simple item, such as a pair of scissors, cannot be located. Likewise, when a lesson plan receives a "boring" response from students, introducing a motivator idea from a *SubPack* can bring a renewed enthusiasm for assignments.

The specific contents of your *SubPack* will be personalized to fit your teaching style and the grade levels you teach most often; however, contents are generally categorized as (1) classroom supplies, (2) personal and professional items, (3) rewards and motivators, and (4) activity materials. Page 45 lists the suggested items that are often used.

SubPack Container

When selecting a container for your *SubPack*, choose one that is easy to carry, large enough to hold all of your supplies, has a secure lid or closure device, and looks professional.

SubPack Contents

Most of the suggested *SubPack* contents listed on page 45 are self-explanatory. The following is a brief explanation of some of the not-so-obvious items:

> A Clipboard is one of the most important items in your *SubPack*.

Clipboard: Carrying a clipboard provides quick access to a seating chart, the roll, and anecdotal records, as well as creates a sense of authority.

Disposable Gloves & Plastic Bags: Whenever you encounter blood or bodily fluids you should wear disposable gloves to help safeguard against many of today's medical concerns. A plastic bag can be used in an emergency when you must dispose of items exposed to blood or bodily fluids.

Estimation Jar: Estimation jars are great motivators for students to behave appropriately and complete assignments efficiently so they can earn guessing tickets (see page 56).

Mystery Box: Place a common item such as a toothbrush or piece of chalk in a small box. Allow students to lift, shake, smell, and otherwise observe the box throughout the day. At the end of the day, have students guess what is in the box and award a small prize to the student who identifies the contents correctly.

Newspaper: A newspaper can be used as the basis for a story starter, spelling review, current events discussion, and a host of other activities (see page 176).

Props: A puppet, magic trick, or even a set of juggling props can capture student interest. Props provide great motivation to complete assignments in order to participate in, learn more about, or see additional prop-related activities.

Tangrams: Tangrams are geometric shapes that can be used as filler activities, as well as instructional material to teach shapes and geometry (see pages 109-114).

Tickets: Tickets are a great way to reward students for appropriate behavior. Students can use tickets to enter an end-of-the-day drawing or redeem them for special privileges and prizes (see pages 57).

Suggested Contents
For Your SubPack

Classroom Supplies

- ❑ Rubber bands
- ❑ Markers and/or colored pencils
- ❑ Ball-point pens (red, blue, black)
- ❑ Pencils and small pencil sharpener
- ❑ Transparent and masking tape
- ❑ Crayons
- ❑ Scissors
- ❑ Glue sticks
- ❑ Paper clips, staples, a small stapler
- ❑ Post-it Notes® (various sizes and colors)
- ❑ Ruler
- ❑ File folders
- ❑ Calculator
- ❑ Lined and blank paper
- ❑ Name badge materials (address labels or masking tape will work)

Rewards/Motivators

- ❑ Tickets
- ❑ Certificates
- ❑ Stickers
- ❑ Mystery Box
- ❑ Stamp and Ink Pad
- ❑ Privilege Cards (get a drink, first in line, etc.)

Personal/Professional

- ❑ Clipboard
- ❑ Substitute teacher report
- ❑ District information (maps, addresses, phone numbers, policies, starting times, etc.)
- ❑ Coffee mug or water bottle
- ❑ Whistle (useful for P.E. and playground duty)
- ❑ Small package of tissues
- ❑ Snack (granola bar, pretzels, etc.)
- ❑ Small bag or coin purse for keys, drivers license, money (enough for lunch), and other essential items. Do not bring a purse or planner with a lot of money, checks, and credit cards (there may not be a secure place to keep it).
- ❑ Band-aids
- ❑ Small sewing kit with safety pins
- ❑ Disposable gloves and small plastic bags

Activity Materials

- ❑ The Substitute Teacher Handbook
- ❑ Tangrams
- ❑ Bookmarks
- ❑ "Prop" (puppet, stuffed animal, etc.)
- ❑ Picture and activity books
- ❑ A number cube or dice for games
- ❑ Estimation jar
- ❑ Newspaper
- ❑ Timer or stopwatch

Verbal Guidance*

Throughout the day a teacher will need to convey instructions, warnings, directions, reprimands, and encouragement to students. Of the many ways to convey these messages, the most common is by speaking directly to the student or students. To be most effective, verbal guidance should be brief, firm, and positive.

SAY:	DO NOT SAY:
Talk in a quiet voice.	Don't shout.
Use both hands when you climb.	You will fall if you don't watch out.
Climb down the ladder.	Don't jump.
Keep the puzzle on the table.	Don't dump the puzzle pieces on the floor.
Turn the pages carefully.	Don't tear the book.
Be sure the ladder is safe.	Be careful, you might fall.
Sit on your chair.	Don't rock in your chair.
Time to go inside.	Are you ready to go inside?

You will find it necessary to acquire techniques that will match your personality. However, the following general rules should be observed.

DO

1. Speak in a calm, kind voice.

2. Speak directly to the student, do not call across the room.

3. Speak in short, meaningful sentences that the student can understand.

4. Try to express your request in a positive way.

5. Keep your voice and facial expressions pleasant.

DO NOT

1. Make fun of the student.

2. Give students a choice if they cannot have one.

3. Compare one student with another, "Look at how many questions Susan has completed."

* Adapted from "Guidance of the Young Child", by Louise M. Langford.

Gifted and Talented Students

Recognizing Gifted and Talented Students

Gifted and talented students usually have above average ability, a high level of task commitment, and highly developed creativity. Many students will excel in one of these areas. Truly gifted students will excel in all three.

You may have a gifted student if s/he...

___ has a vocabulary noticeably above his/her peers

___ is a voracious reader — usually more advanced content

___ has a well-developed sense of humor — gets jokes peers don't understand

___ is intrinsically motivated — works hard with or without teacher approval

___ has a personal standard of quality — independent of others' work

___ thinks at a higher/independent level — often appears to "day dream"

___ is able to go beyond basic lesson concepts — expand, elaborate, and synthesize

Often gifted and talented students seem to be round pegs in square holes. They do not necessarily fit the mold of an "ideal student." They may become bored with class or deeply involved with something unrelated to the lesson. Their friendships and alliances include a need for intellectual peers (often older students or adults) and chronological peers (kids their same age). Moreover, their attention span does not always coincide with the standard time allotments for classroom lessons and activities.

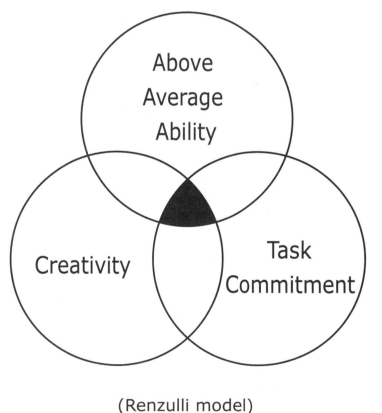

(Renzulli model)

Some Do's and Don'ts When Working with Gifted and Talented Students

Do

✓ Enrichment and extension activities

✓ Puzzles and games

✓ Alternative projects (collages and posters are good)

✓ Comparisons, similes, and analogies

Don't

✗ Make them do things they've already mastered

✗ Give them busywork if/when they finish early

✗ Force them to always work with slower students

✗ Have them memorize, recite, and copy just to fill time

Accelerated

Remember

Some of the activities and lessons in Chapter Six have suggested accommodations listed. Use these accommodations for accelerated learners as appropriate. These accommodations are only suggestions. Think about other possibilities that could be used as you work with diverse learners.

Multiculturalism

The United States is home to a diverse population. No other nation enjoys the rich and varied cultural heritages found within our borders. Since this diversity is reflected in our schools, it only makes sense that our instructional methods should benefit from and be sensitive to the special abilities and needs of people from different groups.

Making your classroom multicultural friendly

- Discuss various groups' heritage, values, and practices/rituals.

- Use local role models from various groups as guest speakers and advisors.

- Plan activities that incorporate materials/objects that reflect various customs and cultures.

- Honor each student's unique background/heritage and how it enhances society's characteristics.

- Encourage discussion of current topics and how they relate to various groups within our society.

- Present stories and/or artifacts from different groups as a basis for various activities.

- Write stories, sing songs, draw pictures, or play games depicting various cultural influences.

- Showcase different groups' contributions and/or participation involving historical events, literary works, art, music, medicine, sports, and industry.

General definitions of terms

- **Ethnic Diversity**: Similarities and differences of groups of people classified according to common traits, values, and heritage. Examples may include food, clothing, music, and rituals.

- **Racial Diversity**: Similarities and differences of groups of individuals with certain physical or genetic features. These features may include skin color, body type, and facial features.

- **Cultural Diversity**: Similarities and differences of groups and/or individuals that align themselves with others based on common racial and/or ethnic characteristics or affiliations. Typical associations often include language, customs, and beliefs.

Alternative Learning Styles

We are all different. We look different and we act differently. We also learn differently. Unfortunately, we tend to teach students as if they were all the same. We all know of people that can't bounce a ball, but can do math story problems in their head — or the person with two left feet that can sing like a bird. No one can do everything, but most of us do excel in one or more areas. It is in these areas that we learn best. By using a variety of teaching methods and activities that incorporate these abilities, we can increase students' ability to stay on-task, pay attention, and enjoy learning.

Here are some main categories of skills and abilities with a few examples of each:

Verbal/Linguistic

Reading/writing

Vocabulary

Speech

Logical/Mathematical

Calculation

Formulas

Codes

Visual/Spatial

Imagination

Patterns/designs

Sculpture/painting

Body/Kinesthetic

Dance

Drama

Sports/games

Interpersonal

Group work

Empathy

Cooperation

Intrapersonal

Self-reflection

Thinking strategies

Reasoning skills

Musical

Rhythms

Sounds/tones

Singing/playing

Using new ways to teach "old" materials might appeal to your students' particular abilities and interests, Here are some ideas.

Math

- Compose a song to help remember a formula
- "Illustrate" the problem on the board
- Solve the problem as a group

Language

- Act out the story
- Write key words using a code
- Listen with eyes closed

History

- Reenact a battle
- Write a commercial for that time period
- Do a mock interview of an historical person

Physical Education

- Research and play an historic game
- Keep score using Roman numerals or fractions
- Skip or hop instead of running

Running out of ideas?

Ask your students how they can turn a writing assignment into a math assignment, or how they can incorporate art into a soccer game. You'll be surprised a the results and your students will enjoy the challenge.

Advice from Students

- Trust us.

- Be fair to everyone.

- Punish only the troublemakers.

- Make learning fun.

- Give us our assignment and let us go to work.

- Allow study time in class.

- Show concern and be willing to help with assignments.

- If I raise my hand, do not ignore me.

- You can be both strict and nice.

- Do not shout.

- Be straightforward with us.

- Be organized.

- Speak quietly and be patient.

- Give us something to work toward.

- Leave your personal life at home.

- Think positively of every student.

- Speak clearly.

- Be reasonable in your expectations.

- Have a sense of humor.

- Follow through with promises and consequences.

101 Ways to Say "Good Job!"

Everyone knows a little praise goes a long way in the classroom. Whether it is spoken or written at the top of a student's paper, praise reinforces good behavior and encourages quality work. But the same traditional phrases used over and over can sound rehearsed and become ineffective. Here are 101 variations of ways to give praise, show interest, and offer encouragement:

1. You've got it made.
2. Super!
3. That's right!
4. That's good!
5. You are very good at that.
6. Good work!
7. Exactly right!
8. You have just about got it.
9. You are doing a good job!
10. That's it!
11. Now you have figured it out.
12. Great!
13. I knew you could do it.
14. Congratulations!
15. Not bad.
16. Keep working on it; you are improving.
17. Now you have it.
18. You are learning fast.
19. Good for you!
20. Couldn't have done it better myself.
21. Beautiful!
22. One more time and you'll have it.
23. That's the right way to do it.
24. You did it that time!
25. You are getting better and better.
26. You are on the right track now.
27. Nice going.
28. You haven't missed a thing.
29. Wow!
30. That's the way.
31. Keep up the good work.
32. Terrific!
33. Nothing can stop you now.
34. That's the way to do it.
35. Sensational!
36. You have got your brain in gear today.
37. That's better.
38. Excellent!
39. That was first class work.
40. That's the best ever.
41. You have just about mastered that.
42. Perfect!
43. That's better than ever before.
44. Much better!
45. Wonderful!
46. You must have been practicing.
47. You did that very well.
48. Fine!
49. Brilliant!
50. Outstanding!
51. Fantastic!
52. Tremendous!
53. Now that's what I call a fine job.
54. That's great.
55. You're really improving.
56. Superb!
57. Good remembering!
58. You have got that down pat.
59. You certainly did well today.
60. Keep it up!
61. Congratulations, you got it right!
62. You did a lot of work today.
63. That's it!
64. Marvelous!
65. I like that.
66. Cool!
67. Way to go.
68. You've got the hang of it!
69. You're doing fine.
70. Good thinking.
71. You are learning a lot.
72. Good going.
73. I've never seen anyone do it better.
74. That's a real work of art.
75. Keep on trying!
76. Good for you!
77. Good job!
78. You remembered!
79. That's really nice.
80. Thanks!
81. What neat work!
82. That's "A" work.
83. That's clever.
84. Very interesting.
85. You make it look easy.
86. Excellent effort.
87. Awesome!
88. That's a good point.
89. Superior work.
90. Nice going.
91. I knew you could do it.
92. That looks like it is going to be a great paper.
93. That's coming along nicely.
94. That's an interesting way of looking at it.
95. Out of sight!
96. It looks like you've put a lot of work into this.
97. Right on!
98. Congratulations, you only missed . . .
99. Super-Duper!
100. It's a classic.
101. I'm impressed!

The Line Up!
30 ways to get elementary students in a row

Line up if you can tell me...

1. a safety rule for home or school: don't play with matches ...

2. the name of a state: Missouri, Kansas, Colorado, New Mexico ...

3. the name of a country: Scotland, Canada, India, Italy ...

4. your favorite subject in school ...

5. your favorite place to visit: the woods, the ocean, the park, the gym ...

6. a book title, author, character, illustrator ...

7. a kind of fruit: banana, plum, grapes ...

8. a kind of vegetable: lettuce, carrots, peas...

9. a type of tree: oak, maple, weeping willow, elm, lilac ...

10. a type of flower: rose, tulip, daisy, iris, marigold ...

11. a hobby or collection: gardening, stamps, stickers, dolls, biking, shells ...

12. an animal in the zoo: ostrich, panda, monkey, rattlesnake...

13. an animal on a farm: rooster, goat, pig, cow, hen, duck ...

14. your address, phone number, birthday ...

15. one thing you learned at school this week ...

Line up if you have...

16. a tooth missing, two teeth, three, four ...

17. blue as your favorite color, purple, orange ...

18. a T-shirt on, short sleeves, long sleeves ...

19. a ribbon in your hair, a watch on your left arm ...

20. a "Z" in your name, a "B," an "F," a "Q" ...

21. a birthday in January, February, March ...

22. sneakers on, boots, sandals ...

23. two people in your family, three, four ...

24. a pet dog, cat, bird, fish, rabbit ...

25. striped socks on, pink socks, brown socks ...

26. helped parents mow the lawn, wash the car, clean the kitchen ...

27. blue eyes, brown eyes, hazel, black ...

28. been to a hospital for tonsils, broken bones, to visit a friend ...

29. written a poem, story, song, play ...

30. stood on your head, played tag, skipped rope, raced ...

Low Cost/No Cost
Rewards and Motivators

In the ideal classroom, all students would be intrinsically motivated to behave appropriately and work hard on every assignment. However, this is not usually the case. Many substitute teachers experience success in motivating classes by providing rewards throughout the day. The following are ideas for low and no-cost rewards and motivators.

- **Certificates** – Photocopy blank certificates (see pages 57-58) to be filled out and given to exceptional students, groups, or the entire class at the end of the day or as prizes for classroom activities.

- **Pencils and Pens** – Colorful variations of these school supply basics are well received at any grade level as contest prizes. They can often be purchased very inexpensively at discount and dollar stores.

- **Stickers** – These can be given intermittently throughout the day to students who are on-task or placed on completed assignments to denote outstanding work.

- **Tickets** – Throughout the day, students can be given tickets for being on-task, cooperating, and following directions. These good behavior tickets are then turned in for a drawing to win a special prize prior to going home (see page 57).

- **Extra Recess Time** – Being allowed five extra minutes of recess can provide tremendous motivation for many students. Be sure to check with the principal or neighboring teacher beforehand to make sure that this reward will not interfere with the schedule of anyone else in the school.

- **Privilege Cards** – Individual students can be rewarded for good work or appropriate behavior with special privileges. You can make privilege cards that entitle students to things such as being first in the line, getting a drink, being the teacher's assistant for an activity, choosing the end of the day activity, etc. (see page 58). Laminate the cards and use a wipe-off marker – when the student redeems the privilege, collect the card and put it back in your *SubPack* for your next assignment.

- **Fun Activity** – The promise of a fun activity later in the day can motivate students for hours. The activity might be a Five-Minute Filler or Short Activity from this book, or any other activity you think they would enjoy. Remember, being "fun" is usually anything that is different from the routine of an ordinary day.

- **Story Time** – One successful substitute teacher uses the promise of a story at the end of the day to motivate classes. She brings to school an old pop-up book about a dinosaur. At the beginning of the day, the word "DINOSAUR" is written on the board. A letter is erased each time the students are off-task or behaving inappropriately. At the end of the day if there is any of the word "DINOSAUR" still left on the board, they get to hear the story. Second-hand book stores are a good place to look for inexpensive books that your students will not have seen before.*

Notes for the Teacher

Establish rewards and motivators not as "bribes to be good," but as "goals" that students can work toward and achieve through good behavior and diligent effort.

* Submitted by Marilyn Machosky of Sylvania, Ohio

- **Estimation Jar** – Fill a jar with pennies, marbles, beans, or rubber bands. Recognize students who are on-task, setting a good example, or working hard, by giving them a slip of paper to write their name and guess the number of items on. The more times they are recognized for good behavior throughout the day the more chances they have to "guess." At the end of the day, reveal the total number of items in the jar and award a prize to the student whose guess was the closest.

- **Talk Time** – Middle school students really like moving to another seat and being allowed to sit and talk with friends during the last five minutes of class. To ensure an orderly classroom, you may need to insist that students select their new seat and then not be allowed to get up until class is over. Elementary students also enjoy this activity while waiting to go to lunch or at the end of the day.

- **Taking Names** – The third principle of human behavior states that students respond better to positive than to negative consequences. Many successful substitute teachers have proven this by taking names of students who are on task instead of those who are off task. This can be done in a few different ways, as the substitute teacher, you can walk around and take names. Or when students complete the assignment, let them sign a piece of paper that will be given to the permanent teacher letting him know who completed the assignment.

Certificate of Award

_____

did an outstanding job _____

today in class!

_____   _____
Date   Teacher

Congratulations!

_____

was a WINNER in the

_____ contest today!

_____   _____
Date   Teacher

TICKET _____ TICKET
Name

TICKET _____ TICKET
Name

TICKET _____ TICKET
Name

TICKET _____ TICKET
Name

TICKET _____ TICKET
Name

TICKET _____ TICKET
Name

TICKET _____ TICKET
Name

TICKET _____ TICKET
Name

TICKET _____ TICKET
Name

Certificate of Award

Presented to

_____

In Recognition of

_____

Date _____   Teacher _____

Privilege Card

The holder of this card
is entitled to

_____

_____

_____

_____

_____

Authorized Signature

_____

Privilege Card

The holder of this card
is entitled to

_____

_____

_____

_____

_____

Authorized Signature

_____

The Professional Substitute Teacher

Chapter Three

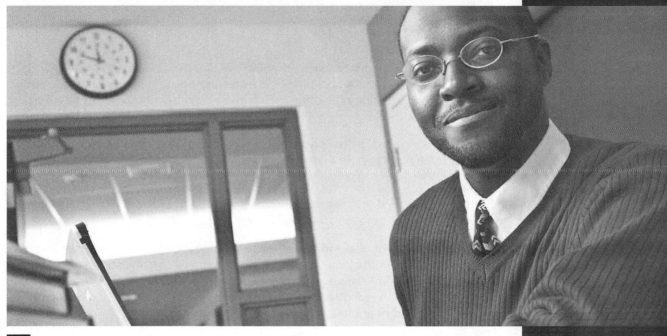

Thousands of surveys, questionnaires, and interviews show that permanent teachers, school administrators, and district personnel unanimously praise and value substitute teachers who are professional in dress, attitude, and presentation.

Being a professional substitute teacher is a full-time job. It involves many aspects of attitude and conduct. In this chapter, these aspects have been organized into the following five time frames:

1. At Home

2. Prior to Entering the Classroom

3. In the Classroom Before School

4. Throughout the Day

5. At the End of the Day

For additional information regarding the Professional Substitute Teacher, visit:

www.stedi.org

The Professional Substitute Teacher

At Home

There are a number of things you can do at home before you ever get that early morning call to substitute teach.

- Prepare a set of note cards, one for each school where you may be called to teach. On each card, list the name of the school, principal, secretary, school phone numbers, start time, address, driving directions, and the approximate time it will take to travel from your house to this location.

- Place a notebook and pencil by the phone you will be using to answer early morning calls. You may even want to note a couple of pertinent questions to ask when the call comes, such as, *"What is the name and grade level of the teacher I will be substituting for?"*

- Assemble a *SubPack* filled with teaching supplies and activity ideas for the grade levels you teach. (For more information about *SubPacks*, see page 44.)

- Designate a section of your closet for substitute teaching clothes. Assemble entire outfits, including shoes and socks, that are ironed and ready to be put on at a moment's notice. Be sure to select comfortable shoes, since as an effective substitute teacher you will be on your feet all day. Have several different outfits ready so that you are prepared to dress appropriately for different grade levels and subject assignments.

- Research shows that teachers who dress professionally command more respect in the classroom than those who dress casually or inappropriately. Gain the respect you deserve by the way you dress.

Appropriate Attire Guidelines for Men and Women

Women: Avoid uncomfortable shoes and clothing. Select outfits in which you can bend down, stoop over, and write on board with ease.

Men: Consider wearing a shirt and tie. You can always remove the tie, undo the neck button, and roll up your sleeves if you find yourself "over-dressed" for the assignment.

As a general rule, jeans, T-shirts, sandals, and other casual clothing are not considered professional or appropriate for the classroom setting. You should always dress at least as professionally as your permanent teacher counterpart.

- When the call comes, answer the phone yourself. A groggy spouse or roommate does not always make a professional impression, and you will be wasting the caller's time while they are waiting for you to wake up and get to the phone.

- After you hang up, take a look at your note card for the school, determine how long it will take you to get there, and plan the rest of the morning accordingly. Remember that you want to be at the school at least 20 minutes prior to either the beginning of class or when students arrive. Get ready and don't forget to grab your *SubPack* as you head out the door.

- Leave all valuables at home or locked in the trunk of your car. Anything you don't want students to have access to shouldn't be in the classroom.

Prior to Entering the Classroom

- Arrive at the school enthusiastic about the day, while serious about your role. If possible, arrive at least 20 minutes prior to the beginning of class. Report to the principal or office to let them know you have arrived, and ask pertinent questions:

    "Will I be responsible for playground, lunch, or other duties?"

    "Do any of the students have medical problems I should be aware of?"

    "If the need arises, how do I refer a student to the office?"

    "How do I report students who are tardy or absent?"

- Obtain any keys that might be necessary.

- Find the locations of restrooms, the teachers' lounge, the cafeteria, the auditorium, the media center, and the nearest drinking fountain before school begins.

- Meet neighboring teachers.

In the Classroom Before School

- Enter the classroom with confidence and your *SubPack*. Put your name on the board, then familiarize yourself with the room. Locate and review the classroom rules and evacuation map.

- Read through the lesson plans left by the permanent teacher and identify books, handouts, and papers that will be needed throughout the day. Study the classroom seating chart. If you can't find a seating chart, get ready to make your own (see page 5).

- Prepare a starter activity if the permanent teacher doesn't already have one planned.

- When the bell rings, stand in the doorway and greet students as they enter the classroom. Be professional, friendly, and enthusiastic about the day. This first impression will take you a long way.

Throughout the Day

- Do your best to follow the lesson plans and carry out the assigned duties left by the permanent teacher. Over 75 percent of permanent teachers report that they spend at least 45 minutes preparing lesson plans and materials for substitute teachers. Having invested both time and energy into these plans, permanent teachers feel very strongly about having them carried out.

- On the other hand, you may enter a classroom where you are unable to locate the lesson plans or necessary materials. In such a case, act quickly, calmly, and confidently. By utilizing materials and ideas in your *SubPack*, you will still have a productive day.

- Whatever situation or challenge you are faced with, always strive to be positive and respectful. Permanent teachers care about the students in their class. They know each student's strengths and weaknesses, and want to see these handled appropriately. They expect the substitute teacher to appreciate the good in their students and bring out the best in them.

- Permanent teachers urge substitute teachers to be aware of how small things, like using a normal voice, giving praise, and having a positive attitude, can affect students. Students resent teachers who talk down to them, make promises or threats they don't intend to keep, and are not fair in administering rewards and consequences. Treating students as individuals is important. Don't blame the whole class or punish the group for the misdeeds of a few. (See Chapter One for suggestions on classroom management.)

- When a substitute teacher uses good judgment, avoids criticism, and adapts to circumstances in a positive way, s/he becomes a professional role model for both the students in the class and other teachers.

At the End of the Day

Being a professional is just as important at the end of the day as it is at the beginning. What you do just before the school day ends will be the impression students take home with them. How you leave the classroom will be the first impression the permanent teacher has of you when s/he returns.

Before the Students Leave

There are several things you should do during the last few minutes of class before the students leave:

- If the teacher has classroom sets (calculators, scissors, books, etc.), make sure they are all returned before the students leave the room. It is much easier to locate a missing calculator in a class of 30 than trying to find it somewhere in the whole school.

- Challenge students to recall, and list on the board, projects and topics they have studied that day. (*Now they will have a positive answer when parents ask what they did in school, instead of the traditional, "Nothing, we had a substitute teacher."*)

- Remind students of homework. Writing homework assignments on the board throughout the day will help both you and the students remember.

- Have students straighten and cleanup the area around their desks.

After the Students Have Left

- After the students have gone, take a few minutes to complete your professional duties as a substitute teacher. Fill out a *Substitute Teacher Report* for the permanent teacher (see sample form on the following page). Write a detailed summary of what was accomplished throughout the day, along with any problems that arose and notes about things that went well, or students that were particularly helpful.

- If, for any reason, you were unable to carry out the plans left by the permanent teacher, make sure you explain why you were unable to carry them out and what you did instead. Leave your name, phone number, and an invitation for the permanent teacher to contact you if they have any questions, or to request you as their substitute teacher again in the future.

- Leave the teacher's desk and assignments completed by students neatly organized. Close windows, turn off lights and equipment, and double check to make sure the room is in good order before you lock the door and head for the office. At the office, return keys, hand in any money collected, express appreciation for assistance provided, and check to see if you will be needed again the next day.

In Conclusion

Teachers have high expectations of others who come into their classroom. By implementing the ideas in this chapter, you can become a professional that meets and exceeds these expectations. Always remember that you are a valued and important part of the educational system. Never diminish your role as a substitute teacher. Teachers appreciate having a person come into their classroom who is caring and capable. By being prepared, poised, and professional, you will greatly reduce the stress on the teacher, students, and yourself. The checklist on pages 66-67 will help you stay on the right track throughout the day. Additional hints and suggestions are found at the end of Chapter One, on pages 23-24.

Substitute Teacher Report

Substitute Teacher: _____ Date: _____

Phone Number: _____ Grade: _____

Substituted for: _____ School: _____

Email address: _____

Notes regarding lesson plans:

I also taught:

Notes regarding behavior:

Terrific helpers:

Students who were absent:

Messages for the permanent teacher:

Please let me know of any areas you feel I can improve to be a better substitute teacher for you.

Substitute Teacher Report

Substitute Teacher: _____   Date: _____

Phone Number: _____   Grade: _____

Substituted for: _____   School: _____

Email address: _____

Lesson	Notes about lessons (see back)	Notes about students (see back)
1		
2		
3		
4		
5		
6		
7		
8		

Messages for the permanent teacher:

Please let me know of any areas you feel I can improve to be a better substitute teacher for you.

Substitute Teacher Report

Dear _____ Date: _____

Over all class behavior:

☐ excellent

☐ good

☐ fair

☐ poor

I follow your lesson plan:

☐ exactly _____

☐ modified _____

☐ changed_____

☐ omitted _____

The students:

☐ remained seated   ☐ did not remain seated

☐ raised hands to talk   ☐ did not raise hands

☐ good listeners   ☐ did not listen well

☐ followed directions   ☐ did not follow directions

☐ stayed on task   ☐ did not stay on task

Chattering level:

☐ at a minimum

☐ somewhat noisy

☐ constant noise

Students had difficulty in:

☐ Reading   ☐ Science   ☐ Social Studies   ☐ Computers

☐ Math   ☐ Health   ☐ English   ☐ _____

☐ Spelling   ☐ P.E.   ☐ Art   ☐ _____

Comments: _____

_____

_____

_____

_____

_____

_____

_____

Sincerely,

Email address:_____

Form created by Sheryl Puckett

Professional Substitute Teacher Checklist

At Home

__ Compile a set of note cards containing pertinent information about the schools where you may be assigned.

__ Keep a notebook and pen by the phone you use to answer early morning phone calls.

__ Assemble a *SubPack*. Keep it well stocked and ready.

__ Organize several appropriate substitute teacher outfits in a section of your closet.

__ Leave early enough to arrive at school at least 20 minutes prior to the beginning of school.

Prior to Entering the Classroom

__ Report to the principal or the office.

__ Ask about student passes, playground rules, bus duty, lunch procedures, and other duties.

__ Ask if there are any special duties associated with the permanent teacher's assignment.

__ Find out how to refer a student to the office.

__ Review the school's discipline policy.

__ Ask if any children have medical problems.

__ Obtain necessary keys.

__ Ask how to report students who are tardy or absent.

__ Find the locations of restrooms, the teachers' lounge, and other important places in the school.

__ Introduce yourself to the teachers on both sides of your classroom.

In the Classroom Before School

__ Enter the classroom with confidence and your *SubPack*.

__ Put your name on the board.

__ Review the classroom rules.

__ Locate and review the school evacuation map.

__ Read through the lesson plans left by the permanent teacher.

__ Prepare starter activity.

__ Locate books, papers, and materials that will be needed throughout the day.

__ Study the seating chart. If you can't find one, be prepared to make your own.

__ When the bell rings, stand at the doorway and greet students as they enter the classroom.

Throughout the Day

__ Greet students at the door and involve them in learning activities quickly.

__ Carry out the lesson plans and assigned duties to the best of your ability.

__ Improvise using the materials in your **SubPack** to fill extra time, enhance activities, or supplement sketchy lesson plans as needed.

__ Be fair and carry out the rewards and consequences you establish.

__ Be positive and respectful in your interactions with students and school personnel.

At the End of the Day

__ Make sure all classroom sets are accounted for.

__ Challenge students to recall projects and topics they have studied that day.

__ Remind students of homework.

__ Have students straighten and clean the area around their desks.

__ Complete a *Substitute Teacher Report* for the permanent teacher.

__ Neatly organize papers turned in by students.

__ Close windows, turn off lights and equipment, and make sure the room is in good order before you lock the door.

__ Turn in keys and any money collected at the office.

__ Thank individuals who provided assistance during the day.

__ Check to see if you will be needed again the next day.

Getting a Permanent Job!

Many substitute teachers are working toward the goal of getting a permanent teaching assignment and classroom of their own. If you are such a substitute, below are some suggestions that might help.

- **Be Proactive**
  Meet with principals and district personnel early in the year to let them know that you are excited about working in the district and hope, at some point, to be offered a permanent teaching position. Let your intentions be known.

- **Be Available**
  Districts are looking for people on whom they can depend. Once you have signed up to substitute, try to be available to teach whenever you are needed. Your willingness to fill in at the "last minute" will make a lasting, favorable impression on those making personnel decisions later in the year.

- **Be Professional**
  You are a teacher in the school district. You should act, dress, and speak appropriately. Arrive early and stay late. Volunteer to help with after school activities. If your intentions to become a permanent teacher are known, you will be evaluated for this position in everything you do and say throughout the school year.

- **Avoid Criticism**
  Anything negative you say about a school, principal, or teacher will eventually come back to haunt you. Stay positive and compliment those around you whenever possible. If you can't say anything nice, don't say anything at all.

- **Be Confident**
  Walk tall, teach with confidence, but don't be overbearing.

- **Evaluations**
  When appropriate, ask for positive evaluation forms or letters of support/recognition to be filed at the district office. Many times only negative evaluations are filled out and sent in.

- **Learn From Experience**
  Don't assume that one bad experience or evaluation will take you out of the running. Learn from the experience and ask for advice from other teachers or principals.

- **Grow Professionally**
  Attend workshops sponsored by the district. Some districts even invite substitute teachers to attend professional development workshops scheduled for permanent teachers. You may also consider subscribing to current education journals or magazines. This illustrates that you are serious about a career in education and want to stay current with what is happening in the profession. Check with media center personnel for subscription information.

- **Get To Know The District**
  One of the most commonly used phrases in prospective teacher interviews is, "Are you familiar with . . ." By illustrating your knowledge of special programs, textbooks, or the mission statement of a district, you show that you are interested and up-to-date with what is going on in the district. Applicants who are familiar with district programs and practices have a better chance at getting a job.

Special Education

Chapter Four

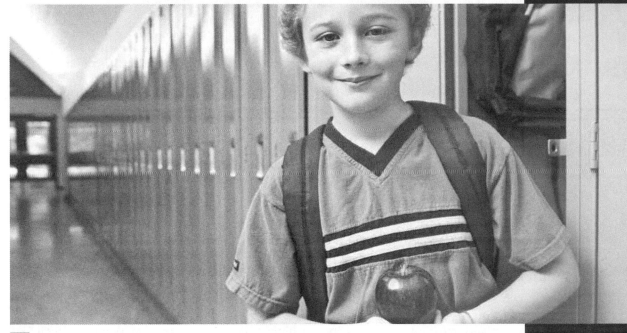

Each day in the United States millions of children go off to school, all with different strengths and weaknesses, abilities and disabilities. Over five million of these children have been identified as having a specific disability such as a learning disability, mental retardation, autism, or emotional disturbance that necessitates some type of special instruction. Teachers of these students need substitutes who can fill in for them while they are away.

Why Substitute in Special Education?

The same desire to help children that prompted you to become a substitute teacher also qualifies you for substitute teaching in special education classrooms. Every child brings unique abilities and possibilities into the school setting. Uniqueness and diversity are the capstones that make special education classrooms so dynamic. Whether or not you have worked with children with disabilities, your presence in special education classrooms is needed and worthwhile. These experiences give you the opportunity to do great work for great people.

There are numerous rewards for substitute teaching in special education classes. Perhaps the strongest is the feeling that you have helped to improve the lives of children with disabilities. Another is that in dedicated special education classes, you rarely work alone. Whereas in traditional classrooms you are isolated, in special education classes many people work together to make the class successful.

Substitute teachers have the opportunity to teach in a variety of special education settings. This chapter outlines how special education service locations are set up, the skills you need to enter these locations with confidence and make your day a great success, and a brief description of various disabilities you may encounter with guidelines to help you make the most of your assignment.

Many thanks to Dr. Robert L. Morgan and Becky Morgan for their invaluable assistance in the development of this chapter on special education.

For additional information regarding substituting in special education classrooms, visit:

www.stedi.org

The Special Education Service Location

Special education is an integrated set of individualized services, not necessarily a location. However, to familiarize you with what special education may look like, here are some possibilities:

- A general education classroom with some students with special needs who spend all or part of their day in the classroom with or without support from paraprofessionals.

- A resource room where students are pulled from their classrooms for small periods of the day.

- The special education teacher spending time in multiple general education classrooms, co-teaching with the general education teacher with mixed groups of students.

- A self-contained classroom with students with similar disabilities (e.g., a classroom with only students with autism).

The diversity may seem challenging, but can be very fun if you are up for encountering an array of experiences throughout your day and from assignment to assignment.

Special Education Skills

No matter what your specific special education classroom may look like, there are several skills that will make your day go smoothly if put into practice. With an understanding of the principles of behavior outlined in Chapter One and the teaching strategies in Chapter Two, you are well prepared for any classroom. In this section, a number of skills are discussed that are particular to a special education setting, including:

- Having an Attitude of Respect

- Working with Paraprofessionals

- Being Familiar with Special Education Terms and Laws

- Instructional Consistency

- Adapting Lessons and Activities

- Knowing Students and Meeting All Their Needs

Having an Attitude of Respect

When you interact with students with disabilities or special needs, be respectful of them as individuals and treat them with dignity. The way you talk *about* them can reveal your attitudes toward them. Use language that refers to the student as a *person with a disability*, not a disabled person. Do not use demeaning words like "crippled," "handicapped," or "retarded."

One Professional to Another

One of the greatest things about the special education classroom is the amount of support generally available from experienced paraprofessionals.

The way you talk to them can also reveal your attitude toward them. Talk directly to the student, not to the paraprofessional or other helper that may be with them. Be welcoming and caring, but don't baby them or feel sorry for them. As with all students, you want to be firm and fair.

Recognize that students with disabilities have individual differences — both from their non-disabled peers and also from other students that have the same or similar disability. Remember that students with disabilities or special needs, like all students, have a lot in common with their peers.

> Be respectful of students in special education classrooms and treat them with dignity.

Confidentiality is particularly important when working in a special education setting. Refrain from talking about students to anyone who does not work with them. Any private details about a student's disability or program that you learn or hear about should remain private.

A good rule of thumb is the term, "Need to Know Basis." Does the person you are about to tell any detail to "need to know" information in order to help the student. If not, don't say anything. For example, a spouse doesn't need to know who is in a resource class. Information to be communicated on a "need to know basis" only applies to school district personnel and parents/guardians. Assume that others do not need to know.

Working with Paraprofessionals

One of the greatest things about the special education classroom is the amount of support generally available from experienced paraprofessionals. Use their individual expertise about classroom procedures and specific students to make your day successful. It is important, however, that *you* remember that you are substituting for the teacher, not the paraprofessional. Be willing to delegate when appropriate.

- *Define your working relationship early*. You are the teacher. You are responsible for ensuring that the lesson plans are carried out.

- *Ask questions to clarify your responsibilities*. After reading the lesson plans, address any questions you have about the classroom routines, students, or specific responsibilities with the paraprofessional. Define what you and the paraprofessional(s) will do in case of emergency. Do not think that asking questions or asking for help makes you appear less capable.

- *Let the paraprofessional do his/her job*. The classroom paraprofessional may be willing and able to assume some degree of authority for conducting classroom activities. Some students may work better with a familiar face. Discuss roles and responsibilities with the paraprofessional before issues develop.

- *Respect the paraprofessional's level of knowledge and expertise*. Be teachable. The paraprofessional knows the classroom and the students. You can value their experience without diminishing your own.

Being Familiar with Special Education Terms and Laws

As a substitute teacher, you need to have a basic understanding of terms and acronyms used in special education situations. The following are some key terms and a brief synopsis of special education law that you need to be familiar with.

Key Terms

- **Assistive Technology:** The use of devices that increase the ability of students to get along in society or that improve their quality of life (wheelchairs, computers, hearing aids, etc.).

- **Behavior Intervention Plan (BIP):** A plan written by the IEP team for an individual student that specifically outlines what procedures and practices will be used to reinforce positive behaviors and decrease undesirable behaviors.

- **Curriculum-Based Assessment (CBA):** The practice of obtaining direct and frequent measures of student performance based on a series of objectives from a classroom curriculum.

- **Individualized Education Plan (IEP):** An individualized, written program that is developed and carried out by the members of the IEP team.

- **IEP Team:** A group of educational and related services personnel who develop, carry out, and evaluate the individual education plan, or IEP.

- **Inclusion:** Involving students with disabilities as active participants in general education classroom activities. Five effective, or attitudinal, benefits of inclusion are 1) the non disabled students learn to be more responsive to others; 2) new and valued relationships develop; 3) non disabled students learn something about their own lives and situations; 4) students learn about values and principles; and 5) students gain an appreciation of diversity in general.

- **Least Restrictive Environment:** A location in which students have a maximum opportunity to interact with students who do not have disabilities.

Public Law 94-142 (Individuals with Disabilities Education Act)

Passed in 1975 and updated most recently in May 2004, "The Education for All Handicapped Children Act" has been amended and is now called "IDEA" or the "Individuals with Disabilities Education Act." It entitles all students with disabilities between the ages of 3 and 21 to free, appropriate public education. Presently, the terms *disability* and *disabled* are used in place of handicap and handicapped.

The law defines individuals with disabilities to include those who are mentally retarded, hard of hearing, deaf, speech-impaired, visually handicapped, seriously emotionally disturbed, or orthopedically impaired; have multiple handicaps; or have other health impairments or learning disabilities and therefore need special educational services.

IDEA also provides ALL students with disabilities with the right to be served in the least restrictive environment — this means that they must be educated and treated in a manner similar to their non disabled peers. This usually consists of placing children with disabilities in the regular classroom.

Who decides how children with disabilities will be educated? IDEA requires that a team consisting of the student, his/her parent(s), teachers, principal, and other professionals develop an individual education plan (IEP) detailing the goals and objectives of the educational services to be provided. The IEP lists all special and regular activities that the student will participate in.

Section 504

This section of the Rehabilitation Act of 1973 prohibits discrimination against people based on their disability. Students may not be left out of a public school activity only because of a disability. The major difference between *Section 504* and IDEA is that the definition of a "disability" is broader under Section 504. In addition to categories of disability mentioned above, it covers students with AIDS, tuberculosis, hepatitis, allergies, asthma, diabetes, heart disease, and many others that may not be covered by IDEA.

Instructional Consistency

You will often be working with students who especially need *structure* and *consistency*, possibly more than their peers without disabilities, when working in the special education classroom. It is extremely important to continue instruction by following the lesson plans left by the permanent teacher. Additionally, be sure to implement the same classroom procedures.

Follow the schedule as outlined by the permanent teacher. Some undesirable behaviors from students can be avoided by maintaining their structured routines. Carefully note the daily schedules for each student. They often have related service personnel (language or hearing specialists, occupational therapists, and physical therapists) come into the classroom. At other times they may leave the classroom to attend classes in other school locations.

It is also important to become familiar with *behavior intervention plans (BIPs)* that are implemented for some students. These plans have been written by the IEP team and must be carried out with precision. There are usually specific things that should happen when a student does something either desirable or undesirable. If the permanent teacher's lesson plans do not mention any students with behavior plans, you may want to check by asking the paraprofessional. In some cases, behavior reports go home daily to parents that detail the behavior of the student throughout the day. Ask for any help you need to continue this system.

As a general guideline for achieving continuity of instruction, if you know the permanent teacher does something, you should *keep doing it* too. Also, let the permanent teacher know in your substitute teacher report what you were or were not able to accomplish with the students so that s/he knows where to continue upon return.

Adapting Lessons and Activities

By knowing a little bit about the students and their diverse needs, you will be able to make appropriate adaptations throughout the day. It will be necessary to make adaptations for students with special needs, especially when they participate in the general education classroom. Making adaptations or accommodations for students with disabilities does not need to be difficult. Remember that students with disabilities already know their capabilities and limits — simply encourage them and be ready to assist if needed. Focus on what they can do. Depending on the lesson plan or guidelines provided by the permanent teacher, it may be acceptable to modify the assignment or activity for the whole group, or just for certain students and not others. Keep the assignment as similar to the rest of the class as possible. Be sensitive — especially with new students or students with new disabilities — and start slowly and develop gradually.

Ideas for adapting lessons/assignments

- Reduce the number of pages or questions.

- Reduce the difficulty of activities/assignments (for students with barriers due to physical or emotional disabilities).

- Read aloud; use overheads; move desk for better hearing, seeing, and monitoring; speak more slowly; speak louder; repeat, rephrase, and redirect instructions and questions.

- Increase confidence, compassion, and cooperation by reinforcing success.

- Use a lot of examples and warm-ups, provide patterns or steps to follow; model, review, practice, practice, practice. Teacher does part and student does part.

- Be patient and smile.

- Provide breaks between tasks or assignments.

- Break a large task into several smaller ones.

- Structure tasks so that the student does an easier task that s/he is more successful at after a difficult task.

Ideas for adapting games/activities

- Reduce the size of the playing area.

- Adjust the boundaries, change the number of players, lower the net.

- Use walls, fences, or designated "helpers" to aid in keeping the ball in-bounds.

- Find bigger/lighter equipment.

- Incorporate plastic bats, rubber racquets, jumbo gloves, enlarged hoops, expanded goals, etc.

Use the suggestions above and the adaptations included with the activities in chapter six to determine what accommodations may be appropriate for students you work with.

Knowing Students and Meeting All Their Needs

Meeting individual student needs requires sensitivity to their behaviors and developing a keen ability to communicate with each student. Some students have specific needs involving medical issues, transportation, materials, and strategies for instruction and behavior. Be as attentive as possible to the students and keep the following guidelines in mind:

- The permanent teacher knows the students, what is required by their IEP (individualized education plan), and has drawn up lesson plans to meet those needs.

- You may need to locate yourself in close proximity to offer assistance and help the students stay focused. A gentle reminder will often suffice.

- Use the student's name first to get his/her attention (e.g., *"Tamara, please place the paper in the trash."* Avoid *"Place the paper in the trash, Tamara."*).

- You may need to repeat yourself more often than usual. Be patient. Check for student understanding (e.g., "Tamara, please tell me what I asked you to do.").

- Be flexible. Schedules can change. Students may be transitioning in and out of the general education setting throughout the day.

- Be aware that some students may have experienced years of failure. Help them find success by recognizing and praising small successes.

- In class discussions, if a student responds with an incorrect answer, provide clues or a follow-up question to help him/her think of the correct answer.

- Look for ways to praise students for their thinking, behavior, and correct answers.

- Deal with a student individually if problems arise. Do not single him/her out in front of the class.

- Present short and varied instructional tasks planned with the students' success in mind.

- Allow students to use learning aids to assist them with their work as directed by the instructions left by the permanent teacher.

- Check with a paraprofessional, the principal, or another teacher before using any specialized teaching equipment or machines.

- Do not hesitate to ask for assistance from the principal or another teacher if you have concerns or questions during the day.

While some special teaching strategies have been identified to appropriately teach students with some particular disabilities, it remains true that good practices apply in most situations. Use the strategies for behavior and instruction as outlined in Chapters One and Two.

Characteristics of Disabilities and Helpful Strategies

You may encounter a variety of disabilities in your special education assignments. Federal legislation has identified specific disability categories that are covered under the Individuals with Disabilities Education Act (IDEA). Several types of disabilities (autism, blindness, deafness, emotional disorders, learning disabilities, mental retardation, multiple disabilities, orthopedic impairment, other health impairments, speech/language impairments, and traumatic brain injury) are described below. Suggestions for working with students facing these challenges are also included.

Autism

Autism is a variable developmental disorder that is characterized by impairment of the ability to form normal social relationships, to communicate with others, and by stereotyped behavior patterns. Autism can affect language, measured intelligence, rate of development, and responses to people, events, and objects. Autism affects each person differently and its characteristics can fall anywhere on a spectrum that ranges from mild to severe. Students with autism may not communicate or socialize in typical ways. They may also preoccupy themselves with objects or items that seem unimportant. You might see other behaviors such as body rocking, head banging, unusual and repetitive hand movements, uncommon posturing, or repeated speech.

Students with autism need explicit assistance in identifying cues for social occasions and responding in ways considered appropriate by others. When interacting with students with autism, use the communication system they use. Many students with autism require a very structured classroom, clear expectations, fast-paced instruction, and positive consequences for acceptable behavior. Keep classroom activities as regular and predictable as possible.

Blindness or Low Vision

Students are legally blind if they can see (with glasses) at 20 feet what other people see at 200 feet. Because of their severely impaired or nonexistent vision, they need assistance in understanding their place in space and may read using the Braille language. Students with low vision may use computers or books with large print.

When working with students who are blind, be sure to keep the classroom environment and layout consistent. Find out what assisting devices the student uses and allow those devices to be readily available. Ask students if you may assist them in moving from one place to the next.

Deaf or Hearing Impaired

Deafness is severe hearing loss to a degree that a student can't hear spoken language even with hearing aids. A hearing impairment is not as severe but still affects classroom performance. Some deaf students or students with hearing impairments may have delays in their speech or language development and may use alternate forms of communication (sign language, communication boards, or computers).

Speak clearly with your face and lips in full view of the student. Do not talk loudly or speak slowly unless the student asks you to. Use the form of communication that the student uses.

Emotional Disorders

Students with an emotional disorder may display a range of behaviors different from those expected in classrooms. The behaviors may include aggression, violence, verbal threats, destruction of property, seeking attention inappropriately, tantrums, hyperactivity, compulsiveness, impulsiveness, irritability, or withdrawal. Students with an emotional disorder seem to be unable to control their behavior. They may appear to have poor memory, a short attention span, and a poor image of themselves.

Give students with emotional disorders genuine praise for their success. Point out the student's successes so s/he can build his/her self-esteem. Make expectations small and achievable. Maintain trust by making eye contact, talking in a straightforward way, and listening carefully.

Learning Disabilities

Generally, students with learning disabilities have deficits affecting information processing (input and output of language), perception (distinguishing letters, numbers, and symbols), memory (auditory or visual), or attention (distractibility). These students may have problems in reading, writing, spelling, math, listening, or speaking. They do not learn at expected rates and may become frustrated, angry, or withdrawn.

Try to understand the student's frustration, but don't accept "I don't know" as an answer. Allow more time to complete the assignment/task and be patient. Teach lessons in small parts and combine auditory and visual information (say it and write it).

Mental Retardation

Sometimes mental retardation is called cognitive impairment or intellectual disability. Intellectual characteristics and adaptive behavior among students with mental retardation are significantly below average. Students are classified with mental retardation before age 18 based on their low IQ score and limited adaptive behaviors (personal and social standards).

Students with mental retardation learn more gradually than their peers and consequently, their skills are often delayed in comparison to their peers without disabilities. If students have mild limitations, they need special instruction but they communicate, respond to instructions, and care for themselves. Students with severe retardation need intensive instruction, have limited communication skills, and require training to care for themselves.

Your interaction with students with mental retardation will depend on the specific student. Use clear and simple language and check for understanding. Get the student's attention (say name and make eye contact) before giving instructions. Break tasks into small parts. Recognize students when they are successful and be specific in your praise. Students will often imitate what they hear and see, so always model appropriate social behaviors.

Multiple Disabilities

The multiple disabilities category is for students with two or more disabilities, like mental retardation and cerebral palsy, or blindness and deafness. Students with multiple disabilities present a considerable challenge and need highly specialized instruction dependent on their specific needs.

Use the appropriate descriptions and helpful tips included in the other categories as you interact with students with multiple disabilities.

Orthopedic Impairments

Physical and neurological disabilities fall into this category. These include cerebral palsy, spina bifida, and muscular dystrophy. Students may use assistive technology devices for mobility, communication, or independence. Characteristics of students vary based on the type and severity of the impairment.

- Students with cerebral palsy experience physical and neurological problems because of damage to the nervous system that occurred before, during, or immediately after birth. The student's muscles may be rigid and contracted. Coordination, mobility, balance, and communication may be affected.

- Students with spina bifida experience a birth defect of damage to the spinal cord. Students may experience motor impairment, muscle weakness, or paralysis.

- Muscular dystrophy is the progressive deterioration of muscles connected to the skeleton so students have limited muscle movement and mobility.

Appropriate interaction depends on the specific characteristics of the student. Some students may require physical lifting or transferring. Be sure that the paraprofessionals or other staff in the classroom handle these procedures. They have been trained in correct body positioning so they do not injure the student or themselves.

Other Health Impairments

These impairments are those that are not covered in the other categories. Students with disabilities are classified here if they experience attention deficit problems, epilepsy, heart conditions, tuberculosis, rheumatic fever, nephritis, asthma, sickle cell anemia, hemophilia, lead poisoning, leukemia, arthritis, or diabetes.

If a student with epilepsy experiences a seizure, remain calm and follow the procedures outlined by the permanent teacher. These may include calling the office or someone for help and recording the time and length of the seizure.

When working with students with attention deficit problems, keep in mind that they have difficulty attending to tasks in the classroom and may appear impulsive or out-of-control. They are easily distracted. It is helpful if you have the student sit where they will not be disturbed by people passing by their desk. Keep instructional materials and manipulatives out of the student's reach until it is time to use them. Describe expectations positively instead of what should not be done. Let the students learn by doing hands-on activities. Keep instruction fast-paced if the student appears bored; slow instruction if s/he appears hyperactive.

Speech or Language Impairments

Speech impairments include articulation (abnormal production of sounds), stuttering (speech fluency), and voice problems (too loud, soft, or hoarse). Language impairments can include receptive (understanding spoken or written communication) or expressive (speaking clearly) problems. Often, these impairments affect academic skills.

Be supportive and reassuring — students are sometimes self-conscious of their disorder and may give up easily. Listen carefully and patiently and use clear and simple instructions.

Traumatic Brain Injury

These students have experienced severe head injuries. Depending on the part of the brain that was injured and the severity of the damage, the student's speech, language, memory, motor function, intelligence, and behavior may be affected.

Use understanding, patience, and encouragement as the student works toward recovering abilities and skills.

In Conclusion

Special education teachers find their jobs very enjoyable and rewarding. As you spend time working with students with special needs, you will also find satisfaction at the end of the day.

Remember, all of the skills presented in this handbook can and should be used in special education settings. The skills presented in the classroom management chapter are based on 35 years of research and trials conducted by a special education professor. They have been used in countless regular and special needs classrooms worldwide and, combined with the additional skills presented in this chapter, will provide you with an effective and rewarding substitute teaching experience.

Other Things You Should Know

110 Administration

Chapter Five is a compilation of important information that you should know as a substitute teacher. While its contents are not comprehensive, it does cover the basics for the following critical aspects of teaching:

- Safe Schools Policy
- First Aid and Safety
- Legal Aspects of the Job
- Child Abuse Reporting
- Sexual Harassment
- Evacuation and Other Out-of-Classroom Activities

As you review this information, you may think of additional questions relating to these or other topics. The information presented is only an overview of general guidelines. **It is important you seek out your district/school policies and procedures relating to the items presented hereafter**. Do not be afraid to ask fellow teachers, school administrators or district personnel about anything you would like to know. Take the initiative to learn about specific district policies and state laws.

For additional information regarding legal issues or school safety, visit:

www.stedi.org

Safe Schools Policy

Most school districts have established a *Safe Schools Policy* to foster a safe environment where learning can take place without unnecessary disruptions. It includes behavior expectations for students, staff, community, neighbors, and visitors.

Although each district has its own version/edition of a Safe Schools Policy, some general guidelines usually apply. School administrators have a school-wide behavior management program, including:

- A variety of positive reinforcements for appropriate behavior

- A variety of consequences for inappropriate behavior

- A plan for serious misbehavior

- High visibility of teachers, staff, and administration

- Early intervention programs

- Special training programs

- Parent involvement

- Written policies on expulsion and suspension

- Accommodations for students with special needs

> Administrators, staff, teachers, and substitute teachers all have the responsibility and liability of ensuring that the Safe Schools Policy is enforced.

Students are expected to foster safe schools by:

- Knowing and complying with the school's rules of conduct

- Complying with all federal, state, and local laws

- Showing respect for other people

- Obeying people in authority at the school

One Professional to Another

Your district's Safe Schools Policy may be included in the information supplied by the school district.

If not, be sure to request a copy from your school district office and review it thoroughly.

First Aid and Safety

Most classroom and playground accidents should be handled with common sense. Students who are injured should be sent to the office where a school nurse or secretary can administer first aid. Don't fall into the trap where students are continually asking to go to the office for band-aids or ice for fake injuries. In the event of a severe injury, **do not** move the student. Remain with the student, send another student or teacher for help, and try to keep the other students calm.

Never give medication to a student, not even aspirin. If a student requires medication, it should be administered through the school nurse, secretary, or other designated medical personnel.

Learn how to handle situations involving blood and other bodily fluids. Listed below are the OSHA Universal Precautions for dealing with these situations. Contact the school district to find out its specific district policies and procedures that should be followed.

OSHA Universal Precautions for Handling Exposure to Blood/Bodily Fluids

1. All blood/bodily fluids should be considered infectious regardless of the perceived status of the individual.

2. Avoid contact with blood/bodily fluids if possible. Immediately notify the school nurse, administrator, or his/her designated first aid person.

3. Allow the injured individual to clean the injury if possible.

4. If it is not possible for the individual to clean the injury, disposable gloves should be worn. Gloves are to be discarded in a designated lined bag or container.

5. Clothing that has been exposed should be placed in a plastic bag and sent home with the individual.

6. Upon removal of gloves, hands should be washed thoroughly with warm water and soap.

7. Surfaces contaminated with blood/bodily fluids should be cleaned thoroughly with disinfectant. The cleaning should be completed by the custodian, administrator, or his/her designated individual responsible for cleanup.

As a general rule: **Do not touch a student who is bleeding even if you use gloves**. If a student has a bloody nose or cut knee, hand him/her the box of tissues or paper towel, instruct him/her to hold it on his/her wound, and then send him/her to the office or infirmary for further care. Students who are bleeding should not be allowed to participate in class activities until the bleeding has stopped and the wound has been cleaned and completely covered.

First Aid and Safety

- Handle accidents with common sense.
- Only the school nurse or other designated personnel should administer first aid, including dispensing medication.
- Do not move a severely injured student.
- Learn and follow school district policy for handling situations involving blood/bodily fluids.
- Always remain with the class and send a student or another teacher to get help when needed.

Advice from School Nurses
for Substitute Teachers*

1. Do not dispense medication (prescription or over-the-counter) to any students. Send them to the office or school clinic where they have a record of the written permission to give the students the medication, the prescribed amount, and a system for recording the times and dosage administered.

2. Refer all students with injuries (even minor ones) to the office so the normal school procedures can be followed. In an emergency, you may need to escort the student to the office. Or, in a less serious situation, have another student accompany the injured student.

3. Carry to school each day a pair of disposable gloves that are waterproof and made of either latex or vinyl for use in the event of an emergency that requires you to come in direct contact with a student's injury.

4. Always wear protective gloves when you come in contact with blood, bodily fluids, and torn skin, or when handling materials soiled with the same.

5. If you come in contact with bodily fluids from a student, throw your gloves away in a lined garbage can. Better yet, seal the soiled gloves in a small plastic bag before depositing them in the trash. After you remove the gloves, wash your hands for 10 seconds with soap and warm running water.

6. Encourage students to wash their hands before meals and when using the restroom to reduce exposure to germs.

7. Do not allow students who are bleeding to participate in class until the bleeding has stopped and the wound has been cleaned and completely covered.

8. Check with the school office when there is a student injury. Some schools may require you to complete an accident report form. If so, leave a copy for the permanent teacher and keep one for your records.

9. Prevention is the best antidote for medical emergencies. Always stay with the students. Contact another adult if you need to leave the students at any time. If you have recess duty, walk around the playground and be proactive about potentially dangerous behavior. Remember, you are the adult in charge.

Submitted by Berks County Intermediate Unit, Reading, Pennsylvania

Legal Aspects of the Job

An overall consideration when substitute teaching is your legal responsibility in the classroom and school. The following are some legal responsibilities you should be aware of. An understanding of these responsibilities requires some questioning on your part as to specific school/district policies.

- **Supervision of Students** — The substitute teacher who has physical control of a classroom has a duty to keep students safe and orderly. In many states, a teacher acts *in loco parentis* — in the place of a parent — and is allowed to use his/her judgement in a manner similar to a parent. The standard is the reasonable use of professional judgment for the safety and orderly education of students.

> Remember to *never* leave your students unsupervised.

- **Due Care and Caution** — A teacher is required to exercise due care and caution for the safety of the students in his/her charge. Essentially, this means acting reasonably and with safety in mind, being able to explain circumstances and your actions, and following school safety policies and procedures.

- **Release of Students** — Due to possible restraints on who may have custody of a child, students should not be allowed to leave the building during the school day without express consent from the office.

- **Administering Medication** — Medication should only be administered by the school nurse or other appropriate health personnel, not the classroom or substitute teacher. If you know of medication requirements of a student, the school health professional should be notified.

- **Confidentiality** — It is unprofessional and against the law in many states to disclose confidential information about your students. Generally, a substitute teacher should avoid comments about individual students that convey private information (e.g., grades, medical condition, learning or discipline problems, etc.).

- **Anecdotal Records** — Maintaining notes on particular incidents in the classroom can protect you in problematic situations. If you feel that a classroom occurrence might be questioned, note the date and time, the individuals involved, the choices for action considered, and the actions taken.

- **Discipline Policies** — A substitute teacher should know the state's position on corporal punishment and the school's policy over various aspects of discipline. Some states require a school to have a policy and often these policies indicate a specific person, such as the principal, as disciplinarian. If in doubt, referring students to the building principal is sound advice. When sending a student to the principal due to discipline matters, the substitute teacher maintains the duties of supervision and due care for both the individual child and the remainder of the class. Proper action may be detailed in the school policy or may require your independent sound judgement. Possible actions include having another child accompany the child, sending another child to bring someone from the office to intervene, or having another teacher watch your class while you take the child to the office.

- **Dangerous Situations** — A substitute teacher is responsible for making sure the physical surroundings are safe. This includes things such as the arrangement of desks so as not to block exits and proper supervision during the use of potentially dangerous classroom equipment. A teacher must also consider the potential for problems in certain kinds of classes. Planned activities in a physical education, science, shop, or sewing or foods lab class may be uncomfortable for the substitute teacher. In such cases, substitute teachers may choose to do an alternate activity that they feel can be conducted safely.

Child Abuse Reporting

Purpose

The purpose of child abuse reporting legislation is to protect the **best interests of children**, offer protective services to prevent harm to children, stabilize the home environment, preserve family life whenever possible, and encourage cooperation among the states in dealing with the problem of child abuse.

Duty to Notify

Any school employee (including substitute teachers) who knows or reasonably believes that a student has been neglected or physically or sexually abused, shall **promptly notify** the building principal, the nearest peace officer, law enforcement agency, or office of the State Division of Human Services.

It is not the responsibility of the school employees to prove that the student has been abused or neglected, or to determine if the student is in need of protection. Investigations are the responsibility of the Division of Human Services. Investigations by education personnel prior to submitting a report should not go beyond that necessary to support a reasonable belief that a reportable problem exists.

Any person, official, or institution required to report a case of suspected child abuse, sexual abuse, or neglect and fails to do so is guilty of a class B misdemeanor.

Remember

Report suspected abuse as *promptly as possible*. Persons making reports or participating in an investigation of alleged child abuse or neglect in good faith are immune from any civil or criminal liability that might otherwise arise from those actions.

Everything you always wanted to know
about sexual harassment*

What is sexual harassment?

Definition: Unwelcome sexual advances, requests for sexual favors, and other verbal or physical conduct of a sexual nature when:

- submission to such conduct is made, either *explicitly* or *implicitly*, a term or condition of a person's employment or a student's academic success

- submission to or rejection of such conduct by an individual is used as the basis for employment or academic decisions affecting such individuals

- such conduct unreasonably interferes with an individual's work or academic performance or creates an intimidating, hostile, or offensive working or learning environment

> Sexual harassment is illegal. Don't do it. Don't tolerate it!

What is a "yardstick" for determining what constitutes sexual harassment?

Sexual harassment is behavior that:

- is unwanted or unwelcome

- is sexual in nature or gender-based

- is severe, pervasive and/or repeated

- has an adverse impact on the workplace or academic environment

- often occurs in the context of a relationship where one person has more formal power than the other (supervisor/employee, faculty/student, etc.)

To whom can I talk about sexual harassment concerns?

- your local principal, superintendent, or personnel/human resources office

- your city or state office of Anti-Discrimination

- your state office of Equal Employment Opportunity Commission (EEOC)

- the Office of Civil Rights, U.S. Department of Education

but were afraid to ask.

What are some examples of verbal, nonverbal, and physical sexual harassment?

The following are behaviors that *could* be viewed as sexual harassment *when they are unwelcome*:

Verbal

- whistling or making cat calls at someone
- making sexual comments about a person's clothing or body
- telling sexual jokes or stories
- referring to an adult woman or man as a hunk, doll, babe, or honey
- spreading rumors about a person's personal sex life
- repeatedly "*asking out*" a person who is not interested

Nonverbal

- paying unwanted attention to someone (staring, following)
- making facial expressions (winking, throwing kisses, licking)
- making lewd gestures
- giving gifts of a sexual nature

> Sexual harassment can be directed at or perpetrated by you, administrators, faculty members, staff members, or students.

Physical

- hanging around, standing close, or brushing up against a person
- touching a person's clothing, hair, or body
- touching oneself in a sexual manner around another person
- hugging, kissing, patting, stroking, massaging

What should I do if I feel I am being sexually harassed?

- Talk to your harasser if possible. Tell her/him that you find the behavior offensive.
- Continue going to work/classes.
- Document all sexual harassment incidents. Record the time, date, place, and people involved.
- Put your objection in writing, sending a copy by registered mail to the harasser and keeping a copy in your file. Say:

    – On "*this date*" you did "*this.*"

    – It made me feel "*this.*"

    – I want "*this*" to happen next (e.g., I want "*this*" to stop).

- Report the harassment to the building administrator and district personnel/human resource director.

Evacuation and Other Out-of-Classroom Activities

In addition to regular classroom management, there are several special situations that you need to be aware of and prepared for. These situations include emergency and evacuation procedures, assemblies, playground and lunchroom duty, field trips, inclement weather days, and bus duty. As you review the following suggestions, keep in mind that you are the teacher and must assume full responsibility for all of the students in your care.

Emergency and Evacuation Procedures

- Ask the district office for information about emergency action plans and protocol. Find out what to do in the event of fire, flood, earthquake, bomb threat, etc.

- Since every building and classroom is different, it is important to know where the nearest exit is and to have a class list available to grab when you evacuate the building.

- If you hear the fire alarm or a message over the intercom, instruct the students to quickly and quietly leave the room in single file, heading for the designated exit door.

- Some classrooms may have an "emergency backpack" hanging by the door. If you see such a backpack, take it with you when you evacuate.

- After evacuating the building, use the class list to account for all of the students in your class.

Remember

Evacuate the students in your classroom and have a class list with you. This will help you determine if anyone is missing after you leave the building.

Assemblies

At first thought, an assembly seems like a pleasant break in the school day routine. However, it can turn into a nightmare for a substitute teacher who does not have a plan for managing students during this activity. Here are some suggestions to help you survive the event with nerves still intact.

- Find out the time and location of the assembly, and whether or not the students will need to bring chairs from the classroom. You should also check to see how the regular class schedule will be altered to accommodate the assembly.

- Talk to neighboring permanent teachers. Many schools have specific procedures for going to and returning from an assembly, as well as assigned seating for each class.

- If such procedures exist, familiarize yourself with them and do your best to follow them.

- If there are no established procedures, devise your own (walk in a single file line down the hall to the assembly, sit together as a class, return in a single file line, etc.).

- Determine and convey the specific behavior you expect during the assembly, with consequences and rewards dependent upon how these expectations are met. Beware of punishing the whole class for the misdeeds of a few. This can create a hostile environment with the students acting out against each other as well as you.

- Teach or review with the students the procedures, expected behavior, and consequences or rewards associated with the activity.

Field Trips

- A field trip is a method of providing students with first-hand learning opportunities. Field trips are often used to introduce or conclude a specific topic of study. You have many duties in order to successfully carry out the planned learning experience when substituting on the day of a field trip.

- Parental permission to participate in the field trip must be secured prior to the trip. Be certain that such permission, usually a signed release/consent form, has been obtained for all of the students in the class.

- Find out the school policy for any students who do not have documented parental permission to participate in the field trip. If a student without permission is required to remain at school, arrange for him/her to attend another teacher's class.

- Student behavior is an important part of any educational experience. Prior to the trip, reiterate with the students some do's and don'ts of expected behavior:

Do	Don't
✓ be courteous	✗ ask personal or irrelevant questions
✓ stay with the group	✗ lag behind
✓ listen attentively	✗ interrupt
✓ follow safety regulations	✗ take samples or touch, unless given specific permission to do so

- Since you will most likely be unfamiliar with the students, create name tags to be worn on students' shirts or coats. If you are visiting a location where there may be many school groups, use a distinctive shape or color for your students' name tags.

- Students should be assigned a travel partner, and chaperones should be given a specific group of students with a list of their names. You may want to consider giving each chaperone's group a different colored name tag.

- Safety precautions must be considered at all times. Take a first aid kit along.

- Count the number of students before leaving the classroom and often throughout the excursion, especially when loading and unloading buses or moving from one area to another.

- Students should have been informed of special things to look for and what they will likely see and hear on the trip. Familiarize yourself with the learning agenda if possible and use this information to facilitate student learning on the trip.

- Means of note-taking may have been planned. This may include using clipboards, taking notebooks, or completing specific note-taking sheets prepared for the trip. Do your best to carry out the plans left by the permanent teacher.

- Follow the planned time frame and sequence for the visit. Set aside time for note taking, questions and answers, or sketching as needed.

- Processing the trip is essential for true learning to take place. On the return trip or back at school, have students share what particular experiences interested them. You may also want to follow up with a writing assignment.

- Remember, you are responsible for the supervision and conduct of your students at all times, including on the bus and at the field trip destination.

Special Duties and Responsibilities

As part of some assignments your responsibilities may include hall, lunch, or bus duty. Specific instructions associated with such an assignment should be explained by the principal/secretary or outlined in the permanent teacher's lesson plans. If not, keep the following in mind:

- Supervisory duties involve more than just being in the vicinity of the students. Your job is to supervise student actions and activities to ensure a safe environment and experience.

- Proactive measures help to successfully deter potential problem situations. Your active presence is usually enough to discourage inappropriate behavior.

  – Be alert and attentive to what students are doing.

  – Remain standing.

  – Move about the area you are supervising as much as possible.

- Should a problem arise, intervene before the situation gets out of control, and don't hesitate to ask for help from another teacher.

- Never leave a group of students unsupervised.

In Conclusion

It has often been said that there is no such thing as a "normal" school day. Fire drills always occur at the least convenient times; assemblies alter usual schedules and routines; field trips, epidemics, and school competitions often result in large numbers of students being absent; and just the fact that you are there as a substitute teacher means that it is not a "normal" day for the students in your classes. Knowledge, flexibility, and a sense of humor are key to making the best out of any situation. Learn all that you can about school policies, procedures, and responsibilities. Recognize that things will rarely go exactly as you or the permanent teacher have planned and be prepared to make accommodations. Lighten up and laugh, including at yourself — it will make it a much better day for everyone.

Fill-In Activities

As a substitute teacher, it can be difficult to see the big picture and how a particular assignment or activity fits into the teacher's overall plan, but the teacher expects students to complete the work and it is your responsibility to see that it gets done. The *Fill-in Activities* and lessons you bring should be used only when the assigned work is completed, or the plans left by the permanent teacher are unable to be carried out.

There will be situations when the permanent teacher, for some reason, cannot leave lessons plans, when the plans left are impossible to decipher; or activities are too short for the time available. These situations leave you with the challenge of filling class time with manageable and worthwhile activities. Every substitute teacher should have some "tried and true" activities that work in a variety of situations. Such activities are found in this book and should be kept in your *SubPack*. Use them to keep the students occupied and learning at the same time.

The activities and lessons in this chapter are not intended to replace the lesson plans of the permanent teacher, but rather to supplement them in three specific ways. *Five-Minute Fillers*, *Early Finishers*, and *Short Activities* are three types of *Fill-in Activities* included in this chapter. *Five-Minute Fillers* are whole-class, teacher directed activities for those few extra minutes that often occur throughout the school day. *Early Finisher Activities* are for when individual students finish assignments early and need something constructive to do. *Short Activities* include lesson plans and activities that can be completed in 15 to 30 minutes.

Visit The Professional
Substitute Teacher
web site and test your
knowledge at:

www.stedi.org

Each type of activity is introduced at the beginning of this chapter. Following the introduction, the chapter is organized according to content area. Note that most activities can be adapted as needed for use as *Five-Minute Fillers*, *Early Finishers*, or *Short Activities*. In many cases, adaptations for students with special needs and accelerated learners are provided.

A *Reference Guide for Activities* listing each activity in the chapter is located on pages 104-106. By familiarizing yourself with a variety of ideas from various disciplines and assembling the necessary materials, you will be prepared for whatever teaching situation you encounter.

Copy some of the activities in this handbook to keep in your *SubPack*. At the beginning of the class, explain that these worksheets will be available for students who finish assignments early. Prepare enough worksheets for each student in the class to have one. As you leave the school at the end of the day, ask the school secretary if you can make copies to replace those the students used.

Suggestions for Implementing Activities and Lessons

- Many of the activities and lessons in this book indicate an approximate time needed to complete the activity. However, these are guidelines only. The time needed to complete each activity varies with the age and ability of the students.

- Contents are arranged by topic, however, many lessons are appropriate for several different subjects. By familiarizing yourself with all of the lessons, you will be able to make the best use of everything this book has to offer.

- The worksheets and activities in this chapter are designed to stimulate thinking, provide experimentation and deduction, as well as to enhance the standard core curriculum. Convey them as an opportunity to learn something new, rather than as an evaluation of what students already know.

- Consider letting students work in groups to complete assignments, or work independently then in groups for the last five minutes. This removes some of the extreme pressure students feel to get the "right" answer.

- When using worksheets, prepare the students with a discussion or brainstorming activity before handing out the worksheets. If their minds are in gear and they are already thinking about the topic, they will learn more as they process the information on the page.

- If you don't have the time or resources to photocopy student worksheets, consider completing them orally. Read the questions aloud and allow students to respond. The material can be adapted to fit any time frame using this presentation style.

- Be specific in your instructions. If the assignment should be done without talking, say, "Work silently." If it needs to be completed in 15 minutes let the students know.

- Allow enough time to check answers or share results at the end of an activity or assignment. If this is not possible, leave an answer key with the permanent teacher for students to check their work the next day.

- Answers for students to check their own work can be provided in a number of ways:

  - The teacher can read them aloud at the end of the activity.

  - An answer key can be taped to a desk or wall for students to consult.

– Answer keys can be photocopied and distributed when students finish the assignment.

- Always evaluate student work before returning it to them. Even a couple of words at the top of the page recognizes student effort and validates the worth of the assignment. If you gave the assignment, it is your responsibility to correct and evaluate the students' work.

- Summarizing the activity helps to ensure that learning has taken place. One simple way to do this is to have students, or groups, take turns stating one new thing they learned from the activity.

- Many of the activities and lessons in this chapter include adaptations for students with special needs and accelerated learners and are indicated by the icons shown here. Additional suggestions for adapting activities to meet the needs of all learners are found in chapters four and five.

Accelerated

Special Needs

A Special Note

In many of the lesson plans that follow, the last procedure is *"hand in work for the teacher evaluation."* It is important that you, the teacher for that lesson, note some type of evaluation on the students' papers. Often it will work out so you can evaluate and return papers to students before they go home. Other times it may take a few minutes after school to make a note on the papers and leave them for the permanent teacher to distribute. In either case, it is important that *you*, the teacher who assigned the work, be the one to mark it. This validates the students' work and helps them feel like the assignment had a purpose. If you simply leave the papers for the permanent teacher they will probably be either handed back without an evaluation or perhaps even thrown away. In either case, the students will come to believe that assignments they do with a substitute teacher are not really important because no one took the time to look at their work and comment about it. A stamp, a sticker, or a few positive words at the top of the page is all it takes to make students feel good about their efforts.

> Evaluating student work validates student effort.

Example:

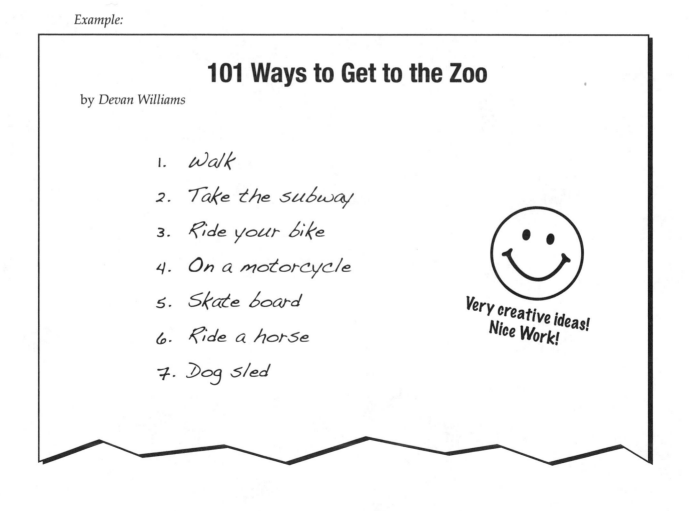

101 Ways to Get to the Zoo

by *Devan Williams*

1. Walk
2. Take the subway
3. Ride your bike
4. On a motorcycle
5. Skate board
6. Ride a horse
7. Dog sled

Very creative ideas! Nice Work!

Sample Activities:
Five-Minute Fillers

This type of filler activity is designed to use critical thinking in order to keep an entire class attentive and involved during those last five minutes, or to get everyone refocused after a break time. Students can complete these sample *Five-Minute Filler* activities independently, in groups, or as a whole class. These fillers can also be developed to introduce, enhance, or compliment the lesson for the day. Many of the activities contained in the content section of this chapter may be used as Five-Minute Filler activities.

Quick Fillers

These lists may be created verbally or in writing. You may have the students brainstorm as a class, or have them create individual lists.

1.   How many different languages can you name?

2.   Scramble five vocabulary words from today's lesson, swap with another student, and unscramble them.

3.   Make a list of the 10 largest animals you can think of.

4.   List as many breakfast cereals as you can.

5.   Write down all of the different places you find sand.

6.   List as many U.S. presidents as you can.

7.   List as many states and their capitals as you can.

8.   Name as many holidays as you can think of.

9.   Write down all of the different flavors of ice-cream you can.

10.   Name as many countries of the world as you can.

11.   List all of the forms of transportation you can think of.

12.   Name as many teachers at the school as you can.

13.   Name the different sections of a newspaper.

14.   Name all of the states that have the letter "e" in them.

15.   Name all of the different types of musical instruments you can.

If I Were A...

This activity can be done while students are sitting in their desks or waiting in a line. Begin by saying, "If I were a..." Have one student name a general topic such as food, sport, plant, animal, etc. Give each student a chance to finish the statement while the rest of the class listens.

Example: *"If I were a food, I would be a pizza."*

Number Phrases

Copy one or more of the abbreviated phrases below on the board, then challenge students to guess the phrase (see answers below).

A. 26 - L. of the A.

B. 7 - W. of the W.

C. 54 - C. in a D. (with the J.)

D. 88 - P. K.

E. 18 - H. on a G. C.

F. 90 - D. in a R. A.

G. 4 - Q. in a G.

H. 24 - H. in a D.

I. 11 - P. on a F. T.

J. 29 - D. in F. in a L. Y.

K. 76 - T. L. the B. P.

L. 20,000 - L. U. T. S.

M. 7 - D. of the W.

N. 12 - E. in a D.

O. 3 - B. M. (S. H. T. R.!)

ANSWERS:

A. 26 letters of the alphabet

B. 7 wonders of the world

C. 54 cards in a deck (with the Joker)

D. 88 piano keys

E. 18 holes on a golf course

F. 90 degrees in a right angle

G. 4 quarts in a gallon

H. 24 hours in a day

I. 11 players on a football team

J. 29 days in February in a Leap Year

K. 76 trombones lead the big parade

L. 20,000 leagues under the sea

M. 7 days of the week

N. 12 eggs in a dozen

O. 3 blind mice (see how they run!)

Sample Activities:
Early Finishers

In every class, every day, there are students who finish assignments early. The following activities are designed to keep "*early finishers*" involved in constructive activities that positively affect the rest of the class. They also provide motivation for students to work hard and finish class assignments. As you select activities from the content section of chapter six to use as *Early Finishers*, remember to adjust each activity to meet the situational and individual needs of students.

At the Back of the Room

- Set up a puzzle that students can work on throughout the day.

- Set up a reading corner where students can go and read silently after they have finished an assignment.

- Tangram puzzles (see page 109).

Name _____

All About Me

1. Draw a picture of your family.

2. Write the names of four friends in your class.

3. Draw three clocks.

   Show:

   A. when you got up.

   B. when you eat lunch.

   C. when you go to bed.

4. Draw a car using only circles.

5. Write the numbers counting by 5's to 50.

6. Write a sentence using six words that start with the letter B.

7. Make a list of everything you ate yesterday.

8. Close your eyes. Listen! Write down six things you hear.

9. What is your favorite color? List five things that color.

10. Write down 10 things you would like to get for your birthday.

11. If you were the teacher what would you do?

12. Write the numbers backwards from 25 to 0.

13. Write down seven things that start with the same letter as your first name.

14. Draw an animal using only triangles.

15. Write down five things you will use today that start with the letter T.

16. How old are you?

17. If you smiled at everyone you saw for one whole day, what do you think would happen?

18. Write the days of the week.

19. What is your favorite animal?

20. If you could do anything you wanted, what would you do today?

Spot 22

Lulu is away at camp. She wrote the following letter to her best friend, after curfew, by the light of a flashlight, under the covers last night. Usually a very good writer, she made a few errors (22 to be exact) in her letter. Can you spot and circle all 22 errors?

Dear Emily;   July 12, 2009

Greatings from camp! You would not believe the awful time I am having! The first day, my bags were run over by the bus as it pulled out of the parking lot. All of the chips I had packed for late night snacks were crushed to dust and deposited throughout my clothes. It was an omen of badd things to come.

That night it rained, and wouldn't you know it, my cot was positioned directly below a leak in the cabin roof? Need less to say I woke up soggy and I've been sneezing ever since. By the time I hanged up my wet blankets and made it to breakfast, the only foold left was cold pancakes and orange juice with unidentified floating objects in it. Ugh!

The first morning we spent most of the time at the lake. Other than the fact that the water was icey cold, our canoe capsized, and my glases are now quietly resting somewhere at the bottom of the Lake Wet. It was tons of fun! That afternoon I went on a nature hike. I can now identify two kinds of pinetrees, a three varieties of wild flowers, an edible berry, and poison oak. The poison oak I studied up close and personal, which left me trying not to scratch for the rest of of the evening.

The secon night passed without incident, unless you want to count the family of mice that spent the dark hours traversing the cabin floor to raid the cookies someone had left out. They were actully kindof cute.

Today it rained so we had to spend the entire day in the lodge. In the morning I tried to make a bird house out of craft sticks. It turned out looking more like a condemmed building than anything a bird would ever want to live in. I spent the afternoon learning how to weave a basket. It was looking great until the person next to me accidentally sat on it. After dinner we learned camp songs. you know, the kind that once you get in your head you can't get rid of. So now I'm breaking curfew to write to you from under my covers to the tune of "Row Row Row You Boat.

Just two more weeks and this joyous adventure will be over! I'll give you a call when I get home, if I survive that long

See you soon,

Lulu

Spot 22

ANSWER KEY

Corrections in **Bold**

Dear Emily**,**   July 12, 2009

Greetings from camp! You would not believe the awful time I am having! The first day, my bags were run over by the bus as it pulled out of the parking lot. All of the chips I had packed for late night snacks were crushed to dust and deposited throughout my clothes. It was an omen of **bad** things to come.

That night it rained, and wouldn't you know it, my cot was positioned directly below a leak in the cabin roof? **Needless** to say I woke up soggy and I've been sneezing ever since. By the time I **hung** up my wet blankets and made it to breakfast, the only **food** left was cold pancakes and orange juice with unidentified floating objects in it. Ugh!

The first morning we spent most of the time at the lake. Other than the fact that the water was **icy** cold, our canoe capsized, and my **glasses** are now quietly resting somewhere at the **bottom** of the Lake Wet. It was tons of fun! That afternoon I went on a nature hike. I can now identify two kinds of **pine trees, a** three varieties of wild flowers, an edible berry, and poison oak. The poison oak I studied up close and personal, which left me trying not to scratch for the rest of **of** the evening.

The **second** night passed without incident, unless you want to count the family of mice that spent the dark hours traversing the cabin floor to raid the cookies someone had left out. They were **actually kind of** cute.

Today it rained so we had to spend the entire day in the lodge. In the morning I tried to make a bird house out of craft sticks. It turned out looking more like a **condemned** building than anything a bird would ever want to live in. I spent the afternoon learning how to weave a basket. It was looking great until the person next to me accidentally sat on it. After dinner we learned camp songs. **You** know, the kind that once you get in your head you can't get rid of. So now I'm breaking curfew to write to you from under my covers to the tune of "Row Row Row **Your** Boat."

Just two more weeks and this joyous adventure will be over! I'll give you a call when I get home, if I survive that long**.**

See you soon,

Lulu

Sample Activities:
Short Activities

There may be occasions when you are faced with empty class time due to insufficient lesson plans or unexpected events. When this occurs, be ready to implement a *Short Activity* designed for the entire class. These activities are usually directed by the teacher and require various lengths of instructional time to complete. Two effective sample *Short Activities* follow this introduction. Additional *Short Activities* and lesson plans are included in the content section of this chapter and are organized by subject area. In many cases, extensions are provided for students who are early finishers or if you are faced with time remaining. Suggestions for integrating the activity into other content areas or adapting for students with special needs and accelerated learners are also provided for some activities.

Poster Creation Review

Subject: Adaptable

Time: 30+ minutes

Materials Needed:

pencil, paper, crayons and other art supplies

Objective:

Students will create a poster that reflects something they have learned in a recent lesson.

Procedures:

1. Review concepts or ideas that students have studied in a lesson that day.

2. List these concepts and ideas on the board.

3. Set a time limit for the posters to be completed.

4. Have students create a poster depicting some aspect of the lesson.

5. Collect posters for teacher evaluation and classroom display.

Extension:

Have volunteers explain their posters to the class.

Bingo Review

Subject: Adaptable

Time: 30+ minutes

Materials Needed:

Bingo Review worksheet (page 103), pencils, small objects to mark the bingo squares (pieces of colored paper, beans, etc.), and prizes for the winners

Advance Preparation:

Identify 25 terms that students have been studying recently. Science, spelling, or vocabulary words work well. Students can help compile this list.

Objective:

Students will review terms or concepts they have been studying.

Procedures:

1. Remind students that participating in this activity is a privilege and that anyone who behaves inappropriately (e.g., flicking their markers across the room or calling out answers), will not be allowed to participate.

2. Distribute one Bingo Review worksheet to each student.

3. List the 25 words on the board and have the students copy them randomly onto their bingo sheet.

NOTE: *Stress the importance of copying the words so that their sheet is like no one else's.*

4. Distribute the bingo markers.

5. Using your own list, randomly select a term and provide the class with a clue or definition of the word.

6. Students raise their hands to guess the answer.

7. When the correct answer is determined, everyone marks that spot on their sheet.

8. Steps 5-7 are repeated until someone has bingo with five squares marked in a row or diagonally.

9. Continue playing until three people have won.

10. Award prizes to the winners.

11. If time allows, have students clear their sheets and play again.

Extension:

At the conclusion of the game, have students turn their sheets over, define each word, and use it correctly in a sentence.

Notes for the teacher:

Be firm, fair, and consistent in maintaining expected student behavior during this activity. It will make it more enjoyable for you and the other students in the class.

If time is limited, alter the game so that three or four in a row constitutes Bingo.

Name _____

Bingo Review

Using the words listed on the board, write one word in each of the 25 squares.

Reference Guide for Activities

Geo Art Gallery

Subject: Art

Time: 30 minutes

Materials Needed:

Several sets of tangrams (ideally one set for each student). These can either be purchased commercially or made using colored card stock and the templates found on page 111.

Advance Preparation.

Objective:

Students will use basic geometric shapes to create a work of art.

Procedures:

1. Divide the class into six groups.

2. Show the class the tangram pieces and explain that they will be using these colored geometric shapes to create a work of art.

3. Stress that any student who behaves inappropriately (e.g., throwing the tangram pieces) will be removed from his/her group and not be allowed to participate in the activity.

4. Allow students to decide if their group wants to work together and use all of the pieces in one big design, or divide the pieces up and make individual designs.

5. Tell the students how much time they will have to create their masterpiece. This will vary depending on the situation, but try to allow at least 10 minutes.

6. Distribute tangram sets to each group. Try not to give any group two sets of the same color.

7. Have students begin working. Provide updates on how much time is left.

8. When the allotted time is up explain that they will spend the last five minutes of the lesson touring the "classroom gallery" and viewing the work of other artists.

9. When touring time is finished, have students separate the pieces back into the original tangram sets. (If each set is a different color, this process is a lot easier!) Ask one student from each group to collect the tangrams and return them to the teacher.

Extension:

Have the students make an artist information card to be displayed next to their work. Things to put on the card may include the names of the artists, the number of each color used, the number of each shape used, the total number of pieces used, and a name for the work of art.

Notes for the teacher:

Classroom management may get a little hectic during the "touring" portion of the lesson. Here are some suggestions of things to do before the tour begins to help keep things under control:

1. Review classroom rules.

2. State the expected student behavior (walking, whispering, look but don't touch, etc.)

3. Ask if anyone in the class has ever been to an art gallery or museum. Discuss the atmosphere and behavior that they observed.

4. Compare the touring time to a trip to the library or school media center.

Tangram Puzzles

Subject: Art

Time: 15 - 30 minutes

Materials Needed:

Tangram sets (page 111) – one for each student or pair of students
(see Notes About Tangrams, page 110)

Tangram Puzzle worksheets (page 112 - 113) – one for each student or pair of students

Advance Preparation:

Photocopy puzzle worksheets

Objective:

Students will practice their spatial thinking skills.

Procedures:

1. Distribute to each student or pair of students a set of tangram pieces and copy of a tangram puzzle such as those found on pages 112 - 113.

2. Encourage students as they rearrange the tangram pieces to construct the puzzle.

3. Students who finish early can make their own puzzles by arranging the tangram pieces on plain paper then tracing around the outside of the design. These student puzzles can be exchanged among class members.

Special Needs

- Work with a partner.

- Match the tangram design using the answer key.

Accelerated

- Create and draw a new tangram design and have a partner try to make it.

- Construct familiar shapes (animals, plants, buildings, etc.) using the tangram puzzle pieces.

Notes About Tangrams

Used in the *Geo-Art Gallery Activity* (page 107) and *Tangram Puzzles* (page 109).

If you choose to make your own tangrams here are a few suggestions:

1. Copy tangrams onto **DIFFERENT COLORS** of **HEAVY** card stock.

2. Be sure the template sheet (page 111) is flat against the copier, otherwise the shapes will be distorted and not fit together properly.

3. Laminate the sheets of printed card before cutting the shapes apart.

4. Take the copied, laminated sheets, along with a few extra pair of scissors to school with you and let students, who finish early, cut them apart. Another option is to turn it into a class project. Have students cut them apart and then experiment making shapes while you read aloud from a good book.

5. Keep sets in sturdy Ziploc bags for storage and distribution purposes.

Purchasing or making tangrams may seem like a lot of work, but they are a versatile tool that can be used for many activities at any grade level and are well worth the effort.

Tangram Puzzles

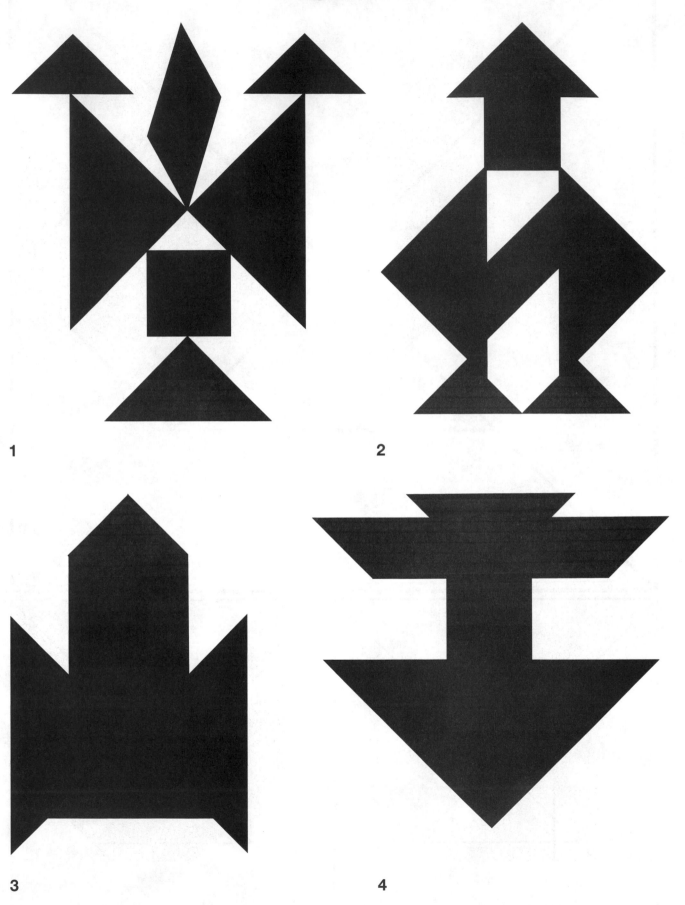

1

2

3

4

Tangram Puzzles

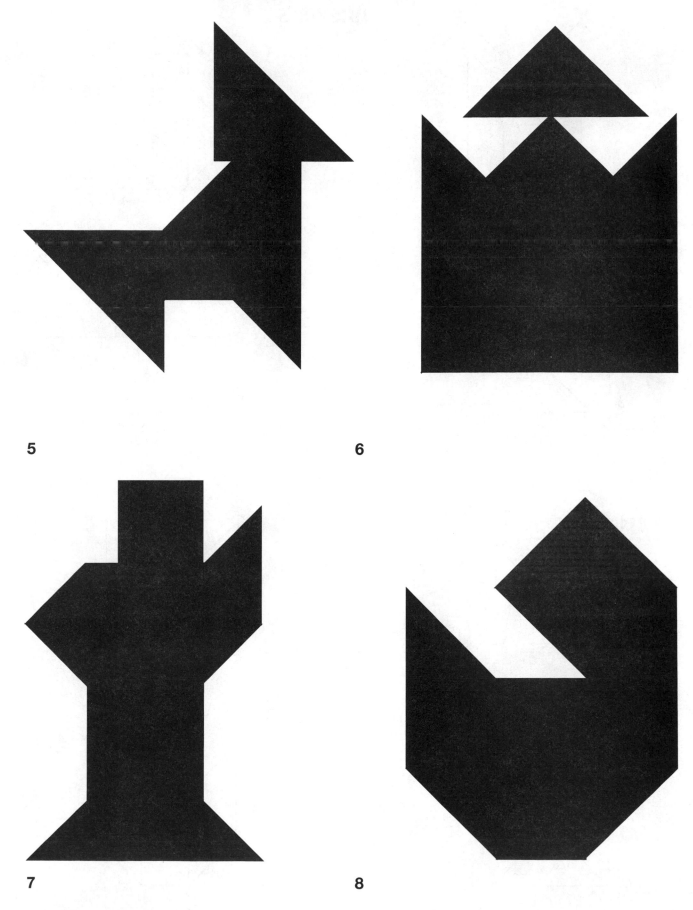

5

6

7

8

Tangram Puzzles
Answers

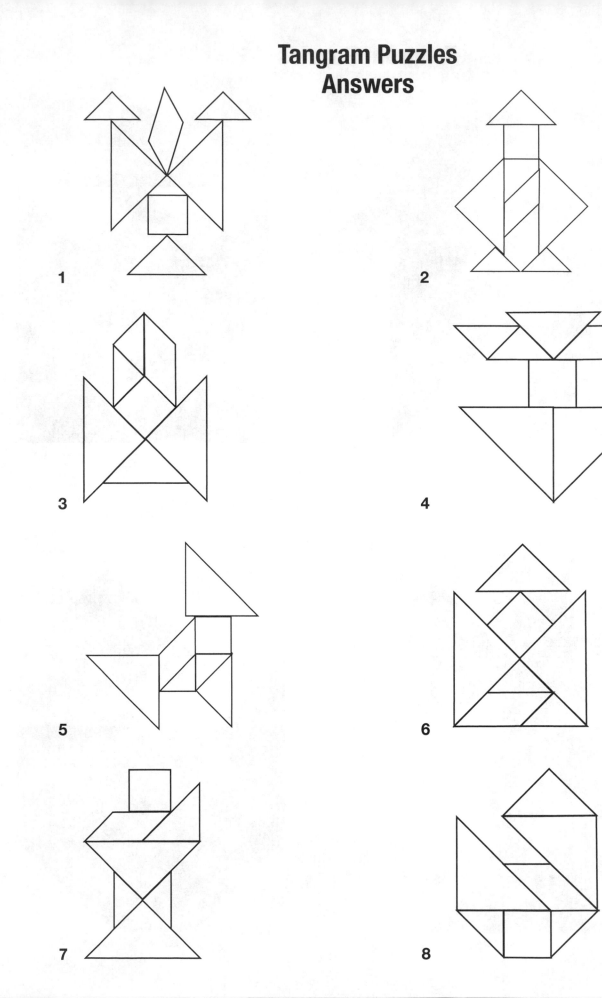

1

2

3

4

5

6

7

8

Hole Punch Art

Directions: Attach this sheet to a piece of colored paper. Use a drawing pin to punch out the dots, then hang the colored paper up in the window!

© STEDI.org

Grid Drawings

Subject: Art

Time: 15 - 30 minutes

Materials Needed:

Pencils, crayons, *Grid* worksheets (page 117 - 120)

Advance Preparation:

Make one copy of each worksheet for each student in the class.

Objective:

Students will use grids to help them complete or enlarge an image.

Procedures:

1. Distribute worksheets.

2. Explain directions and give helpful hints for completing the assignment. (Hints: draw in pencil first, look at the picture block by block, etc.)

3. Have students complete and color worksheets.

4. Turn in drawings for teacher evaluation.

Extension:

Collect student drawings and have students vote for their favorite. Award a prize to the class winner.

Notes for the teacher:

Students often enjoy sitting in small groups and talking quietly while they work on their drawings. If a group gets too noisy they can always be separated.

These worksheets can be copied back to back and students can choose which on they would like to complete. Students who finish early can then turn the paper over and begin working on the other activity.

You may want to create your own *Graph Completion Worksheets* using holiday or lesson content themes and the grid on page 119.

Name _____

Grid Enlargement

Name _____

Grid Drawings

Name _____

Grid Completion

Under Construction

Time: 30 + minutes

Materials: sketch paper, pencils.

Objective:

Students will develop a sketch for a teacher assigned construction project.

Optional Materials:

colored pencils, rulers, compasses, templates, etc.

Advance Preparation:

Determine the specific details of the project to be assigned.

In this activity students will be asked to complete a sketch for a construction project, The details, specifications, areas of emphasis, difficulty level, and nature of the project will be determined by the teacher.

Possible construction projects include the following:

- a kitchen
- a house
- a school
- a shopping mall

- a hotel
- a flower garden
- a new city park
- a new 100 home community

Potential areas of emphasis could include the following:

- drawing to scale
- color schemes
- cost efficiency

- creativity
- practicality

Procedures:

1. Make sure all students are equipped with paper.

2. Explain the nature of the assignment, details of the construction project, and set a time limit.

Example: *Today's assignment is to complete a sketch for a new resort hotel to be built in Las Vegas. The International Boating Association wants to develop a boat - themed resort featuring a 300 - room hotel, swimming pool, tropical aquarium, large sand box, and outdoor restaurant. The resort wants to become "the" place for families to stay in Las Vegas. Your preliminary sketches need to be turned in by the end of the class and will be evaluated on the creativity of incorporating the "boat theme" into the design.*

Distributing copies of the instructions or outlining key information on the board will eliminate the need for repeating the details of the assignment over and over again.

3. Monitor student work.

4. Collect and evaluate the finished projects.

You may want to photocopy or request permission to keep samples of excellent work to use as examples in other classes.

Special Needs

• See a model or example before working.

• Work with a partner

Accelerated

• Use a specified scale (e.g., $1/4'' = 1''$).

• Add more detail to the sketch.

Name _____

The Obscure Words of Art

Like any other discipline, art has a vocabulary of its own. How savvy are you at deciphering its obscure terminology? Try to match the words below with the correct definition or description.

Tools of the Trade:

___ 1. stump
___ 2. rigger
___ 3. rib

___ 4. adze
___ 5. mahlstick

___ 6. spline
___ 7. graver

___ 8. pantograph

A. a rod shaped engraving tool
B. a tool used in shaping ceramic pots
C. cigar shaped tool used to blend or smudge charcoal, pencil, chalk, or crayon
D. a cutting tool used in sculpture to rough shape wood
E. a light wooden rod three or four feet long which painters use as a rest or support when executing detailed work
F. a device used to copy, enlarge, or reduce a work of art
G. narrow strip of flexible, transparent plastic used in mechanical drawing as a ruler for curved surfaces
H. a lettering brush half the width of a standard lettering brush of the same numbered size

Colors of Art:

___ 1. ceruse
___ 2. cyan
___ 3. magenta
___ 4. bistre
___ 5. chay
___ 6. tumeric
___ 7. weld

___ 8. chartreuse

A. a brilliant yellow green
B. a yellow to reddish brown dyestuff
C. a brown pigment made by burning beech wood
D. deep blue
E. white lead
F. deep dark purplish blue, or bluish maroon
G. a natural red dyestuff obtained from the root at an East Indian plant
H. a bright yellow dye

Miscellaneous Art Terms:

___ 1. taboret
___ 2. cachet
___ 3. blot drawing

___ 4. mastic

___ 5. interlace
___ 6. merz
___ 7. putto

___ 8. thumbnail sketch

___ 9. aquarelle

A. a rough sketch of very small proportions
B. small cabinet kept near an artist's drawing table or easel
C. an artistic invention made up of discarded materials (old bus tickets, candy wrappers, etc.)
D. an accidental blot or stain on a paper used to construct an imaginary landscape
E. a monogram or symbol used in place of a signature
F. the technique of painting in transparent water color
G. a chubby nude infant often depicted in art since the 15th century
H. resin obtained from a tree used in the 19th century as a picture varnish
I. a pattern of art in which elements intercross and intertwine with one another

The Obscure Words of Art
ANSWER KEY

Like any other discipline, art has a vocabulary of its own. How savvy are you at deciphering its obscure terminology? Try to match the words below with the correct definition or description.

Tools of the Trade:

C 1. stump
H 2. rigger
B 3. rib

D 4. adze
E 5. mahlstick

G 6. spline
A 7. graver

F 8. pantograph

A. a rod shaped engraving tool
B. a tool used in shaping ceramic pots
C. cigar shaped tool used to blend or smudge charcoal, pencil, chalk, or crayon
D. a cutting tool used in sculpture to rough shape wood
E. a light wooden rod three or four feet long which painters use as a rest or support when executing detailed work
F. a device used to copy, enlarge, or reduce a work of art
G. narrow strip of flexible, transparent plastic used in mechanical drawing as a ruler for curved surfaces
H. a lettering brush half the width of a standard lettering brush of the same numbered size

Colors of Art:

E 1. ceruse
D 2. cyan
F 3. magenta
C 4. bistre
G 5. chay
B 6. tumeric
H 7. weld

A 8. chartreuse

A. a brilliant yellow green
B. a yellow to reddish brown dyestuff
C. a brown pigment made by burning beech wood
D. deep blue
E. white lead
F. deep dark purplish blue, or bluish maroon
G. a natural red dyestuff obtained from the root at an East Indian plant
H. a bright yellow dye

Miscellaneous Art Terms:

B 1. taboret
E 2. cachet
D 3. blot drawing

H 4. mastic

I 5. interlace
C 6. merz
G 7. putto
A 8. thumbnail sketch

F 9. aquarelle

A. a rough sketch of very small proportions
B. small cabinet kept near an artist's drawing table or easel
C. an artistic invention made up of discarded materials (old bus tickets, candy wrappers, etc.)
D. an accidental blot or stain on a paper used to construct an imaginary landscape
E. a monogram or symbol used in place of a signature
F. the technique of painting in transparent water color
G. a chubby nude infant often depicted in art since the 15th century
H. resin obtained from a tree used in the 19th century as a picture varnish
I. a pattern of art in which elements intercross and intertwine with one another

Master of the Trade

You probably recognize the names of the artists listed below. Can you match the artist to one of their well known works and an event or characteristic of their life? In front of the artist column write both the Work of Art letter and Trivia number.

	Artist	Work of Art	Trivia
___ ___	Rembrandt	A. The Marriage of Giovanni	1. A person known as the master of the miniature
___ ___	Monet	B. Sistine Madonna	2. Luncheon guests sometimes waited several house while he painted the cook.
___ ___	Da Vinci	C. Anatomy Lesson of Dr. Tulp	3. He painted more than 100 self-portraits throughout his life.
___ ___	Picasso	D. Book of Victory	4. He always signed his pictures in letters of the Greek alphabet.
___ ___	Degas	E. Water-lily Series	5. The local barber came to the open field and cut his hair while he painted.
___ ___	Renoir	F. The Three Dancers	6. Shot himself in a field and died two days later.
___ ___	El Greco	G. Mona Lisa	7. He was forbidden to see his mother after the age of five.
___ ___	Michelangelo	H. The Dancing Class	8. During World War I he designed scenery for Diaghilev's Ballets Russes.
___ ___	David	I. The Burial of Count Orgaz	9. Before death he walked the streets of Paris alone, blind, and terrified of automobiles.
___ ___	Rousseau	J. David	10. He played the violin for his friends and flute in the French Army Infantry Band.
___ ___	Raphael	K. The Coronation	11. As a nobleman and aristocrat he could not accept money for his work
___ ___	Velazquez	L. Gabrielle With a Rose	12. He worked in Rome off and on for 70 years for seven different Popes.
___ ___	Van Eyck	M. Starry Night	13. Made distant and secret journeys to paint portraits of princesses for Philip the Good.
___ ___	Bihzad	N. The Sleeping Gypsy	14. Drew 10 cartoons depicting scenes from the acts of the apostles; made tapestries.
	Van Gogh	O. The Spinners	15. Twice his wife plead for and gained his freedom from prison.

Master of the Trade
ANSWER KEY

You probably recognize the names of the artists listed below. Can you match the artist to one of their well known works and an event or characteristic of their life? In front of the artist column write both the Work of Art letter and Trivia number.

Artist		Work of Art	Trivia
_C_ _3_	Rembrandt	A. The Marriage of Giovanni	1. A person known as the master of the miniature
_E_ _5_	Monet	B. Sistine Madonna	2. Luncheon guests sometimes waited several house while he painted the cook.
_G_ _7_	Da Vinci	C. Anatomy Lesson of Dr. Tulp	3. He painted more than 100 self-portraits throughout his life.
_F_ _8_	Picasso	D. Book of Victory	4. He always signed his pictures in letters of the Greek alphabet.
_H_ _9_	Degas	E. Water-lily Series	5. The local barber came to the open field and cut his hair while he painted.
_L_ _2_	Renoir	F. The Three Dancers	6. Shot himself in a field and died two days later.
_I_ _4_	El Greco	G. Mona Lisa	7. He was forbidden to see his mother after the age of five.
_J_ _12_	Michelangelo	H. The Dancing Class	8. During World War I he designed scenery for Diaghilev's Ballets Russes.
_K_ _15_	David	I. The Burial of Count Orgaz	9. Before death he walked the streets of Paris alone, blind, and terrified of automobiles.
_N_ _10_	Rousseau	J. David	10. He played the violin for his friends and flute in the French Army Infantry Band.
_B_ _14_	Raphael	K. The Coronation	11. As a nobleman and aristocrat he could not accept money for his work
_O_ _11_	Velazquez	L. Gabrielle With a Rose	12. He worked in Rome off and on for 70 years for seven different Popes.
_A_ _13_	Van Eyck	M. Starry Night	13. Made distant and secret journeys to paint portraits of princesses for Philip the Good.
_D_ _1_	Bihzad	N. The Sleeping Gypsy	14. Drew 10 cartoons depicting scenes from the acts of the apostles; made tapestries.
_M_ _6_	Van Gogh	O. The Spinners	15. Twice his wife plead for and gained his freedom from prison.

Name _____

Business by Design

You have been selected to design the business cards for Tropical Island, a company that grows and sells tropical plants.

The following information must be included on the card:

- Company name
- Company Logo (which you design)
- Employee Name
- Employee Title
- Mailing Address
- Fax Number
- Telephone Number
- E-mail Address

The actual card size is:

2" by 3 1/2" but you can complete your design in the large box below.

Actual Size

Your Design:

Following Directions

Subject: Critical Thinking

Time: 15 - 30 minutes

Materials Needed:

Teacher Directed Instructions (page 129), *Following Directions Activity Sheet* (page 130), crayons, colored pencils, or markers.

Advance Preparation:

Photocopy one *Following Directions Activity Sheet* for each student.

Objective:

Students will follow oral directions and develop their listening skills.

Procedures:

1. Ask the following questions to discuss the importance of following directions:

   A. When is it important to follow directions?

   B. Why is it important to follow directions?

   C. What could happen if you did not follow directions?

2. Hand out a worksheet to each student and have them write their names in the specified place.

3. Distribute crayons to each student.

4. Instruct the students to listen carefully as you read each set of instructions twice. Tell them not to do anything until they have listened carefully both times.

5. Read the instructions 1-5 found on the *Teacher Directed Instructions*. Make sure that students do not begin until the instructions have been read twice.

6. Collect worksheets for teacher evaluation.

Extension:

Hand out blank pieces of paper and have students follow simple oral directions as the teacher gives them (e.g., put your name at the top, draw a circle in the center of the paper, make a line across the bottom of the paper, etc.).

Teacher Directed Instructions

Following Directions:

Distribute to each student a copy of the *Following Directions Activity Sheet* and crayons. Tell them to listen carefully while you read the instructions out loud.

> Say: *Listen carefully to what I say to do. I will repeat each direction only two times. Do exactly what I say.*

1. Find the square with the butterfly in the corner. Put your finger on the butterfly. Color in the triangle with your crayon. Put an X in the circle. Draw a circle inside of the square.

2. Find the square with the umbrella in the corner. Put your finger on the smallest square. Color the umbrella. Write the letter A in the biggest square. Draw a line through the middle square.

3. Find the square with the apple in it. Put your finger on the apple. Now look carefully at the triangle. Draw a line above the triangle. Draw a square inside the triangle. Outline the triangle with your crayon.

4. Find the square with the flower in the corner. Put your finger on the flower. Look carefully at the circles. Draw a triangle inside the top circle. Write the letter your name begins with in the biggest circle. Color the smallest circle.

5. Turn your paper over. Draw a big circle. Make this circle into a happy face.

Special Needs

• Remain in close proximity to students with special needs so they can focus and hear better.

Name _____

Following Directions Activity Sheet

Guess the Object

Subject: Critical Thinking

Time: 30+ minutes

Materials Needed:

pencil and paper

Advance Preparation:

Objective:

Students will practice their listening and oral direction skills.

Procedures:

1. Have the class draw an object as you give an oral description. The object should be simple like a toothbrush, pencil, football, key, flowers, umbrella, etc.

2. Do not identify the object by name until students have had a chance to guess what it is and share their pictures with class members.

3. Repeat the activity with students giving oral directions for the class to draw and guess at.

4. Discuss the importance of listening carefully and giving good directions during this activity.

5. Discuss other situations when it is important to listen carefully or communicate clearly.

Extension:

1. Divide the class into teams of two and get them to practice giving descriptions and listening to one another to guess what is being described.

2. Have students draw a simple picture using geometric shapes (see examples on page 132). If time allows, have them color their pictures.

3. Organize the students into partners and instruct them to sit back-to-back.

4. Have one student give directions about how to draw his picture while the other follows the directions and completes a drawing on the back of his paper.

NOTE: *The student giving directions cannot look at the drawing in progress and the student drawing cannot ask questions.*

5. Have students change roles.

6. When they are finished, have students compare pictures and discuss which directions were easy to follow and which were confusing.

7. Get the students to complete the activity again with a different partner. Compare the second partner's drawing with the one done by the first partner to determine which time they gave better directions.

Notes for the teacher:

Give directions for drawing the object rather than saying it is like something else. For example, if the object was a basketball you could say, "Draw a circle. Draw lines across it and put dots all over the inside of the circle," rather than saying, "It is like a baseball only bigger."

Brain Teasers and Riddles

1. What is full of holes, yet holds water? **A sponge.**

2. What is bought by the yard, yet worn by the foot? **Carpet**

3. What is the longest word in the English language?
   Smiles. There is a mile between the first and last letter.

4. If eight birds are on a roof and you shoot at one, how many remain?
   None. They all fly away.

5. Why can't it rain for two days continually? **Because there is always a night in between.**

6. What speaks every language? **An echo.**

7. Why is a nose in the middle of a face? **Because it is the "scenter."**

8. What table is completely without legs? **A times-table.**

9. What is the difference between a jeweller and a jailer?
   One sells watches, the other watches cells.

10. What is black and white and read all over? **A newspaper.**

11. Can a man living in Chicago be buried west of the Mississippi? **No. He is still alive.**

12. How far can a dog run into the woods? **Halfway. The other half he is running out.**

13. A farmer had seventeen sheep. All but nine died. How many did he have left? **Nine.**

14. A man has two coins in his hand. The two coins total thirty cents. One is not a nickel. What
    are the two coins? **A nickel and a quarter. (The other is a nickel.)**

15. Why is Ireland the wealthiest country? **Because its capital is always Dublin.**

16. If a telephone and a piece of paper had a race, who would always win?
    The telephone, since the paper will always remain stationery.

17. Why should fish be well-educated? **They are found in schools.**

18. Which takes the least amount of time to get ready for a trip: An elephant or a rooster?
    The rooster . . . He only takes his comb, but the elephant has to take a whole trunk.

19. Do they have a Fourth of July in England? **Yes. (But it is not a holiday.)**

20. Take two apples from three apples. What have you got? **Two apples.**

21. Four men can build four boats in four days. How long will it take one man to build one
    boat?
    Four days. (Four men building four boats is the same as one man working sixteen days.)

22. Can you measure out exactly two gallons of water using only two unmarked containers?
    One of the containers will hold eight gallons and the other will hold five gallons. **Pour five
    gallons into the eight gallon can. Then repeat this until the eight gallon can is full. (Two
    gallons remain in the five gallon can.)**

Minute Mysteries

"**Minute Mysteries**" are stories that are told within a minute and then require the listeners to solve a mystery. Students generate questions that can be answered with a simple "yes" or "no" in order to solve the mystery. These stories are fun and teach children to use critical thinking skills while they sort through the information to work out the answer.

1. A cowboy left town on Tuesday and was gone three days, coming back on Tuesday.

   Q. *How is that possible?*

   A. **His horse was named Tuesday.**

2. A man is found dead in a cabin in the ocean.

   Q. *What could have happened?*

   A. **The man is in the cabin of an airplane that crashed into the ocean.**

3. A person lived on the 15th floor of a high-rise building. Everyday he got into the elevator, rode down to the lobby and went to work. Every evening he came home from work, took the elevator to the 13th floor and walked up the stairs to his apartment.

   Q. *Why?*

   A. **The person is very short and can only reach the elevator button to the 13th floor.**

4. A man was lonely and wanted a talking parrot to keep him company. He went to the pet shop and found a beautiful bird that was for sale at a bargain price. He asked the shop owner *if the bird could be trained to talk.* The owner said, *"This bird is absolutely guaranteed to repeat everything it hears."* So the man bought the bird and took it home. But two weeks later he returned to the shop, demanding his money back, saying, *"The bird refused to talk."* The shop owner said, *"I stand by my guarantee and will not give your money back."*

   Q. *How could he say that, considering the bird wouldn't talk?*

   A. **The parrot was deaf.**

Mind Benders

1. The Shopping Trip

One day last week my brother went to town with only $10 in his pocket, but returned in the evening with $20.

He bought a pair of shoes at a sporting goods store and some meat at the meat market. He also had his eyes examined. It so happens that my brother gets paid every Thursday by check and the banks in this town are open on Tuesday, Friday, and Saturday only. The eye doctor is not in his office on Saturday and there is no market on Thursday and Friday. What day did my brother go to town?

2. The Chess Tournament Dilemma

Four men named P.F. Smith, C.J. Smith, Reynolds, and Fellows played in a chess tournament.

The Smiths were the famous Smith brothers, twins who played opposite ends on the Princeton football team.

Reynolds surprised everyone when he defeated Fellows.

The man who finished third said graciously to the winner at the conclusion of the matches, "I've heard a great deal about you and I am happy to meet you. May I congratulate you?"

The runner-up was unable to walk, having had infantile paralysis when he was four years old. He had never married, but had lived a sheltered life with his widowed mother, making chess his chief diversion.

P.F. Smith sometimes talked too much. He had disgraced himself when he was an usher at Fellow's wedding by making the bride's mother late for the wedding.

In what order did the men finish the chess tournament?

3. The Artisans

There are three men, named James, John, and Jake, each of whom is engaged in two occupations. Their jobs classify each of them as two of the following: chauffeur, electrician, musician, painter, gardener, and barber. From the following facts, find in what two occupations each man is engaged.

1. The chauffeur offended the musician by laughing at his long hair.

2. Both the musician and the gardener used to go fishing with James.

3. The painter had the electrician wire his new house.

4. The chauffeur dated the painter's sister.

5. John owed the gardener $5.00.

6. Jake beat both John and the painter at horse shoes.

4. The Stolen Antique

Three men, Mr. White, Mr. Black and Mr. Brown and their wives were entertained at the home of their friend one evening. After the departure of the guests, the host and hostess discovered that a valuable antique had been stolen. It was later discovered that one of the six guests was the thief.

From the facts given, see if you can discover who it was.

1. The spouse of the thief lost money at cards that evening.

2. Because of partial paralysis of his hands and arms, Mr. Brown was unable to drive his car.

3. Mrs. Black and another female guest spent the entire evening doing a jigsaw puzzle.

4. Mr. Black accidentally spilled a drink on Mrs. White when he was introduced to her.

5. Mr. Brown gave his wife half of the money that he had won to make up for her loss.

6. Mr. Black had beaten the thief at golf that day.

Solutions to Mind Benders:

1. The Shopping Trip

My brother went to town on Tuesday.

2. Chess Tournament Dilemma

Winner-C.J. Smith; Runner-up- Reynolds; Third- Fellows; Fourth- P.F. Smith

3. The Artisans

James- barber and painter; John- musician and electrician;
Jake- chauffeur and gardener

4. The Stolen Antique

Mrs. Black was the thief.

The Plimpton Hold Up

If you were present for three minutes at the scene of the hold up pictured below and later were questioned as a witness, how many questions relating to it could you answer? Study this picture carefully for three minutes and without referring to the picture again, answer as many of the questions as you can.

The Plimpton Hold Up Questions

1. In what town did the hold-up occur?
2. What was held up?
3. What is its correct address?
4. On the corner of what two streets is it?
5. Is the thief in the picture?
6. Where is he?
7. How much money did he steal?
8. Did the policeman see the hold-up?
9. What is he doing about it?
10. What is the name of the taxi company?
11. What is the number of the taxi?
12. In what direction is the taxi going?
13. What time did the hold-up take place?
14. What is the date?
15. How many people are shown?
16. How many are aware of the hold-up?
17. What kind of store is next to the bank?
18. Who owns it?
19. What is its correct address?
20. What kind of store is on the corner?
21. Who owns it?
22. What is the number of this store?
23. At the corner of what two streets is it?
24. Which of these two is the one-way street?
25. In what direction does traffic go on this street?
26. Where is the hydrant?
27. What does the sign on 20th Street advertise?
28. What is the price of the advertised product?
29. Is there a postbox shown?
30. On what street are the car tracks?

Special Needs

• Allow more time for students with special needs to view the picture.

Desert Dilemma

Subject: Critical Thinking

Time: 15 - 30 minutes

Materials Needed:

Desert Dilemma worksheet (page 140) for each student or group

Advance Preparation:

Make photocopies of the student worksheets.

Objective:

Students will practice critical thinking skills as they analyze and discuss different priorities in a difficult situation.

Procedures:

1. Distribute to the class the *Desert Dilemma* worksheets, either individually or in small groups.

2. Review the situation and instructions as a class.

3. Allow students 10 minutes to rank the items listed.

4. Have a class discussion on how they ranked the items allowing students to justify or revise their own choices.

Extension:

Get the students to list the objects on the back of their paper and put a star next to each of the objects they plan to carry. Then explain in writing how they plan to use each of these items.

Notes for the teacher:

This activity can be done as a class with one student giving directions, and the other students doing the drawing at their own desks.

Special Needs

• Work with a partner.

Desert Dilemma

Situation:

While driving through the desert you take a wrong turn and drive 50 miles before your car runs out of gas. You are stranded wearing shorts, a T-shirt and tennis shoes. There is nothing around you but cactus and sand. The temperature is about 110° F in the shade. Your only hope for rescue is to make it back to the main road.

You rummage around in the car and find the 20 items listed below. You realize that you will not be able to carry all of them with you so you rank the items according to how important you think they will be in ensuring your survival and rescue. Place the number 1 by the most important item, 2 by the second most important, and so on, with 20 being the least important item.

Remember that you are in the desert and that the three essential things for survival are food, clothing, and shelter. Work individually, and later we will discuss your choices with the rest of the class.

_____ any part of the car

_____ sun glasses

_____ AM/FM radio

_____ blanket

_____ lipstick

_____ a candy bar

_____ box of matches

_____ silk scarf

_____ an apple

_____ a map of the state

_____ sling shot

_____ 50 ft. of nylon rope

_____ boots

_____ first aid kit

_____ pencil and paper

_____ flashlight

_____ plastic garbage bag

_____ hammer

_____ a pack of gum

_____ canteen of water

Word Puzzles 1

Directions:

These puzzles represent common expressions and phrases. Solve them by carefully noticing the positions of the words and letters. Are they under, over, mixed-up, inside, or a certain size?

E K A KISS M	search and	NEFRIENDED	wear ——— long
egsg gesg segg sgeg	S M O K E	GIVE GET GIVE GET GIVE GET GIVE GET	cover agent
NOT GUILTY STANDER	man ——— board	EZ iiii	LM AL EA AE EM ML
BELT ——— HITTING	A S D L A	he {art	T. V.
ar up ms	CHAIR	TIRE	T O W N

Answers found on page 143.

Word Puzzles 2

Directions:

These puzzles represent common expressions and phrases. Solve them by carefully noticing the positions of the words and letters. Are they under, over, mixed-up, inside, or a certain size?

I S O C K	1,000, **1**000	C O S T S	ground feet feet feet feet feet feet
go i g n / a r o d n u	time time	stand I	T O U C H
FRIENDS standing / miss FRIENDS	**WALKING**	**SOUP**	ter very esting
r|e|a|d|i|n|g	b sick ed	LO head/heels VE	knee lights
g r u the block n i n n	everyrightthing	R R O O A D D S S	i 8

Answers found on page 143.

Answers to Word Puzzles

kiss and make up	search high and low	friend in need	long underwear	**Word Puzzles 1:**
scrambled eggs	up in smoke	forgive and forget	undercover agent	
innocent bystander	man overboard	easy on the eyes	three square meals	
hitting below the belt	tossed salad	broken heart	black and white TV	
up in arms	high chair	flat tire	downtown	

sock in the eye	one in a million	rising costs	six feet underground	**Word Puzzles 2:**
going around in circles	time after time	I understand	touchdown	
mis understanding between friends	walking tall	split peas soup	very interesting	
reading between the lines	sick in bed	head over heals in love	neon lights	
running around the block	right in the middle of everything	cross roads	I over ate	

Foreign Language Five-Minute Fillers

Similar to the *Five-Minute Filler Activities* at the beginning of this chapter, the following sponge activities have been adapted to challenge students' foreign language skills. Whenever possible, have students write or speak their responses in the language they are studying.

1. Name as many cities as you can where _____ (language) is spoken.

2. List as many colors as you can.

3. Write the names of the months and days of the week.

4. List the numbers from one to one hundred.

5. Write the alphabet.

6. Describe what you are wearing.

7. List 15 objects you can see from where you are sitting.

8. Write down the names of all of the holidays you know.

9. Suppose a friend who doesn't speak _____ (language) was going on vacation to _____ (country where language is spoken), what would be the 10 most useful words you think they should learn before leaving.

Additional Foreign Language Activities

Beginner's Crossword Puzzle:

Make a crossword puzzle in French, Spanish, German, Latin, or another foreign language you are studying. The clues may be in English.

Advanced Crossword Puzzle:

Make a crossword puzzle in the language you are studying. The clues must be in the same language.

Floor Plan:

Draw the floor plan of a house. Label the rooms, doors, windows, and furniture in Spanish, French, German, or any other non-English language.

"Buzz":

Play a game of "buzz" speaking only German, Spanish, or French. The first person calls out the word for "one" the second, "two", the third "three", and so on around the room. Every time a number that contains seven or is a multiple of seven (e.g., 7, 14, 17, 21) comes up call out "buzz" instead of the number. Remember, "buzz" is the only English word allowed!

Telephone:

Play a game of telephone, using only the language you are studying. The first person chooses a phrase or sentence in Spanish, French, or German and whispers it to the person next to him. That person, without asking him to repeat it, whispers the same phrase, as he understands it, to the next person, and son on. The last person in the row says the phrase out loud and translates it into English.

Calendar:

Make a calendar for this month, using only the foreign language you are studying. No abbreviations are permitted.

20 Questions:

Play twenty questions. One student chooses an object and tells the class whether it is animal, plant, or mineral. The rest of the class takes turns asking questions that can be answered only "yes" or "no" until they guess the object, or until they have asked twenty questions and still can't guess. Both the object and the questions must be stated in the foreign language the class is studying.

Stump the Experts:

Play "stump the experts." Three students volunteer or are chosen as experts. Members of the class take turns giving them words in the foreign language for one of the experts to translate into English. If he can do it, he remains as expert. If he can't, the one who stumped him becomes the expert. Later, class members give words in English and the experts translate it into the language being studied.

Writing Directions:

In the language you are studying, write directions explaining step-by-step how to do a simple task, such as putting on a hat and coat, cooking an egg, or sawing a board. Select a volunteer and without telling him what the task is or using and English, read your directions to him and have him carry out the instructions.

Writing a Limerick:

Write a limerick in the language you are studying. Remember, the first, second, and fifth lines rhyme and the third and fourth lines rhyme.

Spelling Bee:

Select one student as moderator and hold a spelling bee entirely in the language you are studying. Use words from the foreign language text used by the class.

Vocabulary Bee:

Select one student as moderator and hold a vocabulary bee. The moderator, using the foreign language text, gives words in English. Students must translate the words.

About the Country:

In English, write a description of a major country where the language you are studying is spoken. Include any small details you may know.

Display:

Arrange a display of several items from around the room on a desk while a volunteer is out of the room. Have him or her come in and study the display from one minute, then, without looking at it again, list everything on the desk from memory. The student must use the language being studied.

Concentration:

Play "concentration". Divide into teams of two. Cut paper into 3-by-5 inch pieces and make a set of concentration cards, using antonyms in the language you are studying. For instance, if Spanish is your language, one card might read "si", its match would be "no" one card might read "noche," its match "dia," one card might read "caliente," its match "frio," and so on. Make ten to twenty pairs.

To play, spread out all the cards, face down. The first player turns over any two cards and shows them to the other player. If they should be a matching pair of antonyms, he then puts them face up at his side of the table. The first player may then have another try at finding a matched pair. If the first player does not find a match, the second player tries to remember where and what has been turned up and attempts to find a matched pair. Both players must see the cards turned up each time to help them locate matches. The game continues until the last card has been picked up. One point is given for each matched pair. The high score wins.

Traveling Game:

Play a traveling game; Each students must think of some item to go in a suitcase, using only the language being studied. The first person in the first row must pack something beginning with the letter "a," the second with "b," and the third must start with "c," and so on. Begin by saying, "I am going to visit relatives, so I will get out my big suitcase and pack it with my ..."

> *Example in Spanish*:
> First student – "Abrigos"   Second student – "Botas"

If a student makes a correct addition – it doesn't need to be a sensible one – he earns one point. If he cannot think of one, he loses two points.

Super Sentence:

Play super sentence. Let one student choose ten or twelve words from the dictionary in the language being studied and write them on the board. In ten minutes, the rest of the class tries to write a sentence using all the words or as many as they can. Read the sentence aloud.

Slapstick:

Arrange students desks in a circle. Each student is assigned a word in the language they are studying (recent vocabulary lists work great). One student is selected to stand in the center of the circle with a rolled up newspaper. The teacher calls out one of the assigned words and the student to whom the word has been assigned must quickly call out another word before the student in the center can "slap" their desk with the newspaper. Play continues until someone doesn't say a word before having their desk slapped, or mispronounces a work. In either event, the student assumes the role of the person in the center, who returns to their desk. Play resumes until class is over or students lose interest.

In large classes it may be beneficial to create two circles, thus allowing for more students involvement and interaction. Changing the assigned words halfway through the class will help to keep things interesting and challenging.

State Nicknames

Every state in the United States has a nickname. How many states can you correctly match with their nicknames?

		State		**Nickname**
_____	1.	Alabama	A.	The Heart of Dixie
_____	2.	Alaska	B.	Palmetto State
_____	3.	Arizona	C.	The First State or Diamond State
_____	4.	Arkansas	D.	Empire State of the South or Peach State
_____	5.	California	E.	Show Me State
_____	6.	Colorado	F.	Peace Garden State
_____	7.	Connecticut	G.	Badger State
_____	8.	Delaware	H.	The Last Frontier
_____	9.	Florida	I.	The Sunflower State
_____	10.	Georgia	J.	Green Mountain State
_____	11.	Hawaii	K.	Garden State
_____	12.	Idaho	L.	Sooner State
_____	13.	Illinois	M.	Volunteer State
_____	14.	Indiana	N.	Old Line State of Free State
_____	15.	Iowa	O.	The Prairie State
_____	16.	Kansas	P.	The Pelican State
_____	17.	Kentucky	Q.	The Golden State
_____	18.	Louisiana	R.	Sage Brush State or Silver State
_____	19.	Maine	S.	Old Dominion
_____	20.	Maryland	T.	The Hoosier State
_____	21.	Massachusetts	U.	Keystone State
_____	22.	Michigan	V.	Tar Heel State or Old North State
_____	23.	Minnesota	W.	The Grand Canyon State
_____	24.	Mississippi	X.	The Centennial State

		State		**Nickname**
_____	25.	Missouri	Y.	The Gem State
_____	26.	Montana	Z.	North Star State or Gopher State
_____	27.	Nebraska	AA.	Cornhusker State
_____	28.	Nevada	BB.	Granite State
_____	29.	New Hampshire	CC.	Equality State
_____	30.	New Jersey	DD.	The Evergreen State
_____	31.	New Mexico	EE.	Beaver State
_____	32.	New York	FF.	The Bay State or Old Colony
_____	33.	North Carolina	GG.	The Hawkeye State
_____	34.	North Dakota	HH.	The Sunshine State
_____	35.	Ohio	II.	The Constitute State or Nutmeg State
_____	36.	Oklahoma	JJ.	Lone Star State
_____	37.	Oregon	KK.	The Blue Grass State
_____	38.	Pennsylvania	LL.	Mountain State
_____	39.	Rhode Island	MM.	Beehive State
_____	40.	South Carolina	NN.	The Empire State
_____	41.	South Dakota	OO.	Treasure State
_____	42.	Tennessee	PP.	Little Rhody or Ocean State
_____	43.	Texas	QQ.	The Aloha State
_____	44.	Utah	RR.	The Land of Opportunity
_____	45.	Vermont	SS.	The Pine Tree State
_____	46.	Virginia	TT.	Mount Rushmore State or Coyote State
_____	47.	Washington	UU.	Buckeye State
_____	48.	West Virginia	VV.	The Land of Enchantment
_____	49.	Wisconsin	WW.	Magnolia State
_____	50.	Wyoming	XX.	The Great Lakes State or Wolverine State

State Nicknames
ANSWER KEY

		State				State
A.	1.	Alabama		OO.	26.	Montana
H.	2.	Alaska		AA.	27.	Nebraska
W.	3.	Arizona		R.	28.	Nevada
RR.	4.	Arkansas		BB.	29.	New Hampshire
Q.	5.	California		K.	30.	New Jersey
X.	6.	Colorado		VV.	31.	New Mexico
II.	7.	Connecticut		NN.	32.	New York
C.	8.	Delaware		V.	33.	North Carolina
HH.	9.	Florida		F.	34.	North Dakota
D.	10.	Georgia		UU.	35.	Ohio
QQ.	11.	Hawaii		L.	36.	Oklahoma
Y.	12.	Idaho		EE.	37.	Oregon
O.	13.	Illinois		U.	38.	Pennsylvania
T.	14.	Indiana		PP.	39.	Rhode Island
GG.	15.	Iowa		B.	40.	South Carolina
I.	16.	Kansas		TT.	41.	South Dakota
KK.	17.	Kentucky		M.	42.	Tennessee
P.	18.	Louisiana		JJ.	43.	Texas
SS.	19.	Maine		MM.	44.	Utah
N.	20.	Maryland		J.	45.	Vermont
FF.	21.	Massachusetts		S.	46.	Virginia
XX.	22.	Michigan		DD.	47.	Washington
Z.	23.	Minnesota		LL.	48.	West Virginia
WW.	24.	Mississippi		G.	49.	Wisconsin
E.	25.	Missouri		CC.	50.	Wyoming

State Nicknames

Name _____

Locations and Associations Activity One:
Locating the State

Use the list of states below to locate and correctly label as many states as you can on the blank map. Do not "cross-out" the states on the list. You will use the list again in *Activity two*. Use a map to check your work.

Alabama	Louisiana	Ohio
Alaska	Maine	Oklahoma
Arizona	Maryland	Oregon
Arkansas	Massachusetts	Pennsylvania
California	Michigan	Rhode Island
Colorado	Minnesota	South Carolina
Connecticut	Mississippi	South Dakota
Delaware	Missouri	Tennessee
Florida	Montana	Texas
Georgia	Nebraska	Utah
Hawaii	Nevada	Vermont
Idaho	New Hampshire	Virginia
Illinois	New Jersey	Washington
Indiana	New Mexico	West Virginia
Iowa	New York	Wisconsin
Kansas	North Carolina	Wyoming
Kentucky	North Dakota	

Locations and Associations Activity
Two: State Associations

Next to each state on the list in activity one, write down one or two words which you associate with that state. For example you might associate "orange juice" with the state of Florida or "igloos" with the state of Alaska.

When you have finished, share your association words with a partner while they try and guess which state you are referring to. Then switch roles and you try to guess the states from their associations.

How Well Can You Follow Directions?

Start in the United States and follow the directions to see where you end up.

1. Write down: THE UNITED STATES OF AMERICA.

2. Take out all of the E's.

3. Take out every fifth letter.

4. Change the F to an A.

5. Move the S's to the front of the word.

6. Take out all of the T's.

7. Take out the first vowel and the last consonant.

8. Move the fourth and fifth letter to the end of the word.

9. Replace the S's with L's.

10. Remove the sixth, seventh, and eighth letters.

11. Move the double L's to be the third and fourth letters.

12. Where did you end up?_____

Answer: Holland

Name _____

Where In The World?

Listed below are ten famous events and ten well known places. Fill in the blanks as accurately and completely as you can.

Where did it happen?

1. Writing of the Declaration of Independence _____

2. First Olympics held _____

3. Abraham Lincoln died _____

4. Columbus first landed _____

5. Treaty of Versailles signed _____

6. Custer's Last Stand _____

7. President John F. Kennedy assassinated _____

8. Surrender papers of the Civil War signed _____

9. Wright brothers first airplane flight _____

10. Martin Luther King shot and killed _____

Where is located?

1. Westminster Abbey _____

2. Grand Canyon _____

3. Louvre _____

4. Taj Mahal _____

5. Pyramids _____

6. Rodeo Drive _____

7. Leaning Tower of Pisa _____

8. Mount Rushmore _____

9. Eiffel Tower _____

10. Statue of Liberty _____

Where In The World?
ANSWER KEY

Listed below are ten famous events and ten well known places. Fill in the blanks as accurately and completely as you can.

Where did it happen?

1. Philadelphia, PA

2. Olympia in Southern Greece (776 BC)

3. Peterson Boarding House across the street from Ford's Theater in Washington DC

4. a small island in the Bahamas

5. Versailles, France (a suburb of Paris)

6. Indian encampment along the Little Big Horn River in Montana

7. Dallas, TX

8. Mclean House near the Appomattox

9. Kitty Hawk, NC

10. balcony of the Lorraine Motel in Memphis, TN

Where is located?

1. London, Enlgand

2. Arizona

3. Paris, France

4. Agra, India

5. four miles south of Cairo, Egypt

6. Beverly Hills, CA

7. Pisa, Italy

8. South Dakota

9. Paris, France

10. Liberty Island, geographically a part of New Jersey but thought of as belonging to New York

A Citizenship Test

What does it take for a person from a foreign land to become an American citizen? In addition to being a person of good moral character, they must be at least 18 years old, have a solid grasp of the English language, and pass a citizenship test. Each year about one million immigrants take this test. They know their American history. Do you?

Below are 30 questions taken from the Immigration and Naturalization Service (INS) citizenship questions pool. Write down the answer, or your best guess, then check your answers. You need to answer at least 18 of the 30 questions correctly to pass.

1. How many stars are there on out flag?

2. What do the stars on the flag mean?

3. What color are the stripes?

4. What do the stripes on the flag mean?

5. What is the date of Independence Day?

6. Independence from whom?

7. What do we call a change to the Constitution?

8. How many branches are there in our government?

9. How many full terms can a president serve?

10. Who nominates judges of the Supreme Court?

11. How many Supreme Court justices are there?

12. Who was the main writer of the Declaration of Independence?

13. What holiday was celebrated for the first time by American colonists?

14. Who wrote the Star-Spangled Banner?

15. What is the minimum voting age in the United States?

16. Who was president during the Civil War?

17. Which president is called the "Father of our Country?"

18. What is the 50th state in the Union?

19. What is the name of the ship that brought the Pilgrims to America?

20. Who has the power to declare war?

21. What were the 13 original states of the United called?

22. In what year was the Constitution written?

23. What is the introduction to the Constitution called?

24. Which president was the first Commander in Chief of the United States Army and Navy?

25. In what month do we vote for the president?

26. How many times may a senator be re-elected?

27. Who signs bills into law?

28. Who elects the president of the United Sates?

29. How many states are there in the United States?

30. Who becomes president if both the president and vice president die?

A Citizenship Test
ANSWER KEY

1. 50

2. One for each state in the Union.'

3. Red and white

4. They represent the 13 original states.

5. July 4th

6. England

7. Amendments

8. Three

9. Two

10. The president

11. None

12. Thomas Jefferson

13. Thanksgiving

14. Francis Scott Key

15. 18

16. Abraham Lincoln

17. George Washington

18. Hawaii

19. The Mayflower

20. The Congress

21. Colonies

22. 1787

23. The Preamble

24. George Washington

25. November

26. There is no limit at the present time.

27. The president

28. The Electoral College

29. 50

30. Speaker of the House of Representatives.

Name _____

If History Were Altered

1. How would the world be different today if the colonists had not won the Revolutionary War and the new country had remained under British rule?

_____

_____

_____

2. How would the world be different today if electricity had never been invented?

_____

_____

_____

3. How would the world be different today if the atomic bomb had not been used against the Japanese in World War II?

_____

_____

_____

4. How would the world be different today if Columbus and his ships had perished at sea and never reached the American Continents?

_____

_____

_____

5. How would the world be different today if travel by airplane had never been developed?

_____

_____

_____

The Constitution

Ratified in 1788 the Constitution of the United States has served as the basis for U.S. government ever since. It set up a federal government system with three branches, legislative, executive, and judicial, while allowing states to retain many rights and responsibilities. Try to correctly fill in the blanks to complete the preamble to this historical document.

Preamble

We the _____ of the United States, in order to _____ a more perfect _____, establish _____, insure domestic _____, provide for the common _____, promote the general _____, and secure the blessings of _____ to ourselves and our _____, do ordain and _____ this _____ for the _____ States of _____.

Constitutional Amendments

Throughout the 200+ years the constitution has been in place, relatively few amendments have been added to the original document. However, the amendments to the constitution, and rights guaranteed by them, are perhaps the most critical documentation of citizen rights in our society today. Can you match the amendment number and date to the responsibility, right, or law it secures?

_____ Amendment 1 (1791)   A. Voting rights for blacks.

_____ Amendment 2 (1791)   B. Lowered the voting age to eighteen.

_____ Amendment 4 (1791)   C. Prohibition of alcohol

_____ Amendment 5 (1791)   D. Limited presidential terms of office.

_____ Amendment 13 (1865)   E. Presidential succession outline

_____ Amendment 15 (1870)   F. Do not have to testify against oneself.

_____ Amendment 18 (1919)   G. Freedom of religion, speech, press, assembly, and
                                      petition.

_____ Amendment 19 (1920)   H. Right to bear arms.

_____ Amendment 21 (1933)   I. Warrants needed for searches and seizures.

_____ Amendment 22 (1951)   J. Voting rights for women.

_____ Amendment 25 (1967)   K. The repeal of the prohibition amendment.

_____ Amendment 26 (1971)   L. The abolition of slavery.

The Constitution
ANSWER KEY

Preamble

We the **people** of the United States, in order to **form** a more perfect **union**, establish **justice**, insure domestic **tranquillity**, provide for the common **defense**, promote the general **welfare**, and secure the blessings of **liberty** to ourselves and our **posterity**, do ordain and **establish** this **Constitution** for the **United** States of **America**.

Constitutional Amendments

<u>G.</u>   Amendment 1 (1791)

<u>H.</u>   Amendment 2 (1791)

<u>I.</u>   Amendment 4 (1791)

<u>F.</u>   Amendment 5 (1791)

<u>L.</u>   Amendment 13 (1865)

<u>A.</u>   Amendment 15 (1870)

<u>C.</u>   Amendment 18 (1919)

<u>J.</u>   Amendment 19 (1920)

<u>K.</u>   Amendment 21 (1933)

<u>D.</u>   Amendment 22 (1951)

<u>E.</u>   Amendment 25 (1967)

<u>B.</u>   Amendment 26 (1971

Presidential Trivia

Matching

_____ 1. George Washington

_____ 2. John Tyler

_____ 3. Grover Cleveland

_____ 4. Harry S. Truman

_____ 5. Gerald R. Ford

_____ 6. Woodrow Wilson

_____ 7. Theodore Roosevelt

A. Made the decision to use the atomic bomb against Japan.

B. The only president to serve two terms which did not follow each other

C. Became the first President to hold regular press conferences to explain his policies.

D. As president, he created more than one million acres of national forests and parks.

E. Became the first vice-president to take over after a president had died in office.

F. Left school around the age of 14 become a surveyor.

G. The only man to be both president and vice-president without being elected to either office.

True or False

_____ 1. President Lyndon B. Johnson was sworn into office aboard the presidential airplane.

_____ 2. President James Madison is referred to as "the father of the Declaration of Independence."

_____ 3. President John Quincy Adams was a poor public speaker with only an elementary knowledge of English.

_____ 4. President William H. Taft began the tradition of throwing out the first baseball of the major league baseball season.

_____ 5. Prior to becoming president, George Bush served as director of the Central Intelligence Agency.

_____ 6. President James Garfield amazed people by writing Latin with one hand and Greek with the other, at the same time.

_____ 7. President Andrew Johnson spent his childhood evenings reading books by the fire.

Which Does Not Belong?

1. James Monroe	A. Monroe Doctrine	B. Louisiana Purchase	C. Civil War Soldier
2. Abraham Lincoln	A. Cherry Tree	B. Emancipation Proclamation	C. Assassination
3. Ronald Reagan	A. Movie Star	B. Barbara	C. I don't remember
4. John F. Kennedy Oswald	A. Oldest President	B. Bay of Pigs	C. Lee Harvey
5. Dwight D Eisenhower	A. I Like Ike	B. Career Soldier	C. Wheelchair
6. George W. Bush	A. War on Terrorism	B. White House birds	C. Texas

Presidential Trivia
ANSWER KEY

Matching

__F.__ 1. George Washington

__E.__ 2. John Tyler

__B.__ 3. Grover Cleveland

__A.__ 4. Harry S. Truman

__G.__ 5. Gerald R. Ford

__C.__ 6. Woodrow Wilson

__D.__ 7. Theodore Roosevelt

True or False

__T__ 1. President Lyndon B. Johnson was sworn into office aboard the presidential airplane.

__F__ 2. President James Madison is referred to as "the father of the Declaration of Independence."

__F__ 3. President John Quincy Adams was a poor public speaker with only an elementary knowledge of English.

__T__ 4. President William H. Taft began the tradition of throwing out the first baseball of the major league baseball season.

__T__ 5. Prior to becoming president, George Bush served as director of the Central Intelligence Agency.

__T__ 6. President James Garfield amazed people by writing Latin with one hand and Greek with the other, at the same time.

__F__ 7. President Andrew Johnson spent his childhood evenings reading books by the fire.

Which Does Not Belong?

1. James Monroe	A. Monroe Doctrine	B. Louisiana Purchase	~~C. Civil War Soldier~~
2. Abraham Lincoln	~~A. Cherry Tree~~	B. Emancipation Proclamation	C. Assassination
3. Ronald Reagan	A. Movie Star	~~B. Barbara~~	C. I don't remember
4. John F. Kennedy Oswald	~~A. Oldest President~~	B. Bay of Pigs	C. Lee Harvey
5. Dwight D Eisenhower	A. I Like Ike	B. Career Soldier	~~C. Wheelchair~~
6. George W. Bush	A. War on Terrorism	~~B. White House birds~~	C. Texas

This Year in History

Subject: Government/History

Time: 30 minutes

Objective:

Students will attempt to identify the things for which the current year will be remembered.

Materials Needed:

paper and pencils

Optional Materials:

news magazines, newspapers, etc.

Advance Preparation:

Procedures:

1. Divide the class into small groups.

2. List categories in which to identify specific events or fads of the year, such as the ones listed below:

   A. World events

   B. National events

   C. Political events

   D. Music

   E. Commercials

   F. Television shows

3. Have students brainstorm as many items as they can for each category.

4. As a class, compile a master list with one or two items in each category which best represents the time period.

5. Discuss how students think the events and fads of this year will change or affect society in the years to come.

20 Events

Listed below are 20 events that changed American history. Match them with their description on the right.

___ 1. Plymouth Colony

A. This protest set the civil rights movement in motion.

___ 2. Slavery

B. Marked the United States' arrival as a major world power.

___ 3. Declaration of Independence

C. Launched the movement that would help women win full citizenship, including the right to vote.

___ 4. Ratification of the Constitution

D. The establishment of a blueprint for American government.

___ 5. 1800 Election

E. Colonists began importing Africans to meet a severe labor shortage.

___ 6. Louisiana Purchase

F. This legislation closed America's open door to immigrants.

___ 7. Seneca Falls Convention

G. A long bloody war that divided America and helped create a generation that mistrusted the government.

___ 8. Secession

H. Presidential decree abolishing slavery.

___ 9. Emancipation Proclamation

I. The first major confrontation between the federal government and the labor movement.

___ 10. Transcontinental Railroad

J. Pilgrim settlers established a new settlement in North America.

___ 11. Pullman Strike

K. Doubled the size of the United States and accelerated territorial expansion.

___ 12. Spanish-American War

L. A confrontation with the Soviet Union that threatened to turn the Cold War into a nuclear war.

___ 13. Treaty of Versailles

M. Economic crisis which left millions of Americans without jobs, homes, or food.

___ 14. National Origins Act, 1924

N. A decisive election in which the American people rejected big government and the welfare state.

___ 15. The Great Depression

O. The creation of a nation by the South and beginning of a long and terrible war.

___ 16. Attack on Pearl Harbor

P. Proclamation of the independence of a new nation which would be ruled by the people rather than a king.

___ 17. Montgomery Bus Boycott

Q. Marked the official beginning of the two party system with a peaceful, and orderly transfer of power.

___ 18. Cuban Missile Crisis

R. A surprise Japanese attack that brought the United States into a Second World War.

___ 19. Vietnam War

S. Ended the First World War and set the conditions that led to the Second.

___ 20. The Reagan Election

T. Transformed the social and economic life of America by linking the regions of the nation.

Select one of the events from the above list. Turn this paper over and write about how American life would be different today if this event had not occurred, or write a brief summary elaborating on the details of the event. You may want to use your textbook as a reference.

20 Events
ANSWER KEY

  J.   1. Plymouth Colony

  E.   2. Slavery

  P.   3. Declaration of Independence

  D.   4. Ratification of the Constitution

  Q.   5. 1800 Election

  K.   6. Louisiana Purchase

  C.   7. Seneca Falls Convention

  O.   8. Secession

  H.   9. Emancipation Proclamation

  T.   10. Transcontinental Railroad

  I.   11. Pullman Strike

  B.   12. Spanish-American War

  S.   13. Treaty of Versailles

  F.   14. National Origins Act, 1924

  M.   15. The Great Depression

  R.   16. Attack on Pearl Harbor

  A.   17. Montgomery Bus Boycott

  L.   18. Cuban Missile Crisis

  G.   19. Vietnam War

  N.   20. The Reagan Election

Name _____

Are They For Real?

Some literary characterizations have been so vivid that they have almost taken a place in history. On the other hand, some real people have lived such legendary lives that they seem almost fictional. Can you identify the following men and explain if they are fact or fiction?

1. Alexander the Great
2. King Arthur
3. Paul Bunyan
4. Lloyd George
5. Johnny Appleseed
6. Robin Hood

7. Sherlock Holmes
8. Paul Revere
9. Mark Twain
10. Mike Fink
11. Marco Polo
12. Ivan the Terrible

Who Invented That?

Some of the men who invented things you use every day are familiar to you, but some of them may not be at all. Below is a list of familiar items used everyday, as well as a list of inventors. Can you match the inventors with their invention?

1. The sewing machine
2. The phonograph
3. The television
4. The material called plastic
5. The sandwich
6. The pin

Elias Howe

Isaac M. Singer

Thomas Edison

Emile Berliner

John Wesley Hyatt

Alexander Parks

John Montagu

Lemuel W. Wright

Are They For Real?
ANSWER KEY

1. Alexander the Great is fact, he was the King of Macedonia, lived 356-323 B.C., and was considered a military genius for his conquests of Greece, Egypt, and the Middle East.

2. King Arthur is fiction, the legendary King of Britain who presided over the Roundtable.

3. Paul Bunyan is fiction, a tall-tale hero of early-American fiction.

4. Lloyd George is fact, he was the Prime Minister of Great Britain during WWI.

5. Johnny Appleseed's real name was John Chapman. One of the original ecologists, who walked over the American countryside planting apple seeds.

6. Robin Hood is fiction, though some authorities say the legendary charitable bandit of Sherwood Forest was based on a historical person, little evidence has been found.

7. Sherlock Holmes is the fictional detective to whom the solutions to tangled problems were "Elementary, my dear Watson." He was created by Sir Arthur Conan Doyle.

8. Paul Revere is fact, a silversmith and patriot of the American Revolution.

9. Mark Twain is fact, though his real name was Samuel Clemens, he was an American humorist and the author of Tom Sawyer and The Adventures of Huckleberrry Finn.

10. Mike Fink, though based on a real person, had so many tall-tales built around his career as a keel boat man that he must be considered fiction.

11. Marco Polo is fact, he was a Venetian who traveled through most of Asia on his trips in the thirteenth and fourteenth centuries.

12. Ivan the Terrible is fact, he was a Russian Czar who became noted for brutality and tyranny.

Who Invented That?
ANSWER KEY

1. Elias Howe received credit for this invention after a lengthy patent dispute with Isaac M. Singer.

2. Thomas Edison is credited with the invention of the phonograph, but Emile Berliner developed the flat disc record, the lateral-cut groove, and a method of duplicating records.

3. There is no single inventor of television. It is the result of many discoveries in electricity, electromagnetism, and electrochemistry.

4. Celluloid was the first of the synthetic plastics and was invented by John Wesley Hyatt following experiments done by Alexander Parkes. Hyatt was seeking material with which to make a better billiard ball.

5. The sandwich was invented by John Montagu, the Earl of Sandwich, because he was too busy gambling to take time out to eat a regular meal.

6. The ordinary pin with a solid head was first made on a machine invented by Lemuel W. Wright in 1824 in New Hampshire. Until then, the head of a pin was made by twisting fine wire into a ball and soldering it to one end of a sharpened wire.

Literature in the Classroom

Literature can enhance learning at every grade level. When sharing literature books:

- Use creative questioning to keep students interested. A question that requires a single right answer does little to keep students involved. Questions that have a variety of answers will keep students engaged in discussion and move learning forward.

- Have students reflect on what they would do in a similar situation, what else the character might have done, what would be different if the setting or era were changed in the story, etc.

- Ask students to justify actions and evaluate occurrences.

- Have trials of story predators.

- Write letters to the author. If you can get students involved in the story, positive behavior will be a natural result.

For a list of recommended children's literature see page 255.

Name Poetry

Subject: Language Arts

Time: 15-30 minutes

Materials Needed:

pencil and paper

Advance Preparation:

Create an example of a Name Poem to be used to teach the activity.

Objective:

Students will create a poem that is an expression of their own traits and personal characteristics.

Procedures:

1. Discuss different types of poetry. Ask students to share some poems that are familiar to them.

2. Tell the students that today they are going to create a poem about themselves.

3. Demonstrate an example of a Name Poem (acrostic poem) on the board.

Example:

C is for chocolate chip cookies, which are my favorite

Y is for the yellow flowers that grow in my garden

N is for Nika my cat

T is for the tree house I helped build

H is for happy thoughts

I is for ice-cream on my birthday

A is for all of the other things that make up me

4. Ask the students to make a name poem using their own name.

5. Share name poems with the class or in small groups.

6. Collect poems for teacher evaluation and display.

Extension:

Create Acrostic Poems using other topics such as holidays, school subjects, sports, etc. Illustrate the poems by drawing and coloring pictures of the things written about in the poem.

Notes for the teacher:

Younger students may have difficulty in completing this assignment with only one example for instruction. It may be helpful to create a second poem on the board as a class, before they write their own.

Accelerated

• Make the poem rhyme.

• Use first and last name.

• Use 20 descriptive words (adjectives).

Diamanté Poetry

Subject: Language Arts

Time: 30+ minutes

Materials Needed:
pencil and paper

Advance Preparation:
Prepare a Diamanté Poem pattern and example.

Objective:
Students will learn the Diamanté Pattern for poetry and create a poem using this pattern.

Procedures:

1. Talk about a specific topic (holiday, school subject, kind of food, famous person, etc.).

2. Draw a chart on the board with the following categories: Smells, Tastes, Sounds, Sights, and Feelings.

3. Fill in the chart with student suggestions for each category.

4. Tell the students they will now use this information to write a diamanté poem about this topic.

5. Explain the pattern and put it on the board (see example below).

	PATTERN	**EXAMPLE**
Line 1	subject	Fourth of July
Line 2	two adjectives or words that describe the subject	Fire Crackers, Bands
Line 3	three words that show action, usually "ing" words	Marching, Fighting, Picnicking
Line 4	two words that describe the subject	Flags, Sparklers
Line 5	a synonym (other name) for the subject	Independence Day

6. As a class, compose a *Diamanté Poem* about the selected topic using words from the chart on the board.

7. Assign students to choose another topic and write a *Diamanté Poem* on their own.

8. Have volunteers share their poems with the class.

Extension:

Have students write a diamanté about an upcoming holiday, then use the poem as the message in a greeting card.

Notes for the teacher:

Students may have difficulty selecting their own topic to write on. You may wish to assign a specific topic to the whole class or brainstorm possible topics and suggest that students use on of the topics from the brainstorming session.

Writing and Revising

Time: 5-45 minutes

Objective: Students will practice writing and editing skills.

Advance Preparation:

Select a writing prompt for the students. Create a handout, write it on the board, or be prepared to give it verbally.

This activity can fill five minutes or an entire lesson depending on the complexity of the writing prompt, and at which step you want students to stop work and turn in their work for teacher evaluation. There are no right or wrong answers, only an opportunity for students to explore their own thoughts, values, and beliefs. Encourage students to explain and justify their responses. Do not allow students to criticize the thoughts and opinions of others.

Procedures:

1. Provide the class with a writing prompt and time limit for completing the first draft of their work.

2. Get students to exchange papers and edit one another's work for content and technical components.

3. Allow students time to discuss their editorial comments with one another, getting a second opinion from other students, if time permits.

4. After the editing process, get students to complete a second draft of their work and hand it in for teacher evaluation.

Writing Prompts:

A. Write an invitation to a social event, real or imaginary, formal or casual.

B. Write a letter to a national news agency convincing them to cover a recent or upcoming event at your school.

C. Write a menu for a new restaurant in town.

D. Write a chronological report of everything you have done so far today.

E. Write an outline of your life. Include events you anticipate will happen in the future.

F. Write a letter to a music company explaining a billing mistake they made on your last order.

G. Write a brief essay about what life as a street light would be like.

H. Write a description of eating ice cream.

I. Write an evaluation of the pen or pencil you are using.

J. Write a memo to your boss asking him/her for a raise.

K. Write a synopsis of a book you have recently read.

L. Write a newspaper article about current fashion trends or a recent sporting event.

M. If this weekend you could do anything you wanted to, what would you do?

N. If you were a teacher and the students in your class wouldn't stop talking what would you do? What if you did that and they still didn't stop talking?

O. If there was a poster competition coming up, would you rather create a poster all by yourself and get all of the credit, or work with a group and share the credit with the other group members?

P. If you could be invisible for one day, what would you do?

Q. If your parents were going to be living in a foreign country for the next year, would you rather go with them or stay in your own neighborhood with a friend? Why?

R. What would the perfect day at school be like?

S. If you could change just one thing about school, what would you change?

T. Pretend you could only have one pair of shoes for the next year. Would you choose shoes that are really comfortable but look kind of goofy, or shoes that look really cool but are uncomfortable to wear?

U. What are two things you don't like now, but ten years from now you don't think will be so bad?

V. Suppose your dad forgot that he had promised to drive you and a friend to the movies one Saturday afternoon; he went golfing instead. If you could choose a punishment for your dad, what would it be? Do you think it would make him not do this again?

W. What subjects in school do you think are really important to study? Why?

X. If you could pick any age, and be that age for the rest of your life, what age would you want to be? Why?

Y. If you could choose new jobs for your parents, what would you choose and why?

Special Needs

• Write fewer sentences.

• Use more time to complete the assignment.

• Refer to a list of key words to use.

Sparkle

Subject: Language Arts

Time: 10-40 minutes

Materials Needed:

A list of level appropriate words to be used for spelling practice, pencil and paper

Objective:

Students will review the spelling of vocabulary or spelling list words through a group game.

Procedures:

1. This activity can be played as an entire class or in smaller groups. Start by having the students sit at their desks or stand next to them.

2. Give the class a word to spell. (You may choose to have them write the word on a piece of paper.)

3. Going row by row, get them to spell the word one letter at a time. Everyone must listen so they know what letter comes next when it is their turn.

4. After the last letter is said, the following person says "*Sparkle*" and the next person sits down, indicating they are out. If someone misses a letter along the way, they too are asked to sit down.

5. Those who are out will continue to write the words that are given on their paper and check them against those who are still in the game. The game can end at any point, but may continue until there is a final player.

Special Needs

• Refer to a spelling list.

• Write down the word before spelling it.

Name _____

Cold Words

Brr. . . . Can you ~~selbrmacnu~~ unscramble these cold words?

1. anmnsow _____
2. eci beuc _____
3. inretw _____
4. kewosflna _____
5. gidnslge _____
6. odlc _____
7. bdierge _____
8. ngiisk _____
9. leccii _____
10. cie _____

11. lcreiag _____
12. oloig _____
13. eci rcaem _____
14. radzizlb _____
15. strof _____
16. zenorf _____
17. ushls _____
18. cie kasting _____
19. wnos _____
20. lalownsb _____

How many words can you think of that end in "ice?" **There are at least 75!**

_____

_____

_____

_____

_____

_____

_____

_____

Cold Scrambled Words:

1. snow man
2. ice cube
3. winter
4. snowflake
5. sledging
6. cold
7. iceberg
8. skiing
9. icicle
10. ice
11. glacier
12. igloo
13. ice cream
14. blizzard
15. frost
16. frozen
17. slush
18. ice skating
19. snow
20. snowball

The Newspaper

Subject: Language Arts

Time: 15-30 minutes

Materials Needed:

newspaper, pencil, and paper

Advance Preparation:

Objective:

Apply real life examples to learning that occurs in the classroom.

The newspaper can be a lifesaver when substitute teaching. If there are no plans left for a classroom, the newspaper can be used to teach anything!

- In a kindergarten class, students can circle letters of the alphabet to learn upper and lower case concepts.

- In first grade, students could circle words they recognize or discuss the emotions depicted in pictures.

- Students at various grade levels can:

— create a shopping list from ads and use math skills to create a total cost

— forecast weather and discuss climate

— work out statistics for sporting events

— write a classified ad or cartoon to expand writing skills to different audiences

— create a budget using data from job opportunities, apartment rental, and food advertisement sections

Use some creativity and you can teach anything!

My Awful, Terrible, Horrible, No Good, Very Bad Day

Subject: Language Arts

Time: 30+ minutes

Materials Needed:

pencils, paper, a copy of the book *Alexander and the Terrible Horrible No Good Very Bad Day* by Judith Viorst. Available to check-out at most libraries or for purchase at most bookshops.

Advance Preparation:

Objective:

Students will identify and express their experiences and feelings in writing.

Procedures:

1. Read the book *Alexander and the Terrible Horrible No Good Very Bad Day*. If the book is not available you may tell about a time when you had a bad day.

2. Get students to discuss things that have happened and caused them to have a bad day. Try to discourage the discussion of morbid or disturbing events. (To learn more about brainstorming strategies, see page 28.)

3. Ask students to name feelings that they have when things go wrong (you may want to list these on the board).

4. Get students to write about their own *Awful, Terrible, No Good, Very Bad Day*. Remind them to include feelings in their narration.

5. Ask volunteers to share their writing with the class.

6. Collect stories for the teacher to review.

Extension:

Have the students illustrate their writing. With student permission, place the illustrated experiences in a three ring binder for students to read at their leisure.

Notes to the Teacher:

Giving students specific writing guidelines will help ensure quality work. For example, you may require that younger students write at least six sentences and that older students write at least three paragraphs. Providing an example you have written about a bad day of your own will also help to get them started on the right track.

Most students enjoy listening to a good story, so class management should not be much of a problem while you are reading. However, it is always a good idea to explain exactly the kind of behavior you expect during an activity before you begin (feet on the floor, pencils down, eyes on the teacher, facing forward, etc.).

Silly Stories

Time: 15 minutes

Materials Needed: *Silly Story* worksheets (pages 179-180) and pencils

Objective:

Students will practice naming nouns, verbs, adjectives, adverbs, and other words as they work cooperatively to compose *Silly Stories*.

Procedures:

1. Review with students the following parts of speech:

    A. Noun   =   name of a person, place, or thing

    B. Verb =   shows action

    C. Adjective   =   describes a noun (color, size, etc.)

    D. Adverb   =   describes a verb (often ends in ly)

2. Explain that students are going to practice naming examples of these parts of speech as they work with a partner to complete a *Silly Story*.

3. Complete the example *Silly Story* as a class.

4. Read the completed example aloud to the class.

5. Divide the class into partners and distribute the *Silly Story* worksheets.

6. Get one student to provide the words for one story with the other acting as scribe and narrator. Then switch roles to complete the second *Silly Story*.

7. If time allows, students may volunteer to read their *Silly Stories* to the class.

Extension:

Trade partners and reuse the same worksheets to create new stories with a different person's input. Older students may also enjoy writing their own *Silly Story* worksheets for classmates to complete.

Special Needs

• Review and be given examples of the different parts of speech.

• Refer to a written reminder of what the different parts of speech are.

Name _____

Silly Story — Trip to Outer Space

Directions:

Ask a student for the part of speech or type of word as indicated. Write the word on the space provided. Repeat the process until all the spaces are filled. Read the completed Silly Story aloud to the class.

Last night I had a dream about you. At the age of (1) _____ you were good looking and the captain of the spaceship (2) _____. In the dream you and a crew of (3) _____ traveled to the planet (4) _____. The flight began at (5) _____ a.m. "10... 9... 8... 7... 6... 5... 4... 3... 2... 1...(6)_____ ," the controller called as the space ship blasted off from (7) _____. During take off the ship started to (8) _____ but quick action from the crew kept it on course and prevented you from crashing into (9) _____. Outer space was (10) _____ as you (11) _____ past the moon everyone (12) _____ to the windows to take a look. Finally the planet (13) _____ was in sight. After orbiting the planet (14) _____ times, while you were looking for your (15) _____ , the space ship finally landed. Everyone got off and began collecting (16) _____ (17) _____ that were all over the surface of the planet, until you started hearing (18) _____ noises. You were afraid the planet was going to explode so you hurried back on board the ship and took off (19) _____. The last thing I remember is your spaceship heading straight for the (20)_____ in my house. Oh my, was I ever (21) _____ to wake up!

1. number

2. proper name

3. animal (plural)

4. planet

5. time of day

6. exclamation

7. geographical location

8. verb

9. geographical location

10. adjective

11. verb (past tense)

12. verb (past tense)

13. same planet as #4

14. number

15. personal belonging

16. adjective

17. noun (plural)

18. verb ending in "ing"

19. adverb ending in "ly"

20. room in a house

21. feeling

Name _____

Silly Story — Getting to School

Directions:

Ask a student for the part of speech or type of word as indicated. Write the word on the space provided. Repeat the process until all the spaces are filled. Read the completed Silly Story aloud to the class.

You would not believe the (1) _____ time I had getting to school today. First of all my alarm went off at (2) _____ a.m. instead of (3) _____ a.m., which is the time I usually get up. When I (4) _____ my closet to decide what to wear the only clothes I could find were (5) _____ (6) _____ and (7) _____ (8) _____. Luckily the outfit I'd been wearing for the past (9) _____ days was still in the washing basket so I put it on. Then I went to the (10) _____ to eat breakfast but, the only food I could find was (11) _____ and week old (12) _____ so I (13) _____ them together and ate it (14) _____. As if that wasn't bad enough, when I went to brush my teeth (15) _____ came out of the tap instead of water. I was not having a (16) _____ day. Then my (17) _____ couldn't find the (18) _____ to the car, so I had to walk all the way to school carrying the (19) _____ (20) _____ I had made for my (21) _____ class project. Halfway to school a (22) _____ started chasing me so I (23) _____ ran the rest of the way. I rushed inside the front (24) _____ just as the late bell rang. I hope the rest of my day goes (25) _____.

1. adjective

2. time

3. time

4. past tense verb

5. color

6. piece of clothing

7. adjective

8. piece of clothing

9. number

10. room in a house

11. food

12. food

13. past tense verb

14. adverb ending in "ly"

15. liquid

16. adjective

17. member of a family

18. part of a car

19. adjective

20. noun

21. school subject

22. animal

23. adverb ending in "ly"

24. part of a building

25. adverb

Writing for an Audience

Subject: Language Arts

Time: 15-30 minutes

Materials Needed:
pencil, paper, and a classroom object

Advance Preparation:
Make a list of potential audiences and purposes for writing on the chalkboard (see examples below).

Objective:
Students will practice writing for different audiences.

Procedures:

1. Hold up a common object in the classroom (ruler, stapler, key, tablet, etc.).

2. Discuss what the object is and what it is used for.

3. Ask the students to choose an audience and purpose for writing from the board. Give the students a time limit and have them write about the object discussed in procedure 2.

4. Instruct students to not tell anyone the audience they have selected.

5. Get volunteers to read their paragraphs aloud and get the class members to guess which audience they selected.

Examples of Audiences and Purposes:

• Tell a story about the object in procedure 1 to a Kindergarten class.

• Write in a diary as though you were an archeologist who dug up this object two hundred years from now.

• You are from another planet and you are writing home to explain how the object is used on Earth.

• Write a memo to the principal explaining why this object should be purchased for every student in the school.

• Explain to someone who has never seen this object how it is used.

• Write specific details about this object so that the reader could walk into the classroom and pick it out from other similar objects.

Extension:

Get students to select another object in the classroom and write about it without mentioning it by name. Trade papers among class members and have them try to work out what object the person is writing about.

Notes for the Teacher:

Setting specific guidelines for the writing assignment will help with this activity. Specify that it should be at least five sentences or that ten minutes will be all the time available for writing. The younger the students the more specific instructions they will need.

Establishing guessing procedures for step five will help with classroom management. Students will want to call out their guesses as the volunteers read their paragraphs. Establish that no one is to guess until the reader has read their entire paper and that the reader will call on someone who has raised his/her hand when s/he has finished.

Adjective? What Is An Adjective?

 Time: 1 hour

Materials Needed:

- Four-foot piece of heavy newsprint or butcher paper for each group.

- Masking tape or other means of attaching paper to wall.

- A different colored marker for each group.

- A variety of scenic pictures to be mounted on the top of each piece of long paper.

Objective:

Students will learn what an adjective is and how it can be used to make creative writing more interesting, and will use their creative ability and vocabulary to describe a picture.

Procedures:

1. Mount pictures at the top of the long sheets of paper and hang them around the room or in hallways. Students will be writing on them so make sure the surface is smooth, markers do not fade through the paper, and there is enough space for students to stand in front of the picture without bothering other groups.

2. Divide students into workable groups equal to the number of pictures being used. Be sure each group is a different color of markers. Emphasize the need for all students to contribute not just the one who is doing the writing.

3. Students are to make a list of words that describe what they see in the picture. These must be single words not phrases and they can only be used once. For example, the word green may be used to describe the grass and the trees in a picture, not green grass and green tree. Depending on the length of the class period and the follow up activities set a timer for how long you want the students to be at each picture.

4. When time is up groups move to the next picture and continue the word list. The only catch is that they can not use the same words as the previous group. They must come up with original words of their own.

5. Continue the rotation until each group has had an opportunity to evaluate each picture.

6. When the lists are completed the teacher should read through the lists reviewing them with the students. The following are suggestions on what to look for:

   a. Does the word describe the picture?

   b. Is the word listed only once? (If not the second listing is crossed out.)

   c. Is each word found in the dictionary or did students make them up?

   d. Discuss which group made the best and most contributions to the pictures: the group who worked on a picture first or last.

   e. Which pictures were the easiest to describe?

7. The rest of the activity may be done in small groups or individually. Do one or all of the following:

   a. Write a poem about one of the pictures using as many of the adjectives as possible.

   b. Write a story about one of the pictures making sure that none of the words on the list are used. Rewrite the story using appropriate adjectives from the list to see how much more interesting the story becomes.

   c. Have the student become part of the picture then write a story including who, what, when, where, and why format.

   d. Same as above except from the prospective of a news reporter.

Integration:

Math:

1. Use a bar or line graph to show the number of words each group got on each picture. Use the same colors as the markers for easy comparisons.

2. Figure the percentage of words each group had on each page or total number of words. Make a circle graph showing the results.

3. Count the syllables or number of letters in each word and find out what the average number of syllables or letters each word has or which group averaged the highest number.

Study Skills:

1. Look up each adjective in a thesaurus and make a list of synonyms.

2. Arrange the words in alphabetical order or divided into syllables

3. Students may make individual word lists including the group generated ones as well as any they may think of. The process may continue by listing action words and adverbs.

Social Studies:

Instead of scenic pictures, use period pictures or write certain years at the top of the paper. Have students describe the era using single words.

Science:

Place the words: moneran, protist, fungus, plant, and animal on the sheets of paper. Have students list characteristics or examples of each—good review of the classification system or as a research project.

Name _____

Let's Play Baseball

Use the following clues to help you identify 25 words associated with the game of baseball.

1. A summer pest. _____

2. Something you get in a nylon stocking. _____

3. Used to stay cool in hot weather. _____

4. A mistake. _____

5. Type of bird served at a holiday dinner. _____

6. A successful song or CD. _____

7. Container for storing orange juice. _____

8. A good foundation. _____

9. A famous Greek poet, also Bart Simpson's dad. _____

10. Not married. _____

11. To take something that isn't yours. _____

12. A quick visit. _____

13. The man at the dog pound. _____

14. You should slow down for these on a highway. _____

15. Giving up something you really like. _____

16. To multiply by two. _____

17. It flies only at night. _____

18. Used to make pancakes. _____

19. A disguise. _____

20. To boycott going to work. _____

21. The results of a test. _____

22. Not in. _____

23. Used to serve food on. _____

24. Found on the playground. _____

25. An expensive jewel. _____

Lets Play Baseball ANSWER KEY:

1. fly	6. hit	11. steal	16. double	21. score
2. run	7. pitcher	12. short stop	17. bat	22. out
3. fan	8. base	13. catcher	18. batter	23. plate
4. error	9. homer	14. curve	19. mask	24. swing/slide
5. foul	10. single	15. sacrifice	20. strike	25. diamond

Name _____

Pieces of a Puzzle

In many ways a story is like a puzzle. A story can be broken down into individual pieces such as good guys, bad guys, supporting characters, settings, beginning, ending, conflict, etc. Until all of the pieces are arranged correctly they may not make a lot of sense, but skillfully pieced together to form a complete picture, they can tell a powerful story. Choose one story piece from each column in the chart below and then put them together to create an original story of your own.

Protagonist (Good Guy) did it	Antagonist (Bad Guy)	Supporting Character	Setting	Conflict	Conclusion
chef	dentist	doctor	New York City	man vs. self	tragedy
nurse	father	best friend	beach	man vs. nature	to be continued
lawyer	college student	dog	foreign country	man vs. society	happy
teacher	athlete	waitress	hotel	good vs. evil	bad guy wins
cowboy	politician	movie star	ranch	something stolen	everyone dies
computer expert	thief	artist	cemetery	young vs. old	guy gets girl
detective	jockey	zoo keeper	used car lot	man vs. machine	only a dream
author	sister	computer	school	a dying request	the butler did it

Great Minds Think Alike

Time: 30 minutes

Objective: Students will write the ending to a short story then compare their conclusion with that of the original author.

Materials:

Copy of an original short story, paper, pencils

Advance Preparation:

Procedures:

1. Explain to students that you are going to read the beginning of a short story by Guy De Maupassant (or author of your choice) and then have them write the ending to the story. When everyone has finished writing, they will have the opportunity to share their writings and compare them to the conclusion written by the original author.

2. Read the beginning of *The Necklace* (or other short story of your choice) aloud to the class (see page 188).

3. Allow students 15 minutes to write a conclusion to the story.

4. If time permits, invite students to share their conclusions with the class or in small groups.

5. Read aloud the original ending to the story.

6. Ask students to list similarities and differences between their conclusion and the author's conclusion at the bottom of their page and then turn it in for teacher evaluation.

Special Needs

- Give an oral response.

- Dictate response to a scribe.

The Necklace

GUY DE MAUPASSANT

She was one of those pretty, charming young ladies, born, as if through an error of destiny, into a family of clerks. She had no dowry, no hopes, no means of becoming known, appreciated, loved and married by a man either rich or distinguished; and she allowed herself to marry a petty clerk in the office of the Board of Education.

She was simple, not being able to adorn herself, but she was unhappy, as one out of her class; for women belong to no caste, no race, their grace, their beauty and their charm serving them in the place of birth and family. Their inborn finesse, their instinctive elegance, their suppleness of wit, are their only aristocracy, making some daughters of the people the equal of great ladies.

She suffered incessantly, feeling herself born for all delicacies and luxuries. She suffered from the poverty of her apartment, the shabby walls, the worn chairs and the faded stuffs. All these things, which another woman of her station would not have noticed, tortured and angered her. The sight of the little Breton, who made this humble home, awoke in her sad regrets and desperate dreams. She thought of quiet antechambers with their oriental hangings lighted by high bronze torches and of the two great footmen in short trousers who sleep in the large armchairs, made sleepy by the heavy air from the heating apparatus. She thought of large drawing rooms hung in old silks, of graceful pieces of furniture carrying bric-a-brac of inestimable value and of the little perfumed coquettish apartments made for five o'clock chats with the most intimate friends, men known and sought after, whose attention all women envied and desired.

When she seated herself for dinner before the round table, where the tablecloth had been used three days, opposite her husband who uncovered the tureen with a delighted air, saying; "Oh! the good potpie! I know nothing better than that," she would think of the elegant dinners of the shining silver, of the tapestries peopling the walls with ancient personages and rare birds in the midst of fairy forests; she thought of the exquisite food served on marvelous dishes, of the whispered gallantries, listened to with the smile of the Sphinx while eating the rose-colored flesh of the trout or a chicken's wing.

She had neither frocks nor jewels, nothing. And she loved only those things. She felt that she was made for them. She had such a desire to please, to be sought after, to be clever and courted.

She had a rich friend, a schoolmate at the convent, whom she did not like to visit; she suffered so much when she returned. And she wept for whole days from chagrin, from regret, from despair and disappointment.

One evening her husband returned, elated, bearing in his hand a large envelope.

"Here," he said, "here is something for you."

She quickly tore open the wrapper and drew out a printed card on which were inscribed these words:

The Minister of Public Instruction and Madame George Ramponneau ask the honor of M. and Mme Loisel's company Monday evening, January 18, at the Minister's residence.

Instead of being delighted, as her husband had hoped, she threw the invitation spitefully upon the table, murmuring:

"What do you suppose I want with that?"

"But my dearie, I thought it would make you happy. You never go out, and this is an occasion, and a fine one! I had a great deal of trouble to get it. Everybody wishes one, and it is very select; not many are given to employees. You will see the whole official world there."

She looked at him with an irritated eye and declared impatiently:

"What do you suppose I have to wear to such a thing as that?"

He had not thought of that; he stammered:

"Why, the dress you wear when we go to the theater. It seems very pretty to me."

He was silent, stupefied, in dismay, at the sight of his wife weeping. Two great tears fell slowly from the corners of her eyes toward the corners of her mouth; he stammered:

"What is the matter? What is the matter?"

By a violent effort she had controlled her vexation and responded in a calm voice, wiping her moist cheeks:

"Nothing. Only I have no dress and consequently I cannot go to this affair. Give your card to some colleague whose wife is better fitted out than I.

He was grieved but answered;

"Let us see, Matilda. How much would a suitable costume cost, something that would serve for other occasions, something very simple?"

She reflected for some seconds, making estimates and thinking of a sum that she could ask for without bringing with it an immediate refusal and a frightened exclamation from the economical clerk.

Finally she said in a hesitating voice:

"I cannot tell exactly, but it seems to me that four hundred francs ought to cover it."

He turned a little pale, for he had saved just this sum to buy a gun that he might be able to join some hunting parties the next summer, on the plains at Nanterre, with some friends who went to shoot larks up there on Sunday. Nevertheless, he answered:

"Very well. I will give you four hundred francs. But try to have a pretty dress."

The day of the ball approached, and Mme Loisel seemed sad, disturbed, anxious. Nevertheless, her dress was nearly ready. Her husband said to her one evening:

"What is the matter with you? You have acted strangely for two or three days."

And she responded: "I am vexed not to have a jewel, not one stone, nothing to adorn myself with. I shall have such a poverty-laden look. I would prefer not to go to this party."

He replied: "You can wear some natural flowers. At this season they look very chic. For ten francs you can have two or three magnificent roses."

She was not convinced. "No," she replied, "there is nothing more humiliating than to have a shabby air in the midst of rich women."

Then her husband cried out: "How stupid we are! Go and find your friend Madame Forestier and ask her to lend you her jewels. You are well enough acquainted with her to do this."

She uttered a cry of joy. "It is true!" she said. "I had not thought of that."

The next day she took herself to her friend's house and related her story of distress. Mme Forestier went to her closet with the glass doors, took out a large jewel case, brought it,

opened it and said; "Choose, my dear."

She saw at first some bracelets, then a collar of pearls, then a Venetian cross of gold and jewels and of admirable workmanship. She tried the jewels before the glass, hesitated, but could neither decide to take them nor leave them. Then she asked:

"Have you nothing more?"

"Why, yes. Look for yourself. I do not know what will please you."

Suddenly she discovered in a black satin box a superb necklace of diamonds, and her heart beat fast with an immoderate desire. Her hands trembled as she took them up. She placed them about her throat, against her dress, and remained in ecstasy before them. Then she asked in a hesitating voice full of anxiety:

"Could you lend me this? Only this?"

"Why, yes, certainly."

She fell upon the neck of her friend, embraced her with passion, then went away with her treasure.

The day of the ball arrived. Mme Loisel was a great success. She was the prettiest of all, elegant, gracious, smiling and full of joy. All the men noticed her, asked her name and wanted to be presented. All the members of the Cabinet wished to waltz with her. The minister of education paid her some attention.

She danced with enthusiasm, with passion, intoxicated with pleasure, thinking of nothing, in the triumph of her beauty, in the glory of her success, in a kind of cloud of happiness that came of all this homage and all this admiration, of all these awakened desires and this victory so complete and sweet to the heart of woman.

She went home toward four o'clock in the morning. Her husband had been half asleep in one of the little salons since midnight, with three other gentlemen whose wives were enjoying themselves very much.

He threw around her shoulders the wraps they had carried for the coming home, modest garments of everyday wear, whose poverty clashed with the elegance of the ball costume. She felt this and wished to hurry away in order not to be noticed by the other women who were wrapping themselves in rich furs.

Loisel detained her. "Wait," said he. "You will catch cold out there. I am going to call a cab."

But she would not listen and descended the

steps rapidly. When they were in the street they found no carriage, and they began to seek for one, hailing the coachman whom they saw at a distance.

They walked along toward the Seine, hopeless and shivering. Finally they found on the dock one of those old nocturnal coupes that one sees in Paris after nightfall, as if they were ashamed of their misery by day.

It took them as far as their door in Martyr Street, and they went wearily up to their apartment. It was all over for her. And on his part he remembered that he would have to be at the office by ten o'clock.

She removed the wraps from her shoulders before the glass for a final view of herself in her glory. Suddenly she uttered a cry. Her necklace was not around her neck.

Her husband, already half undressed, asked: "What is the matter?"

She turned toward him excitedly:

"I have — I have — I no longer have Madame Forestier's necklace."

He arose in dismay: "What! How is that? It's not possible."

And they looked in the folds of the dress, in the folds of the mantle in the pockets, everywhere. They could not find it.

He asked: "You are sure you still had it when we left the house?"

"Yes, I felt it in the vestibule as we came out."

"But if you had lost it in the street we should have heard it fall. It must be in the cab."

"Yes. It is probable. Did you take the number?"

"No. And you, did you notice what it was?"

"No."

They looked at each other, utterly cast down. Finally Loisel dressed himself again.

"I am going," said he, "over the track where we went on foot, to see if I can find it."

And he went. She remained in her evening gown, not having the force to go to bed, stretched upon a chair, without ambition or thoughts.

Toward seven o'clock her husband returned. He had found nothing.

He went to the police and to the cab offices and put an advertisement in the newspapers, offering a reward; he did everything that afforded them a suspicion of hope.

She waited all day in a state of bewilderment before this frightful disaster. Loisel returned at evening, with his face harrowed and pale, and had discovered nothing.

"It will be necessary," said he, "to write to your friend that you have broken the clasp of the necklace and that you will have it repaired. That will give us time to turn around."

She wrote as he dictated.

At the end of a week they had lost all hope. And Loisel, older by five years, declared:

"We must take measures to replace this jewel."

The next day they took the box which had inclosed it to the jeweler whose name was on the inside. He consulted his books.

"It is not I, Madame," said he, "who sold this necklace; I only furnished the casket."

Then they went from jeweler to jeweler, seeking a necklace like the other one, consulting their memories, and ill, both of them, with chagrin and anxiety.

In a shop of the Palais-Royal they found a chaplet of diamonds which seemed to them exactly like the one they had lost. It was valued at forty thousand francs. They could get it for thirty-six thousand.

Stop reading at this point and assign students to write their own conclusion.

The Necklace – Conclusion

GUY DE MAUPASSANT

They begged the jeweler not to sell it for three days. And they made an arrangement by which they might return it for thirty-four thousand francs if they found the other one before the end of February.

Loisel possessed eighteen thousand francs which his father had left him.

He borrowed the rest.

He borrowed it, asking for a thousand francs of one, five hundred of another, five louis of this one and three louis of that one. He gave notes, made ruinous promises, took money of usurers and the whole race of lenders. He compromised his whole existence, in fact, risked his signature without even knowing whether he could make it good or not, and, harassed by anxiety for the future by the black misery which surrounded him and the prospect of all physical privations and moral torture, he went to get the new necklace, depositing on the merchant's counter thirty-six thousand francs.

When Mme Loisel took back the jewels to Mme Forestier the latter said to her in a frigid tone:

"You should have returned these to me sooner, for I might have needed them."

She did open the jewel box as her friend feared she would. If she should perceive the substitution what would she think? What should she say? Would she take her for a robber?

Mme Loisel now knew the horrible life of necessity. She did her part, however, completely, heroically. It was necessary to pay this frightful debt. She would pay it. They sent away the maid; they changed their lodgings they rented some rooms under a mansard roof.

She learned the heavy cares of a household, the odious work of a kitchen. She washed the dishes, using her rosy nails upon the greasy pots and the bottoms of the stew pans. She washed the soiled linen, the chemises and dishcloths, which she hung on the line to dry; she took down the refuse to the street each morning and brought up the water, stopping at each landing to breathe. And, clothed like a woman of the people, she went to the grocer's, the butcher's and the fruiterer's with her basket on her arm, shopping, haggling to the last sou her miserable money.

Every month it was necessary to renew some notes, thus obtaining time, and to pay others.

The husband worked evenings, putting the books of some merchants in order, and nights he often did copying at five sous a page.

And this life lasted for ten years.

At the end of ten years they had restored all, all, with interest of the usurer, and accumulated interest, besides.

Mme Loisel seemed old now. She had become a strong, hard woman, the crude woman of the poor household. Her hair badly dressed, her skirts awry, her hands red, she spoke in a loud tone and washed the floors in large pails of water. But sometimes, when her husband was at the office, she would sear herself before the window and think of that evening party of former times, of that ball where she was so beautiful and so flattered.

How would it have been if she had not lost that necklace? Who knows? Who knows? How singular is life and how full of changes! How small a thing will ruin or save one!

One Sunday, as she was taking a walk in the Champs Elysees to rid herself of the cares of the week, she suddenly perceived a woman walking with a child. It was Mme Forestier, still young, still pretty, still attractive. Mme Loisel was affected. Should she speak to her? Yes, certainly. And now that she had paid, she would tell her all. Why not?

She approached her. "Good morning, Jeanne."

Her friend did not recognize her and was astonished to be so familiarly addressed by this common personage. She stammered:

"But, Madame — I do not know — You must be mistaken."

"No, I am Matilda Loisel."

Her friend uttered a cry of astonishment: "Oh! my poor Matilda! How you have changed!"

"Yes, I have had some hard days since I saw you, and some miserable ones—and all because of you."

"Because of me? How is that?"

"You recall the diamond necklace that you loaned me to wear to the minister's ball?"

"Yes, very well."

"Well, I lost it.

"How is that, since you returned it to me?"

"I returned another to you exactly like it. And it has taken us ten years to pay for it. You can understand that it was not easy for us who have nothing. But it is finished, and I am decently content."

Mme Forestier stopped short. She said:

"You say that you bought a diamond necklace to replace mine?"

"Yes. You did not perceive it then? They were just alike."

And she smiled with a proud and simple joy. Mme Forestier was touched and took both her hands as she replied:

"Oh, my poor Matilda! Mine were false. They were not worth over five hundred francs!"

How Many are There?

Subject: Math

Time: 15-30 minutes

Materials:
chalkboard and chalk

Advance Preparation:
This lesson works well with *Survey Your Friends* on page 201.

Objective:
Students will categorize and count their classmates in various ways.

Procedures:

1. Discuss ways that class members are alike and different (eye color, hair color, number of siblings, number of places lived, month they were born, number of letters in their name, favorite food, color, candy, book, etc.).

2. Make a grid on the board similar to the one below using one of the categories mentioned above.

3. Complete the grid as a class.

When We Were Born

Jan	Feb	Mar	Apr	May	June
July	Aug	Sept	Oct	Nov	Dec

4. Have students determine which column has the most and which has the least.

5. Summarize by explaining that all things can be categorized in different ways.

6. Get the students to decide another way to categorize the class and complete a second grid.

7. Discuss situations where the information from the grids may be useful.

Extension:

Assign students to independently make a grid categorizing the members of their family in some way.

Notes for the Teacher

Developing an organized method for determining and recording grid information will help significantly with class management during this activity. For example, fill in the columns one by one by having students who should be counted for each column raise their hand as you come to it. Ask another student, who is not being counted, to count the hands raised and enter the number on the grid.

Name _____

Addition Facts

7	4	6	3	5	9	8	6	3	9
+ 5	+ 4	+ 3	+ 2	+ 1	+ 4	+ 6	+ 5	+ 3	+ 8
8	7	3	6	7	5	10	6	7	6
+ 7	+ 7	+ 1	+ 2	+ 4	+ 3	+ 9	+ 6	+ 3	+ 1
5	4	9	10	9	10	8	6	4	10
+ 4	+ 3	+ 2	+ 3	+ 9	+ 6	+ 5	+ 4	+ 2	+ 5
5	8	9	7	8	9	2	7	10	8
+ 5	+ 3	+ 7	+ 6	+ 8	+ 6	+ 1	+ 2	+ 7	+ 4
10	2	9	8	2	10	9	9	10	8
+ 8	+ 5	+ 3	+ 1	+ 2	+ 4	+ 5	+ 1	+ 2	+ 2

Name _____

Subtraction Facts

7	4	6	3	5	9	8	6	3	9
– 5	– 4	– 3	– 2	– 1	– 4	– 6	– 5	– 3	– 8
8	7	3	6	7	5	10	6	7	6
– 7	– 7	– 1	– 2	– 4	– 3	– 9	– 6	– 3	– 1
5	4	9	10	9	10	8	6	4	10
– 4	– 3	– 2	– 3	– 9	– 6	– 5	– 4	– 2	– 5
5	8	9	7	8	9	2	7	10	8
– 5	– 3	– 7	– 6	– 8	– 6	– 1	– 2	– 7	– 4
10	2	9	8	2	10	9	9	10	8
– 8	– 5	– 3	– 1	– 2	– 4	– 5	– 1	– 2	– 2

Multiplication Facts

7	4	6	3	5	9	8	6	3	9
x 5	x 4	x 3	x 2	x 1	x 4	x 6	x 5	x 3	x 8

8	7	3	6	7	5	10	6	7	6
x 7	x 7	x 1	x 2	x 4	x 3	x 9	x 6	x 3	x 1

5	4	9	10	9	10	8	6	4	10
x 4	x 3	x 2	x 3	x 9	x 6	x 5	x 4	x 2	x 5

5	8	9	7	8	9	2	7	10	8
x 5	x 3	x 7	x 6	x 8	x 6	x 1	x 2	x 7	x 4

10	2	9	8	2	10	9	9	10	8
x 8	x 5	x 3	x 1	x 2	x 4	x 5	x 1	x 2	x 2

Division Facts

$5\overline{)35}$ $4\overline{)16}$ $3\overline{)18}$ $2\overline{)6}$ $1\overline{)5}$ $4\overline{)36}$ $6\overline{)48}$ $6\overline{)30}$ $3\overline{)9}$ $8\overline{)72}$

$7\overline{)56}$ $7\overline{)49}$ $1\overline{)3}$ $2\overline{)12}$ $4\overline{)28}$ $3\overline{)15}$ $9\overline{)90}$ $6\overline{)36}$ $3\overline{)21}$ $1\overline{)6}$

$4\overline{)20}$ $3\overline{)12}$ $2\overline{)18}$ $3\overline{)30}$ $9\overline{)81}$ $6\overline{)60}$ $5\overline{)40}$ $4\overline{)24}$ $2\overline{)8}$ $5\overline{)50}$

$5\overline{)25}$ $3\overline{)24}$ $7\overline{)63}$ $6\overline{)42}$ $8\overline{)64}$ $6\overline{)54}$ $1\overline{)2}$ $2\overline{)14}$ $7\overline{)70}$ $4\overline{)32}$

$8\overline{)80}$ $5\overline{)10}$ $3\overline{)27}$ $1\overline{)8}$ $2\overline{)4}$ $4\overline{)40}$ $5\overline{)45}$ $1\overline{)9}$ $2\overline{)20}$ $2\overline{)16}$

Salute

Subject: Math

Time: 5-30 minutes

Materials Needed:

One deck of numbered cards per group. Scratch paper, if needed.

Objective:

Students will enjoy a fast paced review of addition, subtraction, multiplication, and division math facts. Salute is a small-group math facts activity that requires two players and one dealer.

Procedures:

1. Three students work as a group. The dealer holds the deck of cards and deals one card, face down, to each player.

2. Both players "salute" with the card by placing the card face out while holding it on their foreheads. This process should allow the dealer to see both cards and the players to see each others cards, but not his/her own card.

3. After the players "salute," the dealer adds or multiplies the cards together and tells the players the answer.

4. When the players hear the answer, they will use an opposite operation and orally respond with the number on the card s/he is holding.

Graph Art

Subject: Math

Time: 15-30 minutes

Materials Needed:
Graph Art worksheets (page 200), pencils, and crayons

Advance Preparation:
Copy worksheets and determine six points to be used in the art activity.

Objective:
Students will learn to plot points on a graph and create an image that incorporates several plotted points.

Procedures:
1. Teach or review with students how to plot a point on a graph (see *Notes For The Teacher*, page 199).

2. Distribute graph worksheets and get students to plot six pre-determined points.

3. Make sure the points are dark enough to be seen on the back side of the paper.

4. Demonstrate or show examples of graph art (see page 199).

5. Explain the rules for *Graph Art*.

   A. All dots must be connected.

   B. A dot may connect more than once.

   C. All dots must be used.

   D. Other lines may be added to create the picture.

6. Get the students to turn their paper over and use the dots to create their own graph art.

7. If time allows, color the artwork.

8. Turn in artwork for classroom display. It is fun to see different pictures that all contain the same six dots.

Graph Art Examples

Extension:

Number and display pictures without the students' names visible. Have each class member vote by secret ballot for their three favorite works of art. Tally the votes on the board and award a prize to the classroom winner.

Notes for the Teacher

Making copies of or keeping graph art done by previous classes is a great way to collect a portfolio of examples. Often students who finish early are more than willing to make another picture for you to keep and show to other classes.

Background Information On Plotting Points

A point on a graph can be found using a pair of numbers. The number pair for a point is called its coordinates. The first number in the pair tells how far to go right or left. The second number in the pair tells how far to go up or down. Below are examples of how to find points from coordinates.

Name _____

Graph Art

Survey Your Friends

Subject: Math

Time: 30+ minutes

Materials Needed:

pencil and paper

Advance Preparation:

Objective:

Students will survey the class on a topic of interest, create a bar graph to illustrate the results, and develop questions relating to the information collected.

Procedures:

1. Conduct a class survey on a topic of interest. (Favorite candy bar, color, professional football team, etc.)

2. Have students construct a bar graph illustrating the results of the survey (see example on the following page).

3. Have students write three questions that require using the bar graph to determine the correct answer (see examples below).

4. Exchange papers among classmates and get them to answer each other's questions.

5. Make sure that both the student who wrote the questions and the student who answered them are clearly identified on the paper, then hand in for teacher evaluation.

Example Questions and Bar Graph:

1. How many more students voted for Oatmeal than Oreo cookies? _____

2. What is the total number of votes for Peanut Butter and Sugar cookies combined? _____

3. Which kind of cookie received the most votes? _____

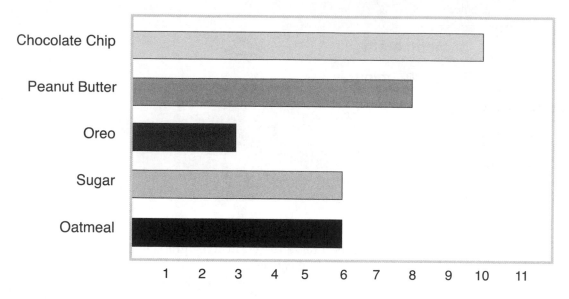

Favorite Cookie

Extension:

Get students to develop individual surveys to conduct outside of class. Assign them to survey 30 people, at lunch, during recess, etc. After the surveys are complete, assign students to construct bar graphs to be compiled in a book or displayed in the classroom for other students to see.

Notes for the teacher:

Finding an organized way to conduct the class survey will help with class management during this activity. One method is to get students to write their answers on a piece of paper. Collect the papers and get one student to read the results while another tallies the information on the board. The students love to participate like this and it leaves the teacher free to monitor the class and deal with any disruptive behavior without interrupting the progress of the lesson.

It is also helpful in classes where students have not had much graph experience to model the bar graph on the board while they construct their own on paper.

Name _____

Calendar Math

January						
S	M	T	W	Th	F	S
						1
2	3	4	5	6	7	8
9	10	11	12	13	14	15
16	17	18	19	20	21	22
23	24	25	26	27	28	29
30	31					

February						
S	M	T	W	Th	F	S
		1	2	3	4	5
6	7	8	9	10	11	12
13	14	15	16	17	18	19
20	21	22	23	24	25	26
27	28	29				

March						
S	M	T	W	Th	F	S
		1	2	3	4
5	6	7	8	9	10	11
12	13	14	15	16	17	18
19	20	21	22	23	24	25
26	27	28	29	30	31	

April						
S	M	T	W	Th	F	S
						1
2	3	4	5	6	7	8
9	10	11	12	13	14	15
16	17	18	19	20	21	22
23	24	25	26	27	28	29
30						

May						
S	M	T	W	Th	F	S
	1	2	3	4	5	6
7	8	9	10	11	12	13
14	15	16	17	18	19	20
21	22	23	24	25	26	27
28	29	30	31			

June						
S	M	T	W	Th	F	S
				1	2	3
4	5	6	7	8	9	10
11	12	13	14	15	16	17
18	19	20	21	22	23	24
25	26	27	28	29	30	

July						
S	M	T	W	Th	F	S
						1
2	3	4	5	6	7	8
9	10	11	12	13	14	15
16	17	18	19	20	21	22
23	24	25	26	27	28	29
30	31					

August						
S	M	T	W	Th	F	S
		1	2	3	4	5
6	7	8	9	10	11	12
13	14	15	16	17	18	19
20	21	22	23	24	25	26
27	28	29	30	31		

September						
S	M	T	W	Th	F	S
					1	2
3	4	5	6	7	8	9
10	11	12	13	14	15	16
17	18	19	20	21	22	23
24	25	26	27	28	29	30

October						
S	M	T	W	Th	F	S
1	2	3	4	5	6	7
8	9	10	11	12	13	14
15	16	17	18	19	20	21
22	23	24	25	26	27	28
29	30	31				

November						
S	M	T	W	Th	F	S
			1	2	3	4
5	6	7	8	9	10	11
12	13	14	15	16	17	18
19	20	21	22	23	24	25
26	27	28	29	30		

December						
S	M	T	W	Th	F	S
					1	2
3	4	5	6	7	8	9
10	11	12	13	14	15	16
17	18	19	20	21	22	23
24	25	26	27	28	29	30
31						

1. How many days are there between March 5th and October 30th? _____

2. How many months have names with four or less letters in their name? _____

3. How many days are in these "short name" months combined? _____

4. How many days are there in the month you were born? _____

5. Laws require that there are 180 days in a school year. If school started on August 15 and you went seven days a week without any days off for holidays or weekends, when would summer vacation begin? _____

6. Suppose there was a law that allowed you to attend school only on odd numbered dates, Monday to Friday. How many days would you attend school in the month of October? _____

7. There are 24 hours in one day. How many hours are there in the month of June? _____

8. There are 365 days in a year (excluding leap year). Work out, as of today, how many days old you are. _____

9. Which months have 30 days?

_____   _____
_____   _____

Which have 31 days?

_____   _____
_____   _____
_____   _____
_____   _____

10. Which month did you not list in the previous question? _____

11. If you left on April 26th for a 14 day vacation to Hawaii, on what day would you return home? _____

12. How many school days are there between February 26 and April 19? _____

13. What is something you remember from last year? _____

14. If school finishes for summer vacation on June 1 and begins again on August 28, how many ddays of summer vacation do you get? _____

15. How many Mondays are there in the month of October? _____

16. How many days are there between Christmas Day and New Year's Day? _____

17. Do any months in the calendar have a Friday the 13th? _____ Which one(s)?

_____
_____

18. How many days are there between Valentine's Day and Independence Day? _____

19. Suppose you only went to school on Monday, Wednesday, and Friday. How many days would you go to school in the month of March? ___

20. Think up your own Calendar Math Question and get someone else to answer it.

Question: _____

_____

_____

Answer: _____

_____

_____

Calendar Math
ANSWER KEY

1. 238 days

2. 3 months

3. 92 days

4. answers will vary

5. February 10

6. 11 days

7. 720 hours

8. answers will vary

9. 30 Days: April, June, September, November
   31 Days: January, March, May, July, August, October, December

10. February

11. May 9

12. 37 days

13. answers will vary

14. 88 days

15. 5 Mondays

16. 6 days

17. Yes; October

18. 140 days

19. 14 days

20. answers will vary

Number Patterns

Find the next three numbers in the sequences below.

1. 150, 200, 250, 300, _____, _____, _____

2. 1, 7, 49, 343, _____, _____, _____

3. 654, 641, 628, 615, _____, _____, _____

4. 13312, 3328, 832, 208, _____, _____, _____

5. 72, 78, 84, 90, _____, _____, _____

6. 23, 27.5, 32, 36.5, _____, _____, _____

7. 123, 234, 345, 456, _____, _____, _____

8. 115, 105, 96, 88, _____, _____, _____

9. 86, 84, 80, 74, _____, _____, _____

10. 2, 3, 4.5, 6.75, _____, _____, _____

11. 99, 98, 96, 93, _____, _____, _____

12. 11, 43, 75, 107, _____, _____, _____

13. 2, 5, 11, 20, _____, _____, _____

14. 842, 759, 676, 593, _____, _____, _____

15. 1, 2, 4, 7, _____, _____, _____

16. 5, 16, 38, 82, _____, _____, _____

17. 12, 18, 27, 40.5, _____, _____, _____

18. 2, 3, 5, 8, 13, _____, _____, _____

19. 4, 13, 40, 121, _____, _____, _____

20. 888, 448, 228, 118, _____, _____, _____

Number Patterns
ANSWER KEY

1.   150, 200, 250, 300, 350, 400, 450   (+ 50)

2.   1, 7, 49, 343, 2401, 16807, 117649   (x 7)

3.   654, 641, 628, 615, 602, 589, 576   (– 13)

4.   13312, 3328, 832, 208, 52, 13, 3.25   (÷ 4)

5.   72, 78, 84, 90, 96, 102, 108   (+ 6)

6.   23, 27.5, 32, 36.5, 41, 45.5, 50   (+ 4.5)

7.   123, 234, 345, 456, 567, 678, 789   drop the first number, add the next consecutive counting number on the end

8.   115, 105, 96, 88, 81, 75, 70   (– 10, – 9, – 8, – 7 …)

9.   86, 84, 80, 74, 66, 56, 44   (– 2, – 4, – 6, – 8, – 10 …)

10.   2, 3, 4.5, 6.75, 10.125, 15.1875, 22.78125   (x 1.5)

11.   99, 98, 96, 93, 89, 84, 78   (– 1, –2, – 3, – 4, – 5 …)

12.   11, 43, 75, 107, 139, 171, 203   (+ 32)

13.   2, 5, 11, 20, 32, 47, 65   (+ 3, + 6, + 9, + 12)

14.   842, 759, 676, 593, 510, 427, 344   (– 83)

15.   1, 2, 4, 7, 11, 16, 22   (+ 1, +2, +3, +4, +5)

16.   5, 16, 38, 82, 170, 346, 698   (+ 3 then x 2)

17.   12, 18, 27, 40.5, 60.75, 91.125, 136.6875   (÷2 then + the original number)

18.   2, 3, 5, 8, 13, 21, 34, 55   (add the two previous numbers together)

19.   4, 13, 40, 121, 364, 1093, 3280   (x 3 then + 1)

20.   888, 448, 228, 118, 63, 35.5, 21.75   (÷ 2 then + 4)

A Dozen Puzzlers

1. A lady goes to the well with two jugs. One holds exactly nine quarts and the other holds exactly five quarts. She needs exactly three quarts of water for her soup. Using only two jugs, which she cannot mark in any way, how can she get the three quarts?

    Answer: She fills the nine-quart jug and pours five quarts from it into the five-quart jug. She empties the five-quart jug and pours the remaining four-quarts left in the nine-quart jug into the five-quart jug. Now she fills the nine-quart jug again and pours one quart in to fill up the five-quart jug. Then she empties the five-quart jug and fills it again with five quarts from the eight quarts that are in the nine-quart jug. And now, she has three quarts left in the nine-quart jug—just enough to make her soup!

2. Five hundred people shopped in a candy store and spent a total of $500. The women each spent $1, the children spent one cent each, and the men each spent $5. How many men shopped in the store? How many women? How many children? There is at least one shopper in each category.

    Answer: Four hundred children, one woman, ninety-nine men.

3. The zoo just bought exactly one ton of animals (2000 pounds): a zebra, a wolf, a Lynx, a peacock, and a buffalo. The zebra makes up forty-five percent of the total weight, and the wolf weighs nine times the combined weight of the Lynx and the peacock. The average weight of the Lynx and the peacock is five-tenths percent of the weight of the zebra. How much does the buffalo weigh?

    Answer: 1,010 pounds.

4. Millie, the marble packer, arranged all her marbles in one solid square and found that she had two hundred marbles left over. She then received a new shipment of one thousand marbles. She increased two sides of her original square by five marbles and found she was twenty-five marbles short of completing the second square. How many marbles did Millie have to start with?

    Answer: 14,600 marbles.

5. If you had just bought the land pictured below and wanted to subdivide it into eight lots, each of the exact same size and shape, how would you do it?

    Answer:

    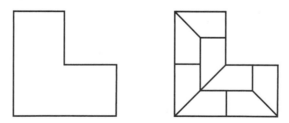

6. Draw a square and divide it into nine smaller squares by drawing two vertical and two horizontal lines. Using each number only once, arrange the numbers one through nine in the squares so that they total fifteen across, down, and diagonally.

    Answer:

2	9	4
7	5	3
6	1	8

7. Without leaving any digit out or repeating a digit, arrange the numbers one to seven so that when added together, they equal one hundred.

   Answer: $15 + 36 + 47 + 2 = 100$

8. Write down any number. Multiply by two. Add eighteen. Divide by two. Subtract your original number. No matter what you started with, your answer is nine!

Answer:	43	x	2	=	86
	86	+	18	=	104
	104	÷	2	=	52
	52	-	43	=	9

9. Write down a three-digit number. Do not repeat any digit within your number. Reverse the number—if you had one hundred twenty-three, write three hundred twenty-one—and subtract the smaller from the larger. Write down the answer. Now reverse the answer and add. Your answer is one thousand eighty-nine, no matter what number you started with!

   Answer: 873

   -378

   495

   +594

   1089

10. If you will tell me which column or columns the age of your car is in, I will tell you how old it is.

A	**B**	**C**	**D**
1	2	4	8
3	3	5	9
5	6	6	10
7	7	7	11
9	10	12	12
11	11	13	13
13	14	14	14
15	15	15	15

   Answer: Add the top number of the columns you find the age in. The total will give you the age.

11. The oldest mathematical puzzle in the world is said to be this four thousand year-old puzzler translated from the Ahmes Papyrus:

There is a number such that if the whole of it is added to one-seventh of it, the result will make nineteen.

Can you work it out?

Answer:	x +	x/7	=	19
	7(x	+	x/7)	=	19 x 7
		8x	=	133
		x	=	16 5/8

12. There are over forty patterns of four squares that add up to thirty-four in Durer's Magic Square. How many can you find?

16	3	2	13
5	10	11	8
9	6	7	12
4	15	14	1

Answer: A few of them are: all rows, all columns, the two diagonals, four corner squares, four center squares. Carry on!

Musical Terms

Match the musical terms below with the correct definition on the right.

_____ 1. Concerto

A. singing on a grand scale often complete with massive choirs and orchestras

_____ 2. Overture

B. a musical composition in honor of the dead

_____ 3. Suite

C. the repetition of a theme with changes in rhythm or style

_____ 4. Chamber Music

D. a long piece of music played by a solo performer and accompanied by a symphony orchestra

_____ 5. Choral Music

E. music to be played in the morning, perhaps to awaken someone

6. Ballet

F. a dance rhythm of one strong beat followed by two lesser beats

_____ 7. Folk Song

G. short orchestral piece designed to precede and set the mood for an opera or play

_____ 8. Quartet

H. a group of pieces either played separately one after the other or as one continuous piece of music

_____ 9. Theme

I. the main melody of a musical work

_____ 10. Variations

J. a traditional song, composer unknown, passed from one generation to the next

_____ 11. Waltz

K. a section of a larger musical work with a distinct beginning and end

_____ 12. Requiem

L. the name given to the highest string on any bowed instrument

_____ 13. Movement

M. a type of classical music played by small groups of musicians without any singing

_____ 14. Aubade

N. a piece of music written for four musicians

_____ 15. Chanterelle

O. an art form that uses dancing, scenery, and music to tell a story

Name _____

Musical Directions

How well do you know your musical directions? The Italian terms below are often used to indicate the tempo, style, or expression with which a composition is to be played. How many can you match with the correct interpretation on the right?

_____ 1. Adagio

_____ 2. Allegro

_____ 3. Andante

_____ 4. Crescendo

_____ 5. Diminuendo

_____ 6. Forte

_____ 7. Fortissimo

_____ 8. Largo

_____ 9. Legato

_____ 10. Maestoso

_____ 11. Mezzo Forte

_____ 12. Mezzo Piano

_____ 13. Pianissimo

_____ 14. Pizzicato

_____ 15. Prestissimo

_____ 16. Presto

_____ 17. Staccato

_____ 18. Vivace

_____ 19. Sotto Voce

_____ 20. Ritardando

_____ 21. Con Brio

_____ 22. Da Capo

_____ 23. Glissando

_____ 24. Piano

_____ 25. Tremolo

A. Get softer

B. Whispered

C. Majestically

D. Pluck the string

E. Repeat the note(s) rapidly (literally "trembling")

F. Moderately soft

G. Medium Speed (literally "at a walking pace")

H. Short, detached notes

I. Fast

J. Play again from the start

K. Smoothly, with long notes

L. Loud

M. Get slower

N. Moderately loud

O. Very, very fast

P. Slow

Q. Get Louder

R. Very loud

S. Slow

T. Very soft

U. Play with sliding notes

V. Soft

W. Lively

X. Very fast

Y. Spirited

Musical Terms
ANSWER KEY

D 1. Concerto

G 2. Overture

H 3. Suite

M 4. Chamber Music

A 5. Choral Music

O 6. Ballet

J 7. Folksong

N 8. Quartet

I 9. Theme

C 10. Variations

F 11. Waltz

B 12. Requiem

K 13. Movement

E 14. Aubade

L 15. Chanterelle

Musical Directions
ANSWER KEY

P 1. Adagio

I 2. Allegro

G 3. Andante

Q 4. Crescendo

A 5. Diminuendo

L 6. Forte

R 7. Fortissimo

S 8. Largo

K 9. Legato

C 10. Maestoso

N 11. Mezzo Forte

F 12. Mezzo Piano

T 13. Pianissimo

D 14. Pizzicato

O 15. Prestissimo

X 16. Presto

H 17. Staccato

W 18. Vivace

B 19. Sotto Voce

M 20. Ritardando

Y 21. Con Brio

J 22. Da Capo

U 23. Glissando

V 24. Piano

E 25. Tremolo

Name that Musical

Time: 30 minutes

Objective: Students will attempt to identify famous stage musicals from information about the music they are best-known for.

Materials Needed:

pencils, paper, Musical Information (see below)

Advance Preparation:

Procedures:

1. Divide the class into small groups.

2. Explain that in this activity you (the teacher) will read some information about a famous stage musical. As a group, they will have two minutes to determine and write down the name of the musical you have described. At the end of the two minute discussion time, each group holds up a piece of paper with the name of a musical on it. If the name is correct, the group gets two points; if it is close, but not quite right, one point may be awarded.

3. Play continues until all of the musicals have been described.

4. Additional information about the musical such as the story line, may be provided by the teacher, to help students identify it, as is appropriate.

5. The group with the most points at the end wins.

Musical Information:

This musical was first performed in New York, 1946. The music and lyrics were both written by Irving Berlin. Best-known songs include *There's No Business Like Show Business and Anything You Can Do I Can Do Better*. What is the title of this musical production? (***Annie Get Your Gun***)

This musical was first performed in London, 1978. The music was written by Andrew Lloyd-Webber, with lyrics by Tim Rice. Best-known songs include *Don't Cry For Me Argentina* and *Goodnight and Thank You*. What is the title of this musical production? (***Evita***)

This musical was first performed in New York, 1972. The music was written by Jim Jacobs, with lyrics by Warren Casey. Best-known songs include *Summer Nights*, *Greased Lightning*, and *Beauty School Drop-Out*. What is the title of this musical production? (***Grease***)

This musical was first performed in New York, 1950. The music and lyrics were both written by Frank Loesser. Best-known songs include *Luck Be A Lady*, *If I Were A Bell*, and *Sit Down You're Rocking The Boat*. What is the title of this musical production? (***Guys and Dolls***)

This musical was first performed in New York, 1957. The music was written by Leonard Bernstein with lyrics by Stephen Sondheim. Best-known songs include *Maria*, *Tonight*, *America*, and *I Feel Pretty*. What is the title of this musical production? (***West Side Story***)

This musical was first performed in New York, 1956. The music was written by Frederick Loewe with lyrics by Alan Jay Lerner. Best-known songs include *The Rain in Spain, On The Street Where You Live*, and *I Could Have Danced All Night*. What is the title of this musical production? (***My Fair Lady***)

This musical was first performed in New York, 1959. The music was written by Richard Rodgers with lyrics by Oscar Hammerstein. Best-known songs include *My Favorite Things, Climb Every Mountain*, and *Do-Re-Mi*. What is the title of this musical production? (***The Sound of Music***)

This musical was first performed in New York, 1967. The music was written by Galt MacDermot, with lyrics by Gerome Ragni and James Rado. Best-known songs include *Aquarius, Manchester England*, and *Good Morning Starshine*. What is the title of this musical production? (***Hair***)

This musical was first performed in New York, 1927. The music was written by Jerome Kern with lyrics by Oscar Hammerstein. Best-known songs include *Old Man River, Can't Help Lovin' Dat Man*, and *Why Do I Love You*? What is the title of this musical production? (***Show Boat***)

This musical was first performed in New York, 1951. The music was written by Richard Rodgers and Oscar Hammerstein. Best-known songs include *I Whistle A Happy Tune* and *Getting to Know You*. What is the name of this musical production? (***The King and I***)

This musical was first performed in New York, 1943. The music was written by Richard Rodgers and Oscar Hammerstein. Best-known songs include *Oh What A Beautiful Morning* and *The Surrey With The Fringe On Top*. What is the name of this musical production? (***Oklahoma***)

This musical was first performed in New York, 1949. The music was written by Richard Rodgers and Oscar Hammerstein. Best-known songs include *Some Enchanted Evening, There Is Nothin' Like a Dame*, and *I'm Gonna Wash That Man Right Out Of My Hair*. What is the name of this musical production? (***South Pacific***)

This musical was first performed in New York, 1945. The music was written by Richard Rodgers and Oscar Hammerstein. Best-known songs include *June Is Busting Out All Over, You'll Never Walk Alone*, and *Mister Show*. What is the name of this musical production. (***Carousel***)

Name _____

Fascinating Facts About Famous Musicians

You probably know that Scott Joplin wrote *The Entertainer* and is considered the father of ragtime music, but did you know he didn't attend school until his teens, college until he was twenty-seven, and that when he died he was buried in an unmarked grave? Listed below are ten famous musicians, a title of their work, and a fascinating fact about their life. Can you place the correct letter of their work and number of the fascinating fact about their life in the blanks before each musician?

____ ___ Vivaldi

____ ___ Bach

____ ___ Mozart

____ ___ Beethoven

____ ___ Chopin

____ ___ Brahms

____ ___ Tchaikovsky

____ ___ Gilbert & Sullivan

____ ___ Stravinsky

____ ___ Gershwin

A. *The Magic Flute*

B. *Four Seasons*

C. *Minute Waltz*

D. *Brandenburg Concertos*

E. *The Pirates of Penzance*

F. *1812 Overture*

G. *Moonlight Sonata*

H. *Rhapsody in Blue*

I. *The Rite of Spring*

J. *Lullaby and Goodnight*

1. He once held his wife's hand during childbirth and with his other hand wrote music.

2. At age seven he begged for piano lessons, but playing the piano made him too excited to sleep.

3. He once composed forty-six pieces of music while spending a month in jail.

4. As a boy he played violin duets with his father at church.

5. When in a new city he always visited the zoo first.

6. When he died one out of ten people in Vienna came to pay their respects.

7. Though not friends, they collaborated, mostly by correspondence for 20 years on 14 operettas.

8. At age sixteen he left school to work 10 hours a day in a music store, by nineteen he was rich and famous

9. He kept his pockets filled with candy and little pictures to give to neighborhood children on his walks.

10. His practical jokes included putting people to sleep with soft music then waking them up with a bang.

Fascinating Facts About Famous Musicians
ANSWER KEY

B.	4.	Vivaldi	*Four Seasons*	As a boy he played violin duets with his father at church.
D.	3.	Bach	*Brandenburg Concertos*	He once composed forty-six pieces of music while spending a month in jail.
A.	1.	Mozart	*The Magic Flute*	He once held his wife's hand during childbirth and with his other hand wrote music.
G.	6.	Beethoven	*Moonlight Sonata*	When he died one out of ten people in Vienna came to pay their respects.
C.	10.	Chopin	*Minute Waltz*	His practical jokes included putting people to sleep with soft music then waking them up with a bang.
J.	9.	Brahms	*Lullaby and Goodnight*	He kept his pockets filled with candy and little pictures to give to neighborhood children on his walks.
F.	2.	Tchaikovsky	*1812 Overture*	At age seven he begged for piano lessons, but playing the piano made him too excited to sleep.
E.	7.	Gilbert & Sullivan	*The Pirates of Penzance*	Though not friends, they collaborated, mostly by correspondence for 20 years on 14 operettas.
I.	5.	Stravinsky	*The Rite of Spring*	When in a new city he always visited the zoo first.
H.	8.	Gershwin	*Rhapsody in Blue*	At age sixteen he left school to work 10 hours a day in a music store, by nineteen he was rich and famous.

Experiments, Tricks, and Activities

The activities in this section can be used in a number of different ways. With little or no preparation they can fill an extra few minutes at the end of the lesson or be presented as part of a comprehensive lesson. The information below provides insights and ideas for comprehensive lesson development.

The Learning Cycle

The learning cycle is a method of instruction that presents three types of activities in a specified order to accomplish effective learning. The three phases of the learning cycle are as follows:

1. **Exploration Phase:** Students explore what they already know about a topic. Questions are raised. Brainstorming and discovery activities are often used.

2. **Concept Development Phase:** This is the "gaining new knowledge" phase. Students learn the names of objects, events, and principles. The teacher gives an explanation and the student does research. This is part of gaining a general understanding of basic concepts.

3. **Concept Application Phase:** Students are asked to apply learned concepts to a new situation. The teacher poses a new problem or situation that can be solved on the basis of previous experiences. Posing a question, determining a possible answer, performing an experiment to verify the answer, then discussing the results are often part of this phase.

The Scientific Method

The scientific method is a structured set of science procedures often used in scientific study. Students will most likely be familiar with the process, but review never hurts.

1. Identify a question or problem.

2. Gather relevant information.

3. Form a hypothesis (an educated guess about the solution or outcome of the problem).

4. Test the hypothesis.

5. Formulate results.

Often the results of one activity or experiment will lead to additional questions. By changing one of the variables and reworking the same basic experiment, additional hypotheses can be tested.

Ideas for Stretching a Science Lesson

- Get students to brainstorm related questions generated by the activity and discuss possible ways of finding the answers.

- Have students write step-by-step instructions for completing the activity portion of the lesson.

- Ask students to list five things that they have learned from the lesson.

- Challenge students to write a short worksheet or quiz for the lesson, then exchange papers and complete.

- Assign students to write about how the world would be different if the scientific principle studied did not exist or was altered.

- Have students use their textbooks or other classroom resources to do further research on the topic and write a brief report.

By selecting a few activities, assembling needed materials, and developing class-length lesson plans ahead of time, you will be prepared to successfully fill empty class time with exciting learning experiences.

The Slippery Bill

Equipment: A dollar bill or piece of paper measuring approximately 3″ x 5″.

Procedures: Hold the bill vertically in your left hand and get ready to catch it with your right thumb and fingers on each side of the bottom edge but not quite touching it. Drop the bill and catch it with your right hand. Easy! Now challenge a student to catch it, poised the same way you were, with thumb and fingers just off the bottom edge, while you hold the note and release it. He will miss it almost every time.

Explanation: When you are both releasing and catching the bill, your brain signals your right hand to catch as it signals your left to release. When someone else is catching, he must rely on a visual clue before he begins to catch, and that almost always takes a little too long.

Not a Knot?

Equipment: Two or three feet of string.

Procedures: Lay the string out on a table. Hold one end in each hand, and pose the problem of how to tie a knot in it without letting go of either end.

Solution: Fold your arms, pick up each end, and unfold your arms. There will be a knot in the string because there was a "knot" in your arms.

Big Things in Small Holes

Equipment: A dime, a quarter, paper, and pencil.

Procedures: Trace around the dime on a small piece of paper and cut out the circle. Now challenge someone to put the quarter through the hole without tearing the paper.

Solution: With the quarter inside, fold the paper in half across the hole. Now just push the coin through. As long as the diameter of the coin is a bit less than half the circumference of the hole, it will go through easily.

White Light

Equipment: A shallow pan or bowl, a pocket mirror, and a flashlight.

Procedures: Fill the bowl with water and put the mirror halfway in at an angle of about 30 degrees to the surface of the water. Shine the flashlight at the mirror. A spectrum of colors will appear on the ceiling.

Explanation: This parallels Isaac Newton's experiment with a prism that proved the "white" sunlight to be made up of many colors. In this case, the water acts as a prism, refracting each wave length at a slightly different angle to form a rainbow on the ceiling. If there is direct sunlight in the room, set a glass of water by a window and a spectrum of colors will appear on the windowsill.

To the Center

Equipment: A glass of water and a cork.

Procedures: Drop the cork in the glass of water. It will float to one side. Challenge someone to make the cork float in the center of the glass. If they are not able to—and the cork will probably head right back to the edge every time—carefully fill the glass with more water until it "bulges" over the top. The cork will move to the center.

Explanation: Surface tension creates the "bulge" and changes the surface of the water into a convex shape. The light cork floats to the center where the water is highest.

Boomerang Spinners

Equipment: Index cards and scissors.

Procedures: Cut a boomerang from an index card—A widespread V with legs about four inches long. Round all the corners slightly. Put the boomerang flat on a book with one leg projecting over the edge. Strike that projecting leg with a sharp forward motion of your pencil along the edge of the book. The boomerang will whirl up and away, then come back to you.

Explanation: The spinning of the boomerang makes it work like a gyroscope. While it spins, it maintains the same rotation plane. As it falls, the force of air on the now inclined blades pushes it back along its own path.

Chimes

Equipment: knife, fork, spoon, string, rubber bands

Procedure One:
Tie the pieces of silverware at intervals on a length of the string so that they do not touch each other. Hold the ends of the string to the ears. As the head is moved the silver pieces will clang together and chimes can be heard.

Explanation: The sounds heard are very much like the sounds of ordinary clanking of the silver, except that each sound lasts longer since the silver is free to vibrate. The string conducts the sounds to the ears, making them louder and more mellow. The vibrations in the individual pieces are at regular frequencies and produce musical tones. Irregular vibrations would make noise.

Procedure Two:
Replace the string with rubber bands tied together. Hold the rubber to the ears as the string was held. There probably will be no sound at all, certainly not chimes. This is because rubber is not elastic in the scientific sense.

Explanation: Vibrations from the silverware are fed into the string, and travel up the string to the ears. The string is elastic enough to transmit the vibrations with a little loss. In the rubber bands the sound energy is absorbed. The sound waves get weaker as they travel up and soon die out completely. The common definition of "elastic" is "stretchable-but-finally-coming-back." So in common usage a rubber band and things woven of rubber are elastic. In the scientific sense, glass and hard steel are very elastic, while rubber is not.

Lemon Fireworks

Equipment: a candle flame, lemon, and flour

Procedure One:
Squeeze the lemon peel near the flame and small displays of "fireworks" may be seen shooting from the flame.

Explanation: As the lemon peel is bent, some of the oil and water in it squirt out into the flame. Some of the oil burns as it passes through the flame, and some of the water vaporizes and sputters.

Procedure Two:
Sprinkle flour on the candle flame. Tiny sparkles will be seen as the flour particles catch fire. The particles must be fine, with a large part of their surfaces exposed to the oxygen of the air, to produce the effect.

The Rising Arms

Equipment: doorway

Procedures: Stand in the doorway with your hands resting at your side. Press outward against the door frame, with the backs of your hands, as if trying to raise your arms. Slowly count to 25. Step away from the door frame and arms will begin to rise mysteriously.

Explanation: This is an example of the workings of mind and muscle. The count to 25 is sufficient to produce a persistent attempt to raise the arms. The door frame prevents this, but as soon as you step out of the doorway, the persistent effort to raise the arms becomes a possible reality.

The Silly Ping-Pong Ball

Equipment: ping-pong ball, hard rubber comb, and a piece of wool cloth

Procedures: Rub the comb briskly against the cloth. Move it in circles around the ping-pong ball, it is not necessary to touch the ball. The ball will follow the comb.

Explanation: Rubbing places a charge of static electricity on the comb. The uncharged ball is attracted by the charge on the comb.

Getting a Lift

Equipment: sheet of paper and two books

Procedures: Suspend the paper by placing the books under each end. Blow straight across, just under the paper, and it will bend downward, not upward as expected.

Explanation: Air in motion exerts less lateral or side pressure than air at rest or moving more slowly. When air is blown under the paper, it exerts less pressure than the still air above it. The still air then pushes the paper down. This is the principle by which airplanes fly.

Things I Like To...

TOUCH

SMELL

SEE

HEAR

TASTE

"Touchy Feely" Scavenger Hunt

Subject: Science

Time: 15-30 minutes

Materials Needed:

paper and pencil

Advance Preparation:

Objective:

The students will be able to identify the five senses, and will become aware of the different textures that make up various objects through a scavenger hunt.

Procedures:

1. Get students to identify the five senses (sight, touch, taste, smell, and hearing).

2. Discuss the sense of touch and how it is used.

3. Brainstorm 15-20 words that describe how things feel (soft, fuzzy, hard, cold, rough, etc.).

4. Get students, either individually or in groups, to list these words on their papers. Then conduct a scavenger hunt around the classroom listing objects that "*feel*" like the word when they "*touch*" it.

5. Discuss the following as a class:

   A.   What was the most difficult "*feel*" to find?

   B.   What textures do you like best?

   C.   Why are different textures used for different things?

Extension:

Conduct a second scavenger hunt outside the classroom such as on the playground. Compare the differences in textures found outside with those found inside.

Extension:

Get students to write a creative story about what the world would be like if everything "*felt*" the same.

Notes for the Teacher

Make sure you remind students of expected class behavior during the scavenger hunt (e.g., walking and talking quietly, keeping hands, feet, and objects to yourself).

Balloon Reactions

Subject: Science

Time: 15 minutes

Materials Needed:

two balloons of the same size, two pieces of string 2 ft. long, wool cloth

Advance Preparation:

Procedures:

1. Inflate balloons and tie the ends with string.

2. Hold the balloons so that they hang about one to two inches apart.

3. Rub one of the balloons with the wool cloth and repeat step two.

4. Observe what happens. (The balloons attract then repel each other after touching.)

5. Rub the other balloon with the wool cloth and repeat step two again.

6. Observe what happens. (The balloons repel each other.)

7. Ask the students if they can explain what they observed.

8. Teach about static electricity to complete or correct student explanations as needed (see Notes For The Teacher/Background Information).

Extension:

Complete the activity again substituting strips of plastic for balloons. Ask the students to predict and explain the outcome of each step.

Notes for the Teacher

Static electricity works best on cool clear days, but success should be attainable, except perhaps on an extremely hot day. As you select the wool cloth for this activity make sure it has not been treated with anti-cling products which would inhibit the production and transfer of static electricity.

Background Information:

As in many other aspects of life, when dealing with static electricity opposites attract. When the balloons in this activity are placed near one another in step two they are both neutral and so there is no reaction. The wool cloth used in step three gives up electrons to the balloon and causes it to be negatively charged. Thus in step four the balloons attract each other until they touch. Upon contact the negatively charged balloon gives up some of its electrons and causes the other to also be negatively charged and so they begin to repel one another. When both balloons have been rubbed with the wool in step five they are both negatively charged and will repel each other.

Eco-Mural

Subject: Science

Time: 30+ minutes

Materials Needed:

four large mural size sheets of paper, *Eco-Cards* (page 227), pencils, and crayons or markers

Advance Preparation:

Copy and cut apart the *Eco-Cards*.

Objective:

Students will learn about the components of different ecosystems as they exist in various environments.

Procedures:

1. Discuss that an ecosystem is a group of things, both living and nonliving, that exist together in an area and help one another to survive.

2. Explain that students are going to work in groups to draw a mural of an ecosystem by depicting the parts of the ecosystem listed on a set of cards given to each group.

3. Explain the rules for the activity.
   A.   Everyone must participate.
   B.   All cards must be represented in the mural.
   C.   Other things that could be found in the ecosystem may be added to the picture.
   D.   The name of the ecosystem must be printed on the mural.
   E.   The names of those who created the mural should also appear on the picture.

4. Divide the class into four groups.

5. Assign a group captain from each group.

6. Distribute the mural paper, pencils, and art supplies to each group.

7. Give the group captain the *Eco-Cards* for each group to distribute among the group members.

8. Assign group captains the responsibility of making sure that everyone participates and that all of the *Eco-Cards* are represented in the mural.

9. Set a time limit for the completion of the murals (students will need 25-30 minutes).

10. Have students complete the *Eco-Murals*.

11. Collect the *Eco-Cards* for future use.

12. Get volunteers from each group to explain their ecosystem.

13. Turn in *Eco-Murals* for classroom display.

Extension:

Discuss what would happen if one or more parts of the ecosystem were destroyed. How would it affect the rest of the ecosystem? Allow the students time to complete a writing activity in which they express what would happen if a piece of the eco-system was removed.

Notes for the Teacher

Students may have difficulty organizing and completing their murals. You may wish to suggest the following steps for groups to follow:

1. Group captain reads the cards out loud.

2. The group decides what kind of an ecosystem they will be drawing.

3. The mural is outlined by placing the cards on the paper where the pictures will be.

4. Everyone then begins replacing the cards with pictures.

Eco-Cards

OCEAN	DESERT	WETLAND	FOREST
sun	sun	sun	sun
water	sand	ponds	waterfall
starfish	rocks	marshy ground	fallen logs
fish	snakes	frogs	deer
sharks	camels	fish	birds
octopus	spiders	birds	chipmunks
seaweed	cactus	tall grass	pine trees
algae	sage brush	water lilies	bushes
whale	lizards	moss covered rocks	lake

Name _____

Weather Words

If you can unscramble these weather words, then you're hot stuff!

1. nira _____
2. hsnusnie _____
3. ucloyd _____
4. fownaslke _____
5. ouownpdr _____
6. nynsu _____
7. dunhtre _____
8. doanort _____
9. ryd _____
10. zaribdlz _____
11. locd _____
12. morthmerete _____
13. yic _____
14. zidzrel _____
15. emarptreuet _____

16. taterpoincpii _____
17. mwra _____
18. owrinab _____
19. idmuh _____
20. hgignnlit _____
21. etw _____
22. toh _____
23. ndywi _____
24. aifanllr _____
25. gogfy _____
26. stacvoer _____
27. wnos _____
28. stacrefo _____
29. ialh _____
30. morts _____

Weather Words Answers:

	24. rainfall	16. precipitation	8. tornado
	23. windy	15. temperature	7. thunder
30. storm	22. hot	14. drizzle	6. sunny
29. hail	21. wet	13. icy	5. downpour
28. forecast	20. lightning	12. thermometer	4. snowflake
27. snow	19. humid	11. cold	3. cloudy
26. overcast	18. rainbow	10. blizzard	2. sunshine
25. foggy	17. warm	9. dry	1. rain

Lost on the Moon

Background Information:

You are in a space crew originally scheduled to rendezvous with a mother ship on the lighted surface of the moon. Mechanical difficulties, however, have forced your ship to crash-land at a spot some 200 miles from the rendezvous point. The rough landing damaged much of the equipment aboard. Since survival depends on reaching the mother ship, the most critical items available must be chosen for the 200 mile trip. Below are listed 15 items left intact after landing. Your task is to rank them in terms of their importance to your crew in its attempt to reach the rendezvous point. Place number 1 by the most important item; number 2 by the second most important, and so on through number 15, the least important.

Materials: ## Answer Differences:

_____Box of matches   _____

_____Food concentrate   _____

_____152.4 meters of nylon rope   _____

_____Parachute silk   _____

_____Portable heating unit   _____

_____Two .45 caliber pistols   _____

_____One case dehydrated milk   _____

_____Two 220 kilogram tanks of oxygen   _____

_____Stellar map (of the moon's constellation) _____

_____Life raft   _____

_____Magnetic compass   _____

_____14.33 litres of water   _____

_____Signal flares   _____

_____First-aid kit containing injection needles _____

_____Solar-powered FM receiver-transmitter   _____

                                                 Total_____

Lost on the Moon Scoring

<table>
<tr><td colspan="2">**Answers:**</td><td colspan="2">**Rank Order of Items:**</td></tr>
<tr><td>15</td><td>box of matches</td><td>4</td><td>food concentrate</td></tr>
<tr><td>4</td><td>food concentrate</td><td>5</td><td>solar power FM receiver-transmitter</td></tr>
<tr><td>6</td><td>152.4 meters nylon rope</td><td>6</td><td>152.4 meters nylon rope</td></tr>
<tr><td>8</td><td>parachute silk</td><td>7</td><td>First-aid kit with needles</td></tr>
<tr><td>13</td><td>portable heater unit</td><td>8</td><td>parachute silk</td></tr>
<tr><td>11</td><td>two .45 cal. pistols</td><td>9</td><td>life raft</td></tr>
<tr><td>12</td><td>one case dehydrated milk</td><td>10</td><td>signal flares</td></tr>
<tr><td>1</td><td>two 220 kilograms tanks oxygen</td><td>11</td><td>two .45 cal. pistols</td></tr>
<tr><td>3</td><td>stellar map (Moon version)</td><td>12</td><td>one case dehydrated milk</td></tr>
<tr><td>9</td><td>life raft</td><td>13</td><td>portable heater unit</td></tr>
<tr><td>14</td><td>magnetic compass</td><td>14</td><td>magnetic compass</td></tr>
<tr><td>2</td><td>14.33 litres of water</td><td>15</td><td>box of matches</td></tr>
<tr><td>10</td><td>signal flares</td><td></td><td></td></tr>
<tr><td>7</td><td>First-aid kit with needles</td><td></td><td></td></tr>
<tr><td>5</td><td>solar power FM receiver-transmitter</td><td></td><td></td></tr>
<tr><td>1</td><td>two 220 kilograms tanks oxygen</td><td></td><td></td></tr>
<tr><td>2</td><td>14.33 litres of water</td><td></td><td></td></tr>
<tr><td>3</td><td>stellar map (Moon version)</td><td></td><td></td></tr>
</table>

Scoring:

Subtract your ranking number for each item from NASA's ranking number. Add these differences. Also do this for the ranking list and compare individual prediction with the group prediction.

Example:

	Your Ranking	NASA's	Difference
Box of Matches	8	15	7
Signal Flares	14	10	4

Explanation:

These are the answers supplied by the NASA scientists. The answers are split into groups — physical survival and traveling to the rendezvous.

The first two items are air and water, without which you cannot survive at all. After that comes the map for locating position and figuring out how to get to the rendezvous. Food comes next for strength on the trip. It is not as necessary for survival as air and water.

The FM transmitter-receiver is for keeping in touch with Earth. In a vacuum, without the ionosphere, radio transmission travels only in line of sight and would be limited on the moon to destination of approximately ten miles. On Earth powerful receivers could pick up messages which would then be relayed to the mother ship. The next item would be the rope for lunar mountain climbing and traversing crevasses on the trip. The next item would be first aid for injuries. Parachute silk would offer excellent protection from sunlight and heat buildup.

The life raft is a carry all for supplies, (the moon's gravity permits heavy loads to be carried), as a shelter, and a possible stretcher for the injured. It also offers protection from micrometeorite showers.

Flares cannot burn in a vacuum but they, as well as the pistols, can be shot. Flares and guns would therefore be excellent propulsive devices for flying over obstructions. The milk is heavy and relatively less valuable.

On the moon overheating is a problem and not cold. Thus the heating unit is useless.

The magnetic compass is useless without a map of the moon's field.

The box of matches is the most useless item.

Compare A Plant Cell to Your School

Teacher Directions:

On the following page students are to compare a plant cell to their school. Listed below are a the definitions of the parts of a plant cell for your reference.

Cell wall
This outer barrier provides extra support for the cell and gives it a shape.

Plasma (Cell) Membrane
The cell membrane encloses the cell. It acts like a gatekeeper – allowing some materials to pass through it, but not others.

Nucleus
This structure, found inside the nucleus, is responsible for making ribosomes, which are then transported to the cytoplasm.

Cytoplasm
Is a gel-like fluid that takes up most of the space inside a cell. Cytoplasm is mostly water, with other substances dissolved in it.

Chloroplast(s)
These food-making structures of plant cells contain the green pigment, chlorophyll.

Mitochondrion
Use oxygen to transform the energy in food to a form the cell can use to carry out its activities. These structures are sometimes called the "powerhouses" of the cell.

Vacuole(s)
These fluid-filled structures temporarily store different substances needed by the cell.

Chromosomes
Are the structures located in the nucleus of a cell, made of DNA, that contains the genetic information needed to carry out cell functions and make new cells.

Ribosome(s)
Are the structure in a cell where proteins are put together.

Special Needs

- Work in a small group or with a partner.

- Use a definition list of the parts of the cell (like the one on this page).

Compare A Plant Cell to Your School

Directions:

In the space provided below, describe the function of each cell organelle and then state what person in your school serves a similar function and why.

Plant Organelle	Function Within The Plant Cell	Who/what at your school has a similar job?
Cell Wall		
Plasma (Cell) Membrane		
Nucleus		
Cytoplasm		
Chloroplast(s)		
Mitochondrion		
Vacuole(s)		
Chromosomes (DNA)		
Ribosome(s)		

What Kind of Energy?

Have you ever been told that you have too much energy? Did you know that energy can change from one form to another. Lets take a close look at the different types of energy.

Motion is known as *kinetic energy*. The wind blowing or any other time when an inanimate object does "work" (e.g., causes an action to occur) would be examples of kinetic energy. *Potential energy* is the energy of anything that could start falling. A rock sitting on the edge of a cliff is an example of potential energy. Potential energy and kinetic energy together are called *mechanical energy*. Any machine is an example of mechanical energy. Friction is the rubbing of one object against another, and that creates *heat energy*.

Listed below are some examples of energy. Next to the example write the form of energy that it uses.

1. Rubbing your hands together _____

2. Walking across a carpet _____

3. Preparing to jump from a tree house _____

4. An airplane taking off_____

5. Riding a bike _____

6. A motorcycle _____

Now list an example for each form of energy.

1. Kinetic energy _____

2. Potential energy _____

3. Mechanical energy _____

4. Heat Energy _____

For the following activity, use these sources of energy: river current, tidal wave, tides, sunlight, sound, heat electricity, magnetism and catapult. Write the source of energy for each of the following:

1. Lifting heavy ships_____

2. Transporting lumber _____

3. Popping a firecracker_____

4. Picking up paper clips_____

5. Wailing sirens _____

6. Light from a lamp _____

7. Demolishing buildings _____

8. Using a microphone _____

9. Growing plants_____

10. Echo _____

Name _____

Interesting Water Facts

Did you know that growing food for one person for one day requires about 1,700 gallons of water? Just think how many gallons are needed to grow the food for all of the students at your school. In completing this worksheet you will compute and learn many interesting facts about water

FACT: Americans use an average of 130 gallons of water, per person, per day.

1. How many gallons would a family of five use in one day?_____

2. How many gallons are used by the people in your household?_____

3. How many gallons will be used by the people in this class today?_____

4. How many gallons would one person use in a year's time?_____

5. Approximately how many gallons have you used in your lifetime? _____

FACT: Water is a bargain.

The average cost for a gallon of water is less than one cent per gallon. The average cost for a gallon of milk is $2.34. Complete the chart below to illustrate how much more daily activities would cost if the price of water was similar to that of milk.

Daily Activity	Water Used	Current Cost	Cost at $2.34 /gal	Difference Between Costs
6. washing a car	100 gallons	< $1.00		
7. doing a load of laundry	47 gallons	< 47 ¢		
8. running the dishwasher	60 gallons	< 60 ¢		
9. brushing your teeth	3 gallons	< 3 ¢		
10. a 10 minute shower	55 gallons	< 55 ¢		

FACT: It takes a lot of water to produce things we use and consume everyday.

Match the amount of water needed for production for each item below.

11. water needed to produce an egg	150 gallons
12. water a cow needs to drink to produce a gallon of milk	6 gallons
13. water used to produce a family car	4 gallons
14. water used to produce a loaf of bread	120 gallons
15. water used to produce french fries	39,000 gallons

Fact: Every drip counts!

16. If a dripping faucet drips a cup of water every hour, how many gallons of water will "drip" down the drain every year? (HINT: THERE ARE 16 CUPS IN A GALLON)_____

17. Many houses in America have toilets that leak. A leaking toilet can waste as much as 60 gallons of water everyday. Suppose that one-third of the students in your class had one leaky toilet in their home. How much water would be wasted in the homes of your classmates every year? _____

18. Turning off the water while brushing your teeth can save as much as two gallons of water every time you brush. If you turn off the faucet as you brush your teeth two times each day, how much water would be saved over the course of one year? _____

Interesting Water Facts
ANSWER KEY

1. 650 gallons

2. no. in household x 130

3. no. in class x 130

4. 47,450 gallons

5. 130 x 365 x age in years

6. $234.00; $233.00

7. $109.98; $109.51

8. $140.40; $139.80

9. $7.02; $6.99

10. $128.70; $128.15

11. 120 gallons

12. 4 gallons

13. 39,000 gallons

14. 150 gallons

15. 6 gallons

16. 547.5 gallons

17. Number in class ÷ 3 x 60 x 365

18. 1,460 gallons

Science Fact and Fiction

Science fiction loves to predict the future. While it often seems impossible that things described in today's science fiction will ever become a reality, many things that science fiction writers wrote about long ago really do exist today. Can you guess the year when science fiction became a reality?

Year	**Invention**	**Predicted By**
_____	1. Air-conditioned Skyscrapers	Jules Verne, *In the Twenty-Ninth Century—The Day of an American Journalist* (1875)
_____	2. Artificial Intelligence	Aaron Nadel, *The Thought Machine* (1927)
_____	3. Atomic Energy	H.G. Wells, *The World Set Free* (1914)
_____	4. Credit Cards	Edward Bellamy, *Looking Backward, 2000-1887* (1888)
_____	5. Lasers	Sir Francis Bacon (1626)
_____	6. Long-distance Submarines	Jules Verne, *Twenty Thousand Leagues Under the Sea* (1870)
_____	7. Microfilm	Hugo Gernsback, *Ralph 125C 41+* (1911)
_____	8. Navigational Satellites	Edward Everett Hale (1870)
_____	9. News Broadcasts	Jules Verne, *In the Twenty-Ninth Century* (1875)
_____	10. Robots	Karel Capek, *R. U. R. (Rossum's Universal Robots)* (1921)
_____	11. Space Suits	Frank R. Paul, *Amazing Stories Magazine* (1939)
_____	12. Spacecraft to take people to the Moon	Jules Verne, *From the Earth to the Moon* (1865) H.G. Wells, *The First Men in the Moon* (1901)
_____	13. Tape Recorders	Hugo Gernsback, *Ralph 125C 41+* (1911)
_____	14. Television	Jules Verne, *In the Twenty-Ninth Century* (1875) H.G. Wells, *The Time Machine* (1895)
_____	15. Test-tube Babies	Aldous Huxley, *Brave New World* (1931)

Science Fact and Fiction
ANSWER KEY

Year	Invention	Predicted By
1930	1. Air-conditioned Skyscrapers	Jules Verne, *In the Twenty-Ninth Century—The Day of an American Journalist* (1875)
1950+	2. Artificial Intelligence	Aaron Nadel, *The Thought Machine* (1927)
1942	3. Atomic Energy	H.G. Wells, *The World Set Free* (1914)
1952	4. Credit Cards	Edward Bellamy, *Looking Backward, 2000-1887* (1888)
1960	5. Lasers	Sir Francis Bacon (1626)
1950+	6. Long-distance Submarines	Jules Verne, *Twenty Thousand Leagues Under the Sea* (1870)
1920	7. Microfilm	Hugo Gernsback, *Ralph 125C 41+* (1911)
1959	8. Navigational Satellites	Edward Everett Hale (1870)
1920	9. News Broadcasts	Jules Verne, *In the Twenty-Ninth Century* (1875)
1920+	10. Robots	Karel Capek, *R. U. R. (Rossum's Universal Robots)* (1921)
1950-60's	11. Space Suits	Frank R. Paul, *Amazing Stories Magazine* (1939)
1960	12. Spacecraft to take people to the Moon	Jules Verne, *From the Earth to the Moon* (1865) H.G. Wells, *The First Men in the Moon* (1901)
1936	13. Tape Recorders	Hugo Gernsback, *Ralph 125C 41+* (1911)
1920's	14. Television	Jules Verne, *In the Twenty-Ninth Century* (1875) H.G. Wells, *The Time Machine* (1895)
1978	15. Test-tube Babies	Aldous Huxley, *Brave New World* (1931)

Extension:

Have students compute the number of years between the science fiction prediction and the actual invention.

Making an Announcement

Time: 30+ minutes

Objective: Students will practice making an announcement to a group of people.

Materials:

Advance Preparation:

Directions:

Assign each student to write a list of four school-related announcements that they will present to the class. Announcements can be fact or fiction, but remind students that they will have to deliver them in a serious and business like manner. Share some examples, and set a time limit (5-10 minutes) for writing the list of announcements.

Randomly select students to exit the classroom, knock on the door, request permission to make an announcement, receive permission, and deliver the announcements they have prepared. Repeat this process until all members of the class have delivered their announcements.

Note: Applause after announcements is appropriate.

Example:

Student exits the classroom and knocks on the door.

Teacher opens the door.

Student: Excuse me Mr./Ms._____, could I make some announcements to your class?

Teacher: Yes. Please come in.

Student: I have been asked to make the following announcements:

1. The French Club wishes to announce their upcoming field trip to Paris next week. Please return parent permission slips to the office.

2. The Calculus Social will be today after school. Remember to bring your graphing calculator.

3. The media center will be closed to all students for the rest of the week.

4. Due to lack of interest, this year's high school graduation has been cancelled.

Applause

An Occasional Speech

Time: 30+ minutes

Objective: Students will prepare and deliver an appropriate speech for a specified occasion.

Materials:

Advance Preparation:

Prepare a scenario for the speech.

Directions:

Explain to students that different events call for different types of speeches. Share the scenario you have selected with the class and discuss the purpose or necessary elements of the speech. For example, does the speech need to persuade, share information, console, express appreciation, etc.

Allow students 10-15 minutes to prepare a short (3 minutes or less) speech for the designated occasion.

As time permits, allow volunteers, or select students at random, to share their speech with the class.

Note: Applause at the end of each speech is appropriate.

Possible Speech Scenarios:

1. An acceptance speech after winning a $1,000,000 sweepstakes contest.

2. A speech given by a city official to announce the construction of a new city park.

3. A speech announcing to employees the closing of the business where they work.

4. A speech to honor the contributions of professional athletes to society.

5. A speech to persuade the school board to only hold classes four days a week.

6. A speech to inform the student body about the dangers of cafeteria food.

7. A speech to announce the assassination of the president of the United States.

Classroom Commercial

Time: 30+ minutes

Objective: Students will prepare a brief presentation designed to sell a product.

Materials:

common classroom objects

Advance Preparation:

Directions:

Arrange students in cooperative learning groups. Explain that each group will be assigned a classroom object and have 15 minutes to prepare a commercial or sales presentation. The goal of the presentation is to convince fellow classmates that they must have the object to be successful, popular, or survive at school.

Assign and distribute a different classroom object to each group of students. Allow students to use the object as a prop in their presentation. Remind students of the preparation time limit.

Get student groups to take turns presenting their presentation/ commercial before the class.

If time permits, discuss how current advertising or promotion campaign strategies were imitated in student presentations.

Note: Applause at the end of each presentation is appropriate.

Classroom Object Ideas:

desk	back pack	chair	pencil sharpener
pencil	chalk	tape	calculator
eraser	pen	stapler	teacher's edition of class textbook

Glossary

Abuse

The physical, sexual, or emotional maltreatment of individuals.

Acknowledge and Restate

Class management strategy that involves verbally acknowledging student protests or outbursts, then restating expected behavior. Acknowledging a student's comment validates them as a person and will often diffuse an emotionally charged situation. Phrases such as, *"I can tell that you"* and *"It is obvious that"* can be used to acknowledge what the student said. Transition words such as *"however," "but,"* and *"nevertheless,"* bring the dialogue back to the expected behavior. Example: *"I can tell that you are not very interested in this topic, nevertheless the assignment is to write a 500 word essay about music and you are expected to have it completed by the end of the lesson."* (See also I Understand.)

Active Response

A questioning response that requires thought, evaluation, or synthesis of information on the part of the student giving the response.

Active Viewer

A student who views a video, DVD, or other audio visual presentation while actively engaging in thought about what they are seeing and hearing. Two forms of active engagement include note taking during the presentation and watching for specific information to answer questions after the presentation.

Anecdotal Records

Records of the date, place, time, names of individuals involved, description of the situation, choices for action considered, action that was taken, and the outcome of specific incidents in which one is involved. Recommended in instances of illness, injury, severe student misbehavior and emotionally volatile situations.

Anecdotal Summary

See Anecdotal Records.

Assistive Technology

Use of devices that increase the ability of students to get along in society or that improve their quality of life (e.g., wheelchairs, computers, hearing aids, etc.).

Authoritarian

Teaching style which demands immediate and unquestioning student obedience to teacher directives.

Behavior Intervention Plan (BIP)

A plan written by the IEP team for an individual student that outlines specific procedures and practices for reinforcing positive behaviors and decreasing undesirable behaviors.

Blood Borne Pathogens

Bacteria, viruses, or other disease-causing agents that can be carried and transmitted from one person to another via blood.

Bloom's Taxonomy

Six levels of thinking organized by Dr. Benjamin Bloom. The levels are organized from the lowest level of thinking to the highest in the following order: knowledge, comprehension, application, analysis, synthesis, and evaluation. These levels of thinking are often used as a basis for developing and presenting thought-provoking questions to students.

Bodily Fluids

Term used for a number of fluids manufactured within the body. Usually used when referring to blood, semen, urine, and saliva.

Brainstorming

Teaching strategy to generate a lot of ideas in a short period of time. A prompt or topic is provided, then ideas are expressed freely and recorded within a given time limit. Evaluation of ideas is not a part of the brainstorming process. This strategy is often used as a springboard or starting point for other activities. (See also DOVE Rules.)

Captain (Cooperative Learning)

Cooperative learning student role of group leader responsible for keeping group members on-task and working towards the objective, sometimes also referred to as the director or manager.

Captivate and Redirect

Two-step strategy for focusing the attention of a group of students. The first step involves capturing the students' attention by whispering, turning out the lights, clapping your hands, ringing a bell, etc. The second step is to immediately provide concise instructions that direct student attention to the desired activity. This strategy is often used at the beginning of the lesson or when making a transition from one activity to the next.

Cleanup Captain (Cooperative Learning)

Cooperative learning student role responsible for supervising the cleanup of the group's area at the end of the activity or project.

Coerce

See Coercive.

Coercive

Interactions with students that attempt to achieve compliance to rules or instructions through the use of threats or force. Methods and practices intended to compel students to behave out of a fear of what will happen to them if they don't.

Common Sense Trap

Behavior management trap which involves trying to motivate students to comply with expectations by restating facts they already know (e.g., "If you don't get started, you're never going to get finished."). Usually unsuccessful because students are not presented with any

real incentive to change their behavior. (See also Traps.)

Concept Mapping

Strategy for organizing information about a central topic or theme. Key words and brief phrases are written down, circled, and connected to the main topic and each other by lines. Concept mapping can be used to introduce a topic, take notes, or summarize what students have learned. "Webbing" is another name for this strategy.

Confidentiality

Keeping personal information about students in confidence (e.g., not discussing student grades, disabilities, and/or behaviors with others, except on a need-to-know basis).

Consequences

A designated action or circumstance, either positive or negative, pre-determined to follow established student behavior (e.g., a student completes his assignment, the consequence is he receive a sticker).

Consequential Behavior

Behavior which has significant impact on student learning or the class learning environment.

Cooperative Learning

Student learning strategy in which students work together in a small group (3-5 students) to complete a project or assignment. Typically each group member has a specific role or assignment and every member must contribute in order for the group to successfully complete the assigned task. Common student roles include captain, materials manager, recorder, procedure director, and cleanup captain. (See also Work Together.)

Correct Individuals

Refers to the philosophy of changing the behavior of individual students by addressing and working with them one-on-one, rather than reprimanding or punishing an entire group of students for the inappropriate behavior of a single person.

Criticism Trap

Classroom management trap that involves criticizing students in an attempt to "shame" them into behaving appropriately. In reality the more students are criticized for a behavior the more likely the behavior is to continue because of the attention students are receiving. Criticism not only perpetuates inappropriate behaviors, but it also creates a negative class atmosphere. (See also Traps.)

Cultural Diversity

Similarities and differences of groups and/or individuals that align themselves with others based on common racial and/or ethnic characteristics or affiliations. Typical associations often include language, customs, and beliefs. (See also Ethnic Diversity and Racial Diversity.)

Curriculum-Based Assessment (CBA)

The practice of obtaining direct and frequent measures of student performance based on a series of objectives from the classroom curriculum.

Despair and Pleading Trap

Classroom management trap where a despondent teacher resorts to pleading with students to behave appropriately. This action communicates to students that the teacher doesn't know how to manage their behavior and that the class has pretty much been turned over to them. Rarely will students be compelled to behave appropriately in order to "help out" the teacher. (See also Traps.)

Disability

Term used in place of handicap in reference to conditions experienced by individuals that result in the individual having special needs. (See also Disabled.)

Disabled

An individual with disabilities such as mental retardation, hard of hearing, deafness, speech impaired, visually impaired, seriously emotionally disturbed, orthopedically impaired, or having other health impairments or learning disabilities such that they need special services or considerations. (See also Disability.)

DOVE Rules (of Brainstorming)

Rules and guidelines for conducting a brainstorming session.

> **D** – Don't judge ideas, evaluation comes later.
>
> **O** – Original and offbeat ideas are encouraged.
>
> **V** – Volume of ideas, get as many possible in the time limit.
>
> **E** – Everyone participates.

(See also Brainstorming.)

Due Care and Caution

The expected level of care and caution that an ordinarily reasonable and prudent person would exercise under the same or similar circumstances.

Early Finisher

Individual student learning activity designated as appropriate for students to be engaged in when they finish an assignment or project earlier than the rest of the class, or prior to the beginning of the next class activity (e.g., crossword puzzles, silent reading, art projects, etc.).

Echo the Correct Response (Questioning/Risk-Free Environment)

Strategy used to generate a positive and risk-free class environment when a student responds incorrectly to a question. The incorrect response is acknowledged, then the question and the student's attention are directed to another student. Once a correct response has been given, the question is redirected to the student who gave the incorrect response. The student can now "echo" the correct response and feel positive about their ability to answer the question.

Emergency Situations

An unexpected situation requiring prompt action to maintain or secure the safety and well being of students (e.g., fire, earthquake, bomb threat, flood, tornado, chemical spill, etc.).

Ethnic Diversity

Similarities and differences between groups of people classified according to common traits, values, and heritage. Examples may include food, clothing, music, and rituals. (See also Cultural Diversity and Racial Diversity.)

Evacuation Map

A map designating the closest and alternative emergency exits, as well as the recommended route for reaching these exits from a given location. Such a map should be posted in every class.

Evacuation Procedures

Specified actions to be taken in the event that students must leave the school building due to fire or other emergency situations. Often such procedures include recognizing the evacuation signal, escorting students out of the building to a designated safe zone, and accounting for students once the evacuation has taken place.

Expectations

Established levels or standards of student behavior. Traditionally referred to as class rules.

Facilitator

One who enables or assists another in accomplishing a goal or objective (e.g., a teacher facilitates student learning by providing instruction, materials, and assistance as needed).

Field Trip

An educational activity in which students travel to a location other than the usual classroom or designated learning area. Often field trips involve the transportation of students to and from school grounds. Special legal considerations and supervision responsibilities are associated with student participation in field trip activities. (See also Permission Slips and Supervision.)

Firm, Fair, and Friendly

Classroom management code of behavior that fosters a positive class atmosphere through firm, fair, and friendly teacher-to-student interactions.

Five-Minute Filler

A whole class learning activity that can be completed in approximately five minutes. Usually teacher directed and often used to fill empty class time while waiting for the bell, lunch, break, etc.

Frequency

The rate at which an event or action occurs and/or reoccurs (e.g., a student leaving her seat to sharpen her pencil three times in twenty minutes).

Gifted and Talented

A student ability classification which indicates exceptional students who demonstrate above average ability, a high level of task commitment, and advanced creativity. These students often function at a higher intellectual level than their peers of the same age. Special programs are often instituted to provide advanced learning opportunities for such students.

Handicap

See Disability.

Higher Level Questioning

Asking questions which require more than a recall of learned facts in response. Higher level questions require students to synthesize, summarize, classify, compare, apply, generalize, and/or evaluate known information before they answer the question.

Homework Assignments

Worksheets, projects, or other assignments which students are supposed to complete at home after school hours. Includes both the completion of assignments started in class and independent "at home" projects.

I Understand

Classroom management strategy used to acknowledge and stop student protests before redirecting the student's attention to appropriate on-task behavior, without becoming emotionally involved in the situation (e.g., Student, "*You are the worst teacher we've ever had.*" Teacher, "*I understand. However as your teacher for today you are expected to follow my directions. Please open your science book to page 132 and begin silently reading the chapter.*") (See also Acknowledge and Restate.)

Individual Education Plan (IEP)

Individual Education Plan established for students with special learning needs. The plan is developed by a team which includes the student, his/her parent(s), teachers, and professionals. It details the goals and objectives of educational services to be provided as well as listing the special and regular activities that the student will participate in.

IEP Team

A group of educational and related services personnel who develop, carry out, and evaluate the individual education plan, or IEP.

Incentives

Student rewards that provide motivation for appropriate behavior. Examples: a fun activity after everyone finishes the assignment, a certificate recognizing student achievement, tickets for a drawing received for being on task or working quietly, etc.

Inclusion

The process of involving students with disabilities as active participants in general education classroom activities.

Inconsequential Behavior

Student behavior, that may or may not be annoying, which does not significantly detract from the learning environment or prevent students from achieving learning objectives and goals.

Instructive Language

Directions, expectations, or rules that instruct students regarding what they are supposed to do or how they are supposed to behave vs. detailing what they are "not" supposed to do (e.g., work silently vs. no talking, walk down the corridor vs. no running, quietly discuss this with your partner vs. don't talk too loud, etc.). (See also Operational, Proactive, or Prohibitive.)

Intrinsic (Motivation)

Motivation based upon an internal and personal reward such as a sense of satisfaction or pride in a job well done.

Intensity

Relating to the degree of concentration or effort required (e.g., the intensity of completing a challenging maths assignment is greater than listening to the teacher read a chapter from a book after lunch).

K-W-L

A learning strategy that begins by identifying what the learner knows about a topic and what the learner wants to know about the topic. A teaching and/or learning experience then takes place and the activity concludes with the learner identifying what they have learned about the topic.

Learning Exercise

An activity, project, lesson or assignment implemented for the purpose of educating students.

Least Restrictive Environment

Regarding the education rights of students with disabilities, referring to their right to be educated and treated in an environment and manner similar to their nondisabled peers. This often involves mainstreaming students with disabilities into regular classes and making individual accommodations as needed to serve these students in a "regular" class environment.

Lesson Plans

A detailed set of instructions which outline class activities for the day, including lessons to be taught, materials to be used, schedules to be met, and other pertinent information relating to student instruction and class management.

Mainstream

The enrollment of a student with disabilities in a regular education class for the purpose of educating them in a least restrictive learning environment. Often involves individual adaptation of activities and assignments according to the specific needs of the student.

Materials Manager (Cooperative Learning)

Cooperative learning student role responsible for obtaining and returning equipment, materials, and supplies necessary for the activity.

Media Resource Room

An updated term for the school library, as it now offers access to information in a variety of ways including video tapes and computers in addition to traditional books and magazines.

Medication

Any substance, either over-the-counter or prescription, used to treat disease, injury or pain.

Monitor

To supervise or keep watch over student actions and behaviors.

Motivators

Consequences which inspire and encourage students to accomplish tasks or behave in an established manner. Motivators can either be tangible objects such as stickers, sweets, and certificates; special privileges such as being first in the queue, talk time, and fun activities; or recognition and acknowledgment of efforts through either verbal or nonverbal communication. (See also Rewards.)

Negative Consequences

Undesirable actions or circumstances that are designated as a punishment when established standards for student behavior are not met

(e.g., a student brings a weapon to school, the weapon is confiscated and the student is expelled).

Negative Interactions

Any teacher/student interaction, either verbal or nonverbal, which is critical, derogatory, unfavorable, or accusatory in nature.

Neglect

A failure to provide a child under one's care with proper food, clothing, shelter, supervision, medical care, or emotional stability.

Non-coercive

Practices and methods that do not utilize force, pressure, criticism, fear, or other negative motivators to achieve desired student behavior.

Nonverbal (Interactions)

Communication which does not involve speaking (e.g., smile of encouragement, written praise, disapproving look, etc.).

Normal Voice

The tone and volume of voice one would use in everyday conversations with friends or family members.

Note Cards

A set of index cards with one card designated for each school where you might be assigned to teach. On the card is listed the name of the school, school address, school telephone number, school start time, name of the head teacher and secretary, driving and parking directions/public transportation routes, and approximate travel time.

Off task

Not engaged in an assigned learning activity (e.g., student is writing a note when they are supposed to be completing a crossword puzzle).

On task

To be actively and appropriately engaged in an assigned learning activity.

Operational (Expectations)

Expectations or rules for student behavior which define a student operation or action (e.g., keep your feet on the floor, follow directions the first time they are given, set your pencil on the table, raise your hand for permission to speak, etc.). (See also Instructive Language.)

Pacing

The speed at which students are expected to complete an assignment or the rate at which a teacher moves from one activity to the next, in order to complete a designated number of activities in a specified amount of time.

Permission Slips

Document signed by the parent and/or legal guardian of a student authorizing permission for the student to participate in a specific activity (e.g., field trip). A signed permission slip must be received before a student can legally leave school property in conjunction with a learning experience. (See also Field Trip and Supervision.)

Physical (Force)

The inappropriate use of one's body to compel a student to behave appropriately or in administering punishment for inappropriate behavior (e.g., hitting, shoving, lifting, spanking, slapping, kicking, etc.).

Physical and Verbal Force Trap

Classroom management trap in which the teacher resorts to physical force or verbal threats and abuse to achieve desired student behavior. Not only are such actions inappropriate but in most situations they are also against the law. (See also Traps.)

Positive Interactions

A favorable action or communication between teacher and student which recognizes student effort or appropriate behavior (e.g., a teacher makes a positive comment about how well a group of students is working together).

Positive Reinforcement

A positive interaction used to acknowledge and compliment appropriate student behavior for the purpose of encouraging the continuation of such behavior in the future (e.g, a teacher verbally praises the class for working diligently and quietly on a writing assignment).

Praise

Positive teacher-to-student interactions that acknowledge and compliment students regarding their behavior or accomplishments (e.g., Teacher, *"It looks like you've put a lot of time and effort into this project, keep up the good work."*).

Preventative Measures

Actions or steps taken to avert the occurrence of inappropriate behavior (e.g., establishing expectations and engaging students in constructive learning experiences).

Proactive (Instruction)

Instructing students regarding their behavior using language which describes the specific actions or activities they should be engaged in. (See also Instructive Language.)

Procedure Director (Cooperative Learning)

Cooperative learning student role responsible for reading instructions, explaining procedures, and making sure that the activity is completed correctly.

Professional Dress

Clean, neat, and appropriate clothing attire for the teaching situation. As a general rule, jeans, t-shirts, sandals, and other casual clothing are not considered professional or appropriate for the class setting. You should always dress at least as professionally as your permanent teacher counterparts.

Prohibitive Language

Words or phrases that detail actions or activities which students are forbidden to participate in. Using prohibitive language in the class may actually increase the occurrence of inappropriate student actions because it draws attention to these types of behaviors (e.g., *"Don't run in the hallway," "Stop tapping your pencil," "Stop being rude,"* etc.). (See also Instructive Language.)

Proximity

The physical distance between student and teacher. Often used in class management, where close proximity or nearness to students encourages appropriate behavior and often stops inappropriate behaviors that are occurring.

Questioning (Teaching Strategy)

An instruction strategy that involves asking topic related questions, and eliciting student responses. Successful and effective questioning involves the utilization of higher level questions, directing questions to a specific student, and allowing appropriate pauses for student responses.

Questioning Trap

Classroom management trap in which the teacher wastes time and is drawn off task by asking a student questions whose answers provide information unnecessary for stopping inappropriate behavior or getting the student on-task. (See also Traps.)

Racial Diversity

Similarities and differences of groups of individuals with certain physical or genetic features. These features may include skin color, body type, and facial features. (See also Cultural Diversity and Ethnic Diversity.)

Recorder (Cooperative Learning)

Cooperative learning student role responsible for recording information regarding the assignment including writing down activity results and other information provided by group members.

Re-evaluate the Situation

To take an objective second look at class circumstances in an effort to determine if there are underlying reasons why students are unable to complete assignments or meet expectations.

Reinforce

To encourage a specific student behavior by providing rewards or attention when the behavior is exhibited.

Reinforce Expected Behaviors

To encourage students to continue to behave in an appropriate or expected manner by providing ongoing praise, rewards, or positive attention when they behave in accordance with expectations.

Removal, Identify, and Redirect

Strategy for dealing with inappropriate student behavior which involves removing the student from the immediate learning environment, acknowledging disapproval of the inappropriate behavior, and providing specific instructions and expectations for future behavior.

Restate (Expectations)

To repeat or explain again student behavior expectations or assignment completion instructions.

Review Technique

A strategy used to recap important events and items students need to remember from the instructional day (e.g., listing homework assignments on the board, brainstorming things learned during the lesson, getting students to construct a concept map of what they learned from a lesson, asking students to name the things they need to remember and bring to class the following day, etc.).

Rewards

Praise, tokens, or tangible items given to recognize student achievement, accomplishments, or attitudes. (See also Motivations.)

Risk-free Class Environment

A class environment where students feel comfortable sharing appropriate ideas and opinions without fear of being ridiculed or criticized for incorrect or original responses.

Safe Schools (Policies)

Policies and/or practices adopted by a school district for the purpose of fostering a school environment that is safe, conducive to learning, and free from unnecessary disruptions.

Sarcasm Trap

Classroom management trap that involves making contemptuous or ironic remarks aimed at belittling students. Usually results in a negative class atmosphere and bad feelings between students and the teacher. (See also Traps.)

Seating Chart

A chart or diagram depicting the arrangement of desks in the class and listing the name of each student in reference to where they sit. A seating chart can be easily made using a file folder and small Post-it Notes®. Get each student to write their name on a Post-it Note® then arrange the notes on the folder to reflect where students sit.

Self-starter Activity

A simple project or assignment typically used at the beginning of the day or class period, which students can complete on their own without instructions or help from the teacher.

Sexual Harassment

Behavior that is unwanted or unwelcome, is sexual in nature or gender-based, is severe, pervasive and/or repeated, has an adverse impact on the workplace or academic environment, and often occurs in the context of a relationship where one person has more formal power than the other (e.g., supervisor/employee, or faculty/student).

Short Activity

Teacher-directed lessons or activities that require 20 minutes to an hour to complete. Often implemented when the lesson plans left by the permanent teacher are unable to be carried out or there is a significant amount of extra class time.

Special Duties

Extra teacher responsibilities or assignments in addition to usual class teaching activities (e.g., hall, lunch, or playground duty).

State the Facts

A direct and to-the-point class management technique that involves clearly and concisely stating student behavior expectations and consequences if the expectations are not met, then immediately instructing students to engage in an assigned task. Appropriate for situations when students are testing the limits, willfully being off-task or making excuses for inappropriate behavior.

Step-by-step Process (Changing Activities)

Providing a clear course of action for students to change from one activity to the next. The process involves instruction regarding what to do about the activity they are currently engaged in, what to do with the materials they are using, what new materials they will need, what to do with these new materials, and how much time they have to make the change (e.g., *"You have one minute to finish your science crossword, put it in your desk, take out your silent reading book, and start reading. Please begin."*).

Stop and Redirect

A classroom management strategy for dealing with inappropriate student behavior. It involves instructing the student to stop the behavior they are currently engaged in and redirecting their actions through further instructions as to what they should be doing (e.g., *"Jason, please stop wandering around the room. Sit down at your desk and spend the rest of the class period working on your homework assignment."*).

Substitute Teacher Report

A report written by a substitute teacher and left for the permanent teacher. It outlines the activities of the day, explains any deviation from the lesson plans, and notes student behavior (including inappropriate behavior the permanent teacher needs to be aware of and information about students who were particularly helpful).

SubPack

A box, bag, briefcase, or rucksack filled with teaching resource materials including personal and professional items, class supplies, student rewards and motivators, and activity materials, which a substitute teacher assembles and brings to teaching assignments.

Supervision (of Students)

To oversee all of the activities and actions of students in one's charge at all times and in all settings and circumstances (e.g., field trips, field trip transportation, break, assemblies, evacuations). (See also Field Trip and Permission Slips.)

Threat Trap

A classroom management trap that involves the teacher verbalising drastic, highly undesirable, and often unrealistic consequences if students do not behave appropriately. The premise of making threats is that students will fear the consequences so much that they don't dare behave inappropriately. Most threats are issued out of frustration and the teacher often loses credibility when students do behave inappropriately because the teacher does not really want to, or cannot, enforce the threatening consequences they have established. (See also Traps.)

Traps

Any of seven classroom management scenarios in which the teacher becomes "trapped" due to poor or improper choices in dealing with student behaviors. Once in a trap the teacher loses some of their ability and authority to direct student actions. (See also Criticism Trap, Common Sense Trap, Questioning Trap, Despair and Pleading Trap, Threat Trap, Physical and Verbal Force Trap.)

Verbal Interactions

Communication or other interactions involving speaking.

Verbal Force

The inappropriate use of language, threats, tone or intensity of voice to compel a student to behave appropriately.

Verbal Recognition

The use of spoken word to praise and/or acknowledge student effort, progress or accomplishments.

Wait Time

The elapsed time or pause between when a question is asked and a response is expected. A recommended wait time is 5-10 seconds. This allows students time to formulate an answer and verbalize a response.

Warm-up/Starter Activity

An introductory activity used at the beginning of a lesson or assignment to engage students, channel their thoughts, or prepare students to achieve the lesson objective.

Whisper

Classroom management strategy in which the teacher uses a very quiet voice to communicate instructions and get the attention of the entire class, rather than speaking loudly or shouting to be heard over the class noise level.

Work Together

Students working together to accomplish a task or complete an assignment. (See also Cooperative Learning.)

Substitute Teacher Professional Reference Guide

Substitute Teacher Handbook: Elementary for Grades K-8, 6th Edition, ISBN 189056317X, Substitute Teaching Institute, Utah State University, 2004.

Substitute Teacher Handbook: Secondary for Grades 6-12, 6th Edition, ISBN 1890563188, Substitute Teaching Institute, Utah State University, 2004.

Classroom Management for Substitute Teachers CD, Effective classroom management techniques on a 2-CD audio set, ISBN 1890563412, Substitute Teaching Institute, Utah State University, 2004.

SubInstructor, Interactive computer CD for use with the Substitute Teacher Handbooks, ISBN 1890563374. Substitute Teaching Institute, Utah State University, 2005.

SubOrientation Video, An introduction to the world of substitute teaching. Substitute Teaching Institute, Utah State University, 1999.

Getting Started: Self-Study Materials for Substitute Teachers, ISBN 1841854670, Department for Education and Skills, 2002.

Core Subjects in Primary Schools: Self-Study Materials for Substitute Teachers, ISBN 1841854700, Department for Education and Skills, 2002.

Core Subjects in Secondary Schools: Self-Study Materials for Substitute Teachers, ISBN 1841854719, Department for Education and Skills, 2002.

Classroom and Behavior Management: Self-Study Materials for Substitute Teachers, ISBN 1841854697, Department for Education and Skills, 2002.

Filling the Gaps: Self-Study Materials for Substitute Teachers, ISBN 1841854689, Department for Education and Skills, 2002.

Effective Supply Teaching: Behavior Management, Classroom Discipline and Colleague Support, ISBN 0761942270, Paul Chapman Publications, 2003.

†*Enhancing Skills of Paraeducators: A Video-Assisted Training Program, Second Edition*, Robert L. Morgan et al, 2001. ISBN 1-931975-19-1, Technology, Research, and Innovation in Special Education (TRI-SPED), Utah State University.

The Guest Teacher: A Fresh Approach to Substitute Teaching, Barbara L. Goldenhersh, 2001. ISBN 1890563250, Substitute Teaching Institute, Utah State University.

Mastering the Art of Substitute Teaching, S. Harold Collins, 1995. ISBN 0931993024, Garlic Press.

Classroom Management for Substitute Teachers, S. Harold Collins, 1982. ISBN 0931993032, Garlic Press.

Instant Success for Classroom Teachers, New and Substitute Teachers, Barbara Cawthorne, 1981. ISBN 0960666605, Greenfield Publications.

The First Days of School, How to be an Effective Teacher, Harry K. Wong & Rosemary Tripi Wong, 1998. ISBN 0962936006, Harry K. Wong Publications.

Substitute Teaching: A Handbook for Hassle-Free Subbing, Barbara Pronin, 1983. ISBN 0312774842, St. Martin's Press.

Super Sub: A Must-Have Handbook for Substitute Teachers, Cary Seeman & Shannon Hofstrand, 1998. ISBN 0673363805, Goodyear Pub Co.

A Handbook for Substitute Teachers, Anne Wescott Dodd, 1989. ISBN 0398060975, Charles C Thomas Pub Ltd.

Substitute Teaching: Planning for Success, Elizabeth Manera, Marji Gold-Vukson & Jennifer Kapp, 1996. ISBN 0912099062, Kappa Delta Pi Publications.

*Available from the Substitute Teaching Division, 925 W 200 N, Logan, UT 84321, www.stedi.org.
†Available from Technology, Research, and Innovation in Special Education (TRI-SPED), Utah State University, 6523 Old Main Hill, Logan, UT 84322-6523, www.trisped.org.

Classroom and Behavior Management Resources

The Acting-Out Child, Coping with Classroom Disruption, Hill M. Walker, 1995, 420 pages. Sopris West, 1140 Boston Avenue, Longmont, CO 80501, ISBN 1570350477

Antisocial Behavior in School: Strategies and Best Practices, Hill M. Walker, Geoff Colvin, Elizabeth Ramsey, 1994. Brooks/Cole Publishing Company, A division of International Thomson Publishing Inc., ISBN 0534256449

Bringing Out the Best in People, How to Apply the Astonishing Power of Positive Reinforcement, Aubrey C. Daniels, 2000. McGraw-Hill, Inc., ISBN 0071364099

Classroom Management for Substitute Teachers CD, Effective classroom management techniques on a 2-CD audio set, ISBN 1890563412, Substitute Teaching Institute, Utah State University, 2004.

Coercion and its Fallout, Murray Sidman, 1989. Authors Cooperative, Inc., Publishers, P.O. Box 53, Boston, MA 02199, ISBN 0962331112

Discipline with Dignity, Richard L. Curwin and Allen N. Mendler, 1988. Association for Supervision and Curriculum Development, Alexandria, VA, ISBN 0871201542

The First Days of School, How to be an Effective Teacher, Harry K. Wong and Rosemary Tripi Wong, 1991. Harry K. Wong Publications, 1030 W. Maude Ave., Ste 501, Sunnyvale, CA 94086, ISBN 0962936006

Talented But Troubled, Reclaiming Children and Youth, Journal of Emotional and Behavioral Problems, Vol. 6, No. 4 Winter 1998, Pro-Ed Journals, 8700 Shoal Creek Blvd., Austin, TX 78757-6897

The Teacher's Encyclopedia of Behavior Management, 100 Problems/500 Plans, for Grades K-9, Randall S. Sprick and Lisa M. Howard, 1995. Sopris West, 1140 Boston Avenue, Longmont, CO 80501, ISBN 1570350310

School Supply Companies

ATCO School Supply	1-888-246-ATCO to request a catalog. Providing quality and value in Home Schooler's Education Products. www.atco1.com
Canter	1-800-262-4347 to request a current catalog. Professional development programs for today's teachers. www.canter.net
Cuisenaire	1-800-445-5985 to request a current catalog. K-9 materials for Mathematics and Science. www.etacuisenaire.com
Delta Education	1-800-442-5444 to request a current catalog. Hands-On Math activity books and supplies; Hands-On Science activity books and supplies. www.delta-education.com
Glenco	1-800-334-7344. 6-12 Science materials. www.glencoe.com
Nasco	1-800-558-9595 to request a current catalog. Health, Arts & Crafts, Math, Science, Language Arts, Social Studies, and Music Materials. www.enasco.com
Schoolmasters	1-800-521-2832 to request a current catalog. Science materials. www.schoolmasters.com
Stenhouse Publishers	1-800-988-9812 to request a current catalog. Professional resources for teachers. www.stenhouse.com
Summit Learning	1-800-777-8817 to request a current catalog. K-9 Math, Language Arts, Science; Early Childhood. www.summitlearning.com

Education Activity Books

Read It With Bookmarks, Barbara L. Goldenhersh, 1992. ISBN 1882429079, Classroom Catalyst Press.

Substitute Ingredients, Grades 3-8, S. Harold Collins, 1974. ISBN 0931993016, Garlic Press.

Substitute Teacher's Reference Manual, Carol A. Jones, 1998. ISBN 088280135X, Etc Publications.

Substitute Teacher's Handbook Activities and Projects, Mary F. Redwine, 1970. ISBN 822466007, Lake Pub Co.

Teacher (Substitute) Survival Activities Kit Vol. 1, Thomas J. Randquist, 1998. ISBN 1884239218, Nova Media Incorporated.

At Your Local Bookstore

Monster Mad Libs, Roger Price & Leonard Stern, ISBN 0843100583. Commercial version of the Silly Stories found in this handbook.

I SPY, Walter Wick & Jean Marzollo, ISBN 0590450875. A picture book of riddles.

The Mammoth Book of Fun and Games, Richard B. Manchester, ISBN 0884860442. Over 400 games, jokes, and puzzles.

The Giant Book of Games, Will Shortz, ISBN 081291951. Games and puzzles compiled from Games magazine.

Kids' Giant Book of Games, Karen C. Anderson, ISBN 0-12921992. Games and puzzles compiled from Games magazine.

Word Games For Kids, Robert Allen. ISBN 1559585935. Word puzzles for kids divided into four levels of difficulty.

Brain Bafflers, Robert Steinwachs, ISBN 0806987871.

Puzzles Perplexities & Obfuscations, George Hardy, ISBN 0806982101.

More Two Minute Mysteries, Donald J. Sobol, ISBN 0590447882. Over 60 mysteries to read and solve in two minutes or less.

More 5 Minute Mysteries, Ken Weber, ISBN 156138058X. Mysteries to read and solve in five minutes or less.

1000 Crazy Jokes For Kids, Ballantine Books, ISBN 0345346947. Jokes for children of all ages.

Smart Alec's Knock Knock Jokes For Kids, Ballantine Books, ISBN 0-345-35196-7. Knock Knock jokes kids love.

Recommended Children's Books

Adventures of a Taxi Dog .... Debra Barracca

Alexander and the Terrible, Horrible, No Good, Very Bad Day .... Judith Viorst

Amelia Bedelia .... Peggy Parrish

Anansi and the Moss-Covered Rock .... Eric Kimmel

Animals Should Definitely Not Wear Clothing .... Ron Barrett

Brown Bear, Brown Bear, What Do You See? .... Bill Martin Jr.

The Butter Battle Book .... Dr. Suess

Charlie Parker Played Be Bop .... Chris Raschka

Cloudy With a Chance of Meat Balls .... Judi Barrett

Cremation of Sam McGee .... Robert Service

The Day Jimmy's Boa Ate the Wash .... Trinka H. Noble

Eleventh Hour .... Grahame Base

Faithful Elephants .... Yukio Tsuchiya

The Frog Prince Continued .... Jon Scieszka

George and Martha .... James Marshall

Giraffe and a Half .... Shel Silverstein

The Giving Tree .... Shel Silverstein

Grandfather Tang's Story .... Lee Tompert

Harold and the Purple Crayon .... Crockett Johnson

Henny Penny .... Paul Galdone

Horton Hatches the Egg .... Dr. Seuss

If You Give a Mouse a Cookie .... Laura J. Numeroff

It Could Always Be Worse .... retold by Margot Zemoch

Koala Lou .... Mem Fox

Lily's Purple Plastic Purse .... Kevin Henkes

Lyle, Lyle, Crocodile .... Bernard Waber

Mike Mulligan and His Steam Shovel .... Virginia L. Burton

Miss Nelson is Missing .... Harry Allard & James Marshall

The Most Important Book .... Margaret Wise Brown

The Napping House .... Audrey Wood

*This book would also work well to teach a moral in upper level classrooms.

Substitute Teacher Report

Substitute Teacher:_____   Date: _____

Phone Number: _____   Grade: _____

Substituted for:_____   School:_____

Email address: _____

Notes regarding lesson plans:

I also taught:

Notes regarding behavior:

Terrific helpers:

Students who were absent:

Messages for the permanent teacher:

Please let me know of any areas you feel I can improve to be a better substitute teacher for you.

Substitute Teacher Report

Substitute Teacher:_____   Date: _____

Phone Number: _____   Class:_____

Substituted for:_____   School: _____

Email address: _____

Messages for the permanent teacher:

Lesson	Notes about lessons (see back)	Notes about students (see back)
1		
2		
3		
4		
5		
6		
7		
8		

Please let me know of any areas you feel I can improve to be a better substitute teacher for you.

Journal of Lessons Taught

Date	School	Permanent Teacher	Subject Taught

Learn More About Substitute Teaching
Register for more information and worksheets.

WITH THE PURCHASE of this handbook, you gain access to some of the most useful tools in substitute teaching, these tool will help you succeed in the classroom.

When you register online you will receive:

- Monthly tips and suggestions from STEDI's SubMentor.

- Monthly podcasts which includes interviews with successful substitute teachers.

- Access to video and audio resources, and best of all, you can participate in up-to-date blogs and chats to ask and answer questions.

Since you or your district purchased this handbook, these tools are FREE! Register today to enjoy these additional benefits.
www.stedi.org